INVESTING
SIMPLIFIED®

INVESTING
SIMPLIFIED®

WHAT YOU DON'T KNOW CAN HURT YOU

CHUCK PRICE, CRFA

WITH 9 CONTRIBUTING EXPERTS

Advantage®

Published by Advantage, Charleston, South Carolina.
Member of Advantage Media Group.

ADVANTAGE is a registered trademark and the Advantage colophon is a trademark of Advantage Media Group, Inc.

Printed in the United States of America.

ISBN: 978-159932-524-8
LCCN: 2014953454

This publication is designed to provide accurate and authoritative information in regard to the subject matter covered. It is sold with the understanding that the publisher is not engaged in rendering legal, accounting, or other professional services. If legal advice or other expert assistance is required, the services of a competent professional person should be sought.

Advantage Media Group is proud to be a part of the Tree Neutral® program. Tree Neutral offsets the number of trees consumed in the production and printing of this book by taking proactive steps such as planting trees in direct proportion to the number of trees used to print books. To learn more about Tree Neutral, please visit **www.treeneutral.com**. To learn more about Advantage's commitment to being a responsible steward of the environment, please visit **www.advantagefamily.com/green**

Advantage Media Group is a publisher of business, self-improvement, and professional development books and online learning. We help entrepreneurs, business leaders, and professionals share their Stories, Passion, and Knowledge to help others Learn & Grow. Do you have a manuscript or book idea that you would like us to consider for publishing? Please visit **advantagefamily.com** or call **1.866.775.1696**.

ACKNOWLEDGEMENTS

This book has taken me over 4 years to complete because I am not a writer, but I really felt I had something important to share and that is why I wrote this book.

It doesn't really matter how much you have or don't have at the end of our journey we call life, we all go out the way we came in with nothing, except we do take our memories and relationships. The ONLY thing that is really important is family, real and extended. I thank God for my blessing to have married the love of my life and my best friend Jackie. We were blessed with four children and nine grandchildren and our great grandson that makes up our family.

The extended part is for my clients that have become like family, many of them have been with me for over 30 years and in some cases, we have worked with three generations of their family and in many ways they have become like family and to me they are my extended family.

I have truly been blessed and thankful to have met and worked with every one of them and their families.

In addition I would like to thank the following in alphabetical order for their contributions to this book: Rick Dimick, Michael Dougherty, Mark Eshelman, Karen Kane, Janelle Markovich, Jerry Murphey, Mei Wong.

I would also like to thank:

Roccy DeFrancesco,
JD and Founder of *The Wealth Preservation Institute*

Mike Chirko and Sean Hanlon of *Hanlon Investments*

Drew Horter and his fabulous staff at *Horter Investments*

Jenelle McCleary, Jaclyn Stewart and Jennifer Thomas
Partners at *Jurevicious Studios*

Special thanks to my two partners on our weekly radio show
"Investing Simplified®"
and contributing Authors, Estate Planning Attorney Carl Jepsen
and Keven Steege, CPA

TABLE OF CONTENTS

Appendix

CHAPTER 1

THIS BOOK IS FOR MAIN STREET, NOT WALL STREET

It is important that you understand this is not a book to sell you annuities, life insurance, mutual funds, managed investments, or anything; instead, this book is designed to help you understand investments and do your own investing or work with a professional team of experts to help you plan and reach your financial goals. We designed this book to inform you about what is really going on in the world of investing and the related services you will need as an investor. It will show you how to make sure your financial professionals are putting you first, unlike many books that try to sell you annuities or life insurance. There are many books that tell you not to buy annuities or life insurance and, unfortunately, all these books tell you half-truths or they have a slanted point of view to try and sell you something.

The goal of this book is to reveal the good, the bad, and the realities of investing and planning your financial life. Once you know the facts, you can decide for yourself, since there is no one individual investment that solves every investor's needs.

Now, I know I am going to upset a lot of life insurance and annuity salespeople, but there is more to life than making a commission, and the same can be said for the stockbroker, the financial advisor, the CFP, CPA, CRFA, CSA, CRC, or insurance agent, or whatever title or name the salesperson goes by.

The problem is that everyone has a different axe to grind and gets paid in different ways for different products. Some can sell some things, and others cannot. So, how do you know what is best for you and how can you trust that the advisor is really putting your needs first?

For example, if your insurance agent only gets paid for selling insurance products like annuities and life insurance, how can your insurance agent get paid if you keep your mutual funds, stocks, bonds, or managed account? What training does your insurance agent have on these other products and services? You need to ask your insurance agent about their investment training; do they actually have any?

In addition, if your stockbroker or financial advisor sells securities and isn't trained in annuities or life insurance or is restricted by their broker-dealer or company regarding what can be sold and serviced for you, what is your stockbrokers incentive to advise you to keep those other products, which may actually be in your best interest?

The fact is that this industry's players are designed to feed off one another, and the consumer gets caught in the middle. The complexity of the licensing requirements between the states, the **Securities Exchange Commission** (referred to as the **SEC**, a government agency), and **Financial Industry Regulatory Authority** or called (**FINRA**, a self-regulating authority for the securities industry or, in their own words: **FINRA is the largest independent securities**

regulator in the United States and our chief role is to protect investors by maintaining the fairness of the US capital markets.)

FINRA does maintain historical information on licensed securities advisors and you can go to www.brokercheck.finra.org/ to check out anyone who talks to you about securities. Every State Insurance Department or Agency has a similar system and you can verify if they have ever had a complaint or have been fined by either system, or just check to see if they are licensed to talk about what they are talking to you about.

Knowledge is power, and the more knowledge you have about investments, the better off you will be in your buying decisions—and the same is true about the person you are working with.

In this book we will cover many things and you will find that it offers ideas and concepts that will save you—or make you—thousands of dollars over your investing life. Here is an example of things we will discuss:

THE 10 BIGGEST MISCONCEPTIONS AND MYTHS OF INVESTING AND RETIREMENT PLANNING AND IMPLEMENTATION

1. **Real estate always goes up:** If we have learned anything since 2008, it's that this is just not true. Many of us realized this fact back in the late '70s and early '80s as well, but for the younger generation, these last six years have been a new awakening. In my opinion, it is not over yet; the trend is our population is decreasing and families

are having fewer children and, more than ever, some are deciding not to have any children. If there are going to be less people to buy real estate, what happens to the price?

2. **Work for a company with a good pension plan and stay with it until you retire to secure all the income you need:** In today's world, most companies have stopped pension plans altogether and now offer 401(k) plans that put the investment responsibility back on the employee's shoulders.

3. **Mutual Funds are managed portfolios, so buy and hold on to them:** There is a big difference between active and passive management, and you, the investor, pay for it. Do you really know the difference? Read Chapters 6, "Funds," and Chapter 7, "What You Don't Know Can Hurt You."

4. **Social Security is an entitlement and you will always have it:** This is a big lie, spread by politicians who have stolen your money without a gun. They did this simply by changing the nation's rules and laws and calling the result a tax. Does this sound familiar? See Chapter 11 for more.

5. **All annuities are bad:** Have you ever heard people say they got rich investing in annuities or life insurance? Neither have I, because they are not investments. What are annuities actually designed to do? Why should anyone own an annuity? What you don't know could really hurt your retirement planning. What is best for us is not always what we have been brainwashed to believe. Get straight talk; see Chapter 8.

6. **All advisors are the same:** This is patently false. See Chapter 14, the chapter your advisor does not want you

to read. What you don't know can hurt you and may have already done so!

7. **Demographics mean nothing when it comes to investing:** Does it make sense to you that the more people who are working and saving and investing, the better the markets should be? Ten thousand aging baby boomers turning 65 every day just might create higher demand for hearing products or retirement communities or healthcare services. Demographics are actually the key to long-term investing. Look into the future before you get there; do you think you could make some good investments if you knew what was happening with Americans future spending habits?

8. **It's not timing the market but time in the market:** The new century has torn apart that theory that lasted 80 years, and the times, they are a-changing. Read Chapter 6 and Appendix A, "The Four Principles of Risk-Intelligent Investing," the keys to managing your downside risk. This chapter should save you or make thousands of dollars into the future if you use it.

9. **Low fees means better results:** Only investments that have poor performance can justify low fees! Many annuity sales people use this to sell their annuities, but the reality is that annuities are not investments; look at the real numbers and you'll see they say something different. When you invest, you want the best performance for the fees you pay, and that is called net return or profit.

10. **Your average annual return (AAR) measures how much you have made on your investment for a period of time:** This is the biggest myth of them all. Read chapter

7, "What You Don't Know Can Hurt You." Every investor should be mad and join my demand that this be changed immediately—unless you like being lied to. This chapter will make you a very wise investor.

Investing Simplified is for all those who are looking to become better, smarter investors, and it is designed as an investors guide that can be used from your first job all the way to, and through, the retirement years. Some of the things we will cover include:

- Individual Stocks and Bonds
- Mutual Funds and 401(k)s and IRAs and Roth IRAs
- Annuities and Life Insurance
- Managed Portolios
- Fee-Based Investing
- Estate Planning
- Long-Term Care
- Reverse Mortgages
- Hidden Veteran Benefits
- Taxes, How to Pick a CPA
- Retirement Investing and Living off Your Investments
- Medicare Benefits
- Health Insurance
- Social Security Benefits
- Risk Investing
- How to Find an Advisor

I consider myself a financial doctor. The family doctor is very similar; I review my clients' needs and wants, analyze their situation, and then refer them to any specialist they might need. If your advisor does it all, you have a fool for an advisor and if you have an advisor who's not a team player and does not work with other professionals, then, for your benefit, you need to read this book and change advisors.

No one advisor has all the answers. Some just think they do, and I know I do not. I know what I don't know, but I know other professionals who have those answers.

The most amazing thing about financial planning is that everyone has ideas, and there are no black-and-white answers; there are many shades of grey, depending on who you are talking with, so how do you decide which one is best for you? You can find out by reading this book.

Does your advisor work with CPAs or attorneys or other experts in other fields? If not, you need to ask, why don't they? By having a team of several professionals, including a CPA or an attorney and a financial advisor, you create a system of checks and balances and they review each other's work. On the other hand, if your CPA and your advisor are the same person, who checks up on that person? When it comes to your money, you need a team of professionals with different areas of expertise, not a jack-of-all-trades. The public can be divided into two basic investment categories:

THE "DO-IT-YOURSELF" INVESTOR

This investor represents about 7 percent to 10 percent of the population and usually they invest all of their investable dollars. We will explain in plain language how a particular investment works, including fees and expenses, and I believe this knowledge will empower you to gain better returns and a greater understanding of what you are investing in. If you are a do-it-yourself investor, you can move on to Chapter 6, since you already know the basics.

Also, remember that even though you do it yourself, this does not mean you don't pay fees, or how could Charles Schwab pay himself in excess of $20 million a year and pay all of his employees and not charge you fees to invest? The same is true of Scottrade, Etrade, and any other self-service brokerages; everyone has to make money to stay in business and there is no free lunch or really free investing!

You may have been born at night, but it wasn't last night was it? Do you know anybody who works for free? We all understand that there is always a cost and the key to being a successful do-it-yourself investor is to be logical, not emotional, about your investments, and really understand how to figure out your real return and account for your time.

The fact is that some day all of us will need help with our investments because if we live long enough, there will come a time we can't mentally or physically take care of them on a daily basis. In fact, many of my clients used to invest for themselves, but once they retired and realized they had better things to do like travel, play golf, or just watch their grandchildren grow up, they started using a fee-based advisor.

THE "I NEED HELP TO INVEST" INVESTOR

The remaining 90 percent to 93 percent of the population realize they need help to invest and they should work with an advisor. This book will explain how to hire one. Yes, I said, "Hire one", and not get sold by one! I will explain how advisors are paid and the fact that many of them just sell certain products and services because of incentives and commissions that are seen or unseen, but do you know the difference?

This is where you need to have a little common sense and ask questions. I will provide the questions and answers for you, but the common sense and the willingness to ask questions is your responsibility; after all, this is your money, not your advisor's.

EVERYONE ENDS UP AT THE SAME POINT IN LIFE AND IT'S CALLED RETIREMENT

Whether you are still a few years from retirement or you are already there, chances are good that you have thought about many of the things and worries that afflict retirees. There is a great deal to process when you retire and the more help you have, the better.

If we live long enough, we will all get there, and **most people will have three main concerns:**

1. **Running out of money or income**
2. **Living too long and ending up in a long-term-care facility**
3. **Medical expenses, the great unkown**

However, the first thing you should be concerned with is if your investment portfolio is managed to your risk tolerance at retirement. Taking big hits during retirement will be one of the most costly things you will encounter and you need a strategy to minimize the effect.

We will try to answer these concerns for you, but you need to prepare for it and you need to work at it. Remember these words: Prepare for the worst and pray for the best.

CHAPTER 2

A BRIEF INTRODUCTION
TO INVESTING

I have over 42 years of experience in helping people live with their retirement planning, or lack thereof, and what I have seen has convinced me that investing is the thing that makes the biggest difference for a comfortable retirement. Investing Simplified® is designed to take you from where you are now to where you want to be, and if you are already retired, this book will make you think about the steps you can take to keep you from outliving your money (see **Chapter 12, "How Much Money Do You Need to Retire,"** and **Chapter 13, "Common Retirement Concerns,"** and to make sure your estate is in good order, see **Appendix B).**

Before you start investing, it is important to lay the proper foundation and establish some rules: The first rule to live by is known as the 90/10 Rule: When applied to your income, the rule states that 90 percnet of your income is for your living expenses, while 10 percent of it goes to work for you. Before that 10 percent can go to work for you, though, you need to make it available by adjusting your budget so that your expenses account for only 90 percent of your income, then start setting aside 10 percent in a savings account at a bank or credit union. Look for a savings account, not a checking account—this is savings and is not to be touched.

Dave Ramsey, host of a national radio talk show, focuses on helping people live within a budget and free themselves of debt. Check out **www.daveramsey.com** if you can't do it yourself; his expertise is worth your time and you need to take advantage of it sooner rather than later!

You will need to purchase a home, but only after you have accumulated the equivalent of six months of your earnings in savings. There is no question that it is better to own than rent; are you trying to build up your assets or your landlord's? If you have a family, you should strongly consider purchasing term life insurance to provide for them in case something happens to you; it's just common sense to own life insurance.

Meeting with a financial professional like an independent life insurance agent can help you determine how much life insurance you need, based on a number of factors related to your situation. A good rule of thumb for life insurance is 10 to 20 times your annual earnings. Be sure to check with several independent insurance agents who can offer more than one insurance company so you get the lowest rate for your term insurance.

Get into the habit of making donations to your church or a charity of your choice; it helps create the discipline that is needed to achieve a comfortable retirement and it feels good. Saving and investing takes a lot of work and effort with strong discipline to achieve your goals and it is a long-term process, like a marathon race that never ends.

Once you get a home and have six months of living expenses in savings for your emergency needs, it is time to move to the 80/20

Rule. This means living on 80 percent of your income and saving and investing the other 20 percent. It takes time, but if you do this, you will never be poor as long as you stay debt free, of course. We must walk before we start running,and we call this period of your life the working and accumulation phase of life.

THIS IS A GOOD TIME TO TAKE STOCK OF WHERE YOU ARE BY FIGURING YOUR NET WORTH AND THERE ARE THREE EASY STEPS

1. **Add up your assets:** This includes everything that has value. Your home's market value, life insurance value, savings, investments (stocks, bonds, funds, cash, real estate that isn't your home, retirement accounts), and managed assets are all assets.

2. **Add up your liabilities:** This includes all of your debt obligations. All of your loans, mortgages, and other obligations including back taxes, medical bills, and credit cards are liabilities.

3. **Subtract your liabilities from your assets:** If your assets add up to $300,000 and your liabilities are $250,000, then your net worth is $50,000. If you have a new mortgage and a great deal of debt, it may be that your net worth is negative. The goal is to create a plan that allows you to pay down debt and start working toward a positive net worth as you begin investing.

Next, figure out all of your monthly expenses. Doing this in list form can help you avoid missing something. Here is a checklist you can use to get started:

- Savings of 10 percent to 20 percent (yes, you should plan this in your budget as the first item)
- Rent or mortgage
- Loan payments (including credit cards)
- Utilities (water, sewer, power, heat, garbage, etc.)
- Cable or satellite TV
- Internet
- Phone (land line and cell phone, iPod, whatever you use)
- Life, home, auto, and health insurance premiums (If paid every six months, divide the premium by six to get a monthly estimate)
- Groceries
- Transportation (gas, bus passes, etc.)
- Household and personal items
- Entertainment (having fun can actually help you live longer; moderation is the key)
- Clothing
- Child care
- Charity or church donations
- Miscellaneous expenses

Compare your monthly expenses to your monthly income. If your expenses exceed your income, it is clear that you need to cut back on some of your spending. Look at your outflows to determine where you can cut back and consider opportunities to increase your income. It may mean making tough choices in order to get to the point where you are living on 90 percent of your income, but this sort of planning is vital to a prosperous retirement. Unfortunately, we cannot print money like the government does, so you need to budget. This is not an option.

You should make a plan to get out of debt and set a goal to be completely debt free, including mortgage free, by the time you retire, and a qualified financial planner can help you with this. The biggest reason people fail to do this is that they are too proud and think they can do it by themselves, or they just don't know who to go to for advice. If you know someone like that, give them a copy of this book and it will be the best thing you have ever done for them.

Once you have a home, life insurance for family protection, six months of savings, and are living on 90 percent of your net income for a minimum of 6 months, it is time to start investing and move to the 80/20 Rule, living on 80 percent of your income and investing the other 20 percent. Follow the 80/20 up to the last five years you work, then go back to the 90/10 Rule based on your estimated retirement income for the rest of your life.

The 80/20 rule provides extra protection against high inflation and unforeseen cost. Never forget Murphy's Law: "Whatever can go wrong, *will* go wrong." Be a good scout and always be prepared; plan for the worst and pray for the best!

While it's never too late to begin investing, it's important to note that the earlier you start, the better, because time is always an asset and the amount of time you have to take advantage of compounding earnings can make a big difference in investing for your future. It is important to do what you can to arrange your finances so you are living within your means and not using credit cards to make excess purcheses, unless you can pay them off quickly.

THE IMPORTANCE OF INVESTING

You are going to be responsible for your own retirement success. Social Security was never meant to replace income, and if nothing changes with our government's spending practices and habits, then Social Security benefits will be reduced in the near future.

The Social Security Board of Trustees released its annual report on the long-term financial status of the Social Security and Medicare trust funds on July 28, 2014. As has been projected for some time, the combined asset reserves of the Old-Age, Survivors and Disability Insurance (OASDI) trust funds are projected to have insufficient funds to pay out all benefits on a monthly basis by 2033. At that time, 77 percent of benefits will be payable. The report also reiterated that the Disability Insurance (DI) Trust Fund, which is kept separate from the Old-Age and Survivors (OAS) Trust Fund, will become depleted by 2016, at which time only 81 percent of benefits will be payable to disability beneficiaries. This projection also remains unchanged from last year's report.

Social Security's cost exceeded its tax income in 2013 and also has exceeded its noninterest income, as it has since 2010. So where are the funds coming from? Does anyone really read this report?

With 10,000 people turning 65 every day and we have had no changes?

According to the Senior Citizens League information, sent to me on June 26, 2014, "A well-known **US Supreme Court ruling known as Fleming v. Nestor**, makes it clear that **Congress can cut or change the Social Security benefits you and I receive at any time, and that Americans do not have a right to Social Security benefits**, no matter what Congress or the Social Security Administration or our President may have promised, no matter how much you have paid in and no matter how much you may be hurt by cuts. **To make things worse, if the USA/Mexico Social Security Totalization Agreement is signed into law, it will mean that millions of Mexican Citizens and their dependents who are covered under this agreement will have almost bulletproof protection against Social Security cuts and changes such as those currently being discussed in Washington.**

Seniors, have you ever heard about this from **AARP** (formally called the American Association of Retired Persons)? Why isn't the **AARP** knocking on the doors of Congress and the President and on TV and NPR yelling about this? Because, in my opinion, **AARP** is nothing more than a wing of the Democratic Party, or why wouldn't they be bringing this to the attention of every senior in America? If you don't believe me, please go to my website www.AsktheFinancial-Doctor.com and read it for yourself. Click on Social Security Facts or e-mail me for a copy at info@askthefinancialdoctor.com, and we will e-mail you a copy.

In order to enjoy a comfortable retirement, it is necessary for you to invest your money on a regular and consistent basis. Investing allows your money to grow and work for you so that you have a better chance of your assets outliving you.

The younger you are when you start, the better, so putting compound returns to work on your behalf is one of the best ways to accumulate wealth. If all you do is simply stash your cash somewhere you think is safe, chances are you will have a very difficult time accumulating the nest egg you need for a comfortable retirement. The right investments are necessary to allow your money to grow at a rate that is adequate to help you maintain the lifestyle you desire, while at the same time overcoming the damaging effects of inflation or deflation and downturns in the markets.

There are many different types of investments available for your use. This book is designed to provide an overview of the following types of investment:

- Cash, money market, savings accounts
- Bonds, taxable and tax free
- Stocks, preferred and common and stock options
- Mutual funds, ETFs
- Managed accounts and fee-based advisors
- Real estate, residential and commercial (REITS)
- Annuities, immediate and deferred, or tax-sheltered annuities
- Additional investments
- 401(k), 403(b), IRA, or Roth IRA
- Deferred compensation

We will also explore how different investments can be combined to create a well-managed portfolio that meets your needs according to the individual retirement income goals that you set. This includes determining how much money you need in order to retire in your preferred manner, as well as addressing how you can make a plan for withdrawing your money (which is just as important as making a plan for how you save and grow it), and different options for protecting your assets and possibly passing them on to others through your estate.

A basic knowledge of how different investments work, as well as an understanding of some basic strategies for managing your assets, can ensure that you have an active role in controlling the future of your retirement.

UNDERSTANDING YOUR CORE CAPITAL

One of the many reasons people invest is to help their money outlive them during retirement. This book is primarily aimed at this group of people, although others should find it useful as well. Before you begin investing, you need to determine how much core capital you require to generate a comfortable income just from the interest you earn from putting the capital to work. Core capital is money that you never intend to spend. Core capital should be carefully invested in order to generate interest or dividends that you can live on, or in some cases, a lifetime income benefit.

You need to start thinking about your money in terms of providing conditions in which it will outlive you. If you plan to have your money support you in a comfortable manner, an investment plan is a necessity, as is the proper protection for what you have accumulated.

Ideally, you will plan in such a way that you will not have to tap into your core capital, or if you do have to use your principal, it will be only a very small amount. Money that just sits there earning interest is doing very valuable work for you when you are retired.

The objective is to ensure that your core capital earns the highest possible rates with a reasonable amount of risk due to market fluctuations. Preservation of principal investments that meet your personal degree of risk is highly recommended when you are retired.

This book is designed to give you a basic understanding of your options, so that you can make informed decisions about how your core capital can best be put to work on your behalf. After all, the last thing you want to worry about when you retire is money, right?

Your medical doctor brings in specialists when necessary, and as your financial doctor, I too bring in other professionals to deal with particular conditions, and if your financial advisor does not work with other professionals, ask, why not?

This book is designed to make you start thinking for yourself and to give you backup information to succeed in your investing. Whether you are investing for yourself or with an advisor, remember that knowledge is power.

You should ask your advisor how they keep up with current economic and market trends and cutting-edge tax planning and investing and tax strategies.

I attend annual educational classes with Ed Slott & Company, which is without challenge the top company that CPAs and financial planners go to for advice on tax strategies that are actually legal. I also attend Ed Slott's monthly webinars to stay up to date with the latest tax laws.

Economist and author Harry S. Dent Jr. has annual economic summits and monthly webinars to stay current on what is going on from an economic point of view, and I have been a lifetime member of Harry Dent Advisors that attend these meetings.

Be sure to ask your advisors what they do to stay current on economic and tax strategies.

CHAPTER 3

CASH INVESTMENTS

Most people don't think of their savings accounts as investments. However, your savings account can be considered an investment, albeit one with a rather low rate of return. Any time you earn a return for letting your money sit somewhere, it can be considered an investment.

It is far better to have your money in cash than to suffer from a large decline in the market; for example, when the S&P 500 index dropped nearly 37 percent in 2008, it would require gains of 58 percent to get back the loss. It took the S&P almost five and a half years to get back to even—a cash account would have looked pretty good compared to that kind of loss, wouldn't it?

The problem is determining when you should be in cash and when you should be invested. Cash products include savings accounts, interest-paying checking accounts, money market accounts, certificates of deposit (CDs), treasuries, and savings bonds. In general, these products are highly liquid, which means that they are easy to access, and relatively easy to exchange with others.

For the sake of this discussion we are going to divide bank accounts into two categories:

1. **Liquid:** Money market and savings and checking accounts are liquid.
2. **Nonliquid:** CDs are not liquid since they have a penalty if you cash them out before the maturity date—usually six months, or one, two, or five years.

Bank products, which are a form of cash products, are generally considered very safe. You put your cash into a savings vehicle, and you are usually able to get out what you put in, with interest, by exerting very little effort or risk. Bank deposits and savings that are insured by the Federal Deposit Insurance Corporation will be referred to as FDIC up to $250,000.

Most CDs, checking accounts, savings accounts, and some money market accounts, when opened at a financial institution that is FDIC-insured, are protected. This means that if the bank fails, you still get your money back, up to the per-account limit. Watch out for money market mutual funds, which, though cash investments, are not insured by the FDIC[1]. Some were briefly backed during the financial crisis of 2008, but this is not a general practice. Before opening any account at a bank or credit union, double-check that your account is properly insured. If you handle these transactions through a credit union, the insurance entity is the National Credit Union Administration (refeferred to as **NCUA**), rather than the **FDIC** that is for banks.

A quick note on credit unions: Many people are beginning to prefer credit unions for their lower fees, more generous yields, and

---

1An investment in the fund is not insured or guaranteed by the FDIC or any other government agency. Although the fund seeks to preserve the value of your investment at $1 per share, it is possible to lose money by investing in the fund.

especially, their personal service. Many credit unions are part of national networks, so you can access fee-free ATMs even outside your local area, and they also allow you to take advantage of other banking services away from home. Credit unions are becoming more adept at offering competitive financial prices with local service. You can learn more about credit unions and the NCUA by visiting www.ncua.gov.

Make sure that you do not exceed the insured limit in any one account so that you are not caught with exposed assets. If you are worried, check out Bankrate.com, which has a list of at-risk banks for closure or failure. You can open different accounts in different institutions so that no one account has "too much money in one bank." In the banking crisis of 2007 and 2008, as well as the years after, many customers received less than 35 percent of the amount they had in bank accounts because their funds were over the insured limit when their bank was taken over by the FDIC. The FDIC only covers up to the insured limits of $250,000, and if your funds exceed the insured limit, they will come out of the bank's assets, and that was why some customers only received 35 percent of the amount over the insured limit.

You are responsible for your accounts and there is no regulation that requires banks or credit unions to warn you about the fact that you might have exceeded the insured amount in your accounts at their institution. Until laws are enacted requiring banks and credit unions to warn you, it is up to you to be vigilant in protecting all of your assets as much as possible; this is referred to as **CYA** (cover your assets).

Isn't it amazing that so-called senior advocacy groups such as AARP have never asked the government to enact a law to protect senior savings accounts and require banks and credit unions to provide full disclosure when their savings exceed the limits? Why hasn't AARP demanded this protection for seniors? In my opinion, AARP is way too involved in politics to worry about real individual senior issues.

The security associated with cash or bank products comes with a price, most cash or bank products earn a very low rate of return. Bankrate.com keeps track of a number of interest rates and yields, and most traditional savings accounts pay something between 0.10 percent and .95 percent as quoted at BankRate.com on October 2, 2014. Online savings accounts offer higher rates than those of local banks. Before the financial crisis of 2008, some online banks were offering yields of more than 5 percent on savings accounts.

Interest checking and money market accounts can offer even higher yields than online savings; in some cases rewards checking accounts are features of local banks and credit unions. To get the best yield on these banking products, it is a good idea to shop around. CDs can provide higher yields, and though you often have to put in more money and keep them for longer maturities, they pay higher rates[2].

Unlike many other cash products, CDs do come with penalties. Unless you have a penalty-free CD, you will be charged a fee if you withdraw your money before the maturity date arrives. Credit union accounts can sometimes result in higher rates of return and some local and regional banks may also offer higher rates of return than their national counterparts. It can be profitable to shop around for the best rates, whether at local banks or credit unions, and look for banks that offer bonuses when you sign up for an account. CDs

---

2Bankrate.com. Accessed April 3, 2010. Available online at http://www.bankrate.com/funnel/cd-investments/cd-investment-results.aspx?local=false&prods=26&tab=CD&ic_id=OA_RateSearch_1_CDs_26_5_Yr_Jumbo_CD_compare-rates.aspx_

issued by fully FDIC insured banks can be purchased through some brokers or registered investment advisors as well[3].

The low rate of return on most liquid cash investments over time erode in value from inflation that eats into your earnings from any investment. However, when that investment has a low rate of return, the effects of inflation are more apparent. For most of the 20th century (1914 to 2000), some estimates figure that inflation averaged about 3.5 percent annually[4]. And we can use this as a guide going forward. Inflation erodes the buying power of your money and reduces your actual returns. When you subtract inflation from your investment earnings, you end up with what economists call "real returns." We will discuss this term a lot in later chapters.

You may think that you are earning 4 percent on your CD, let's look at the facts:

$10,000.00 at 4 percent = $ 400.00 earnings, and inflation of 2.5 percent = - $250.00

The minimum federal tax rate is 15 percent and you earned 4 percent = .60 percent, or $60.00

So you got $400.00 minus $250 and - $60 so your NET RETURN = $90.00

Your Real Rate of Return is 0.90 percent($ 90.00), less than 1 percent

---

3Redeeming a brokered CD prior to maturity may result in a loss of principal due to fluctuations in the interest rate, lack of liquidity, or transaction costs. There is no FDIC insurance coverage for any principal losses that may be incurred.
4"Facts on Policy: Historical Inflation Rates," Hoover Institution, Stanford University. Available at http://www.hoover.org/research/factsonpolicy/facts/4804201.html.

If you are currently earning 1 percent or less on a savings account, once you factor in the loss of buying power due to inflation of 2.5 percent and income taxes of 15 percent, you are, in fact, losing money. How is that working for you?

THE EFFECT OF INFLATION ON PURCHASING POWER

As you can see, at the end of the year, you have more money in your account, but inflation has eroded the "real" value of that money and limited what you can purchase with it. The same is true even if you have a CD with a 5 percent annual rate, as you can see in the diagram below called: **Cash Investment Inflation Erosion**.

(Chart 3.1)

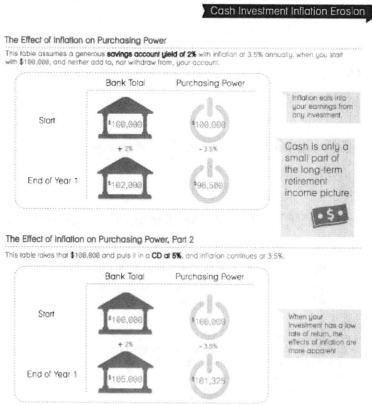

Cash Investment Inflation Erosion

The Effect of Inflation on Purchasing Power

This table assumes a generous **savings account yield of 2%** with inflation at 3.5% annually, when you start with $100,000, and neither add to, nor withdraw from, your account.

	Bank Total	Purchasing Power	
Start	$100,000	$100,000	Inflation eats into your earnings from any investment.
	+ 2%	- 3.5%	
End of Year 1	$102,000	$96,500	Cash is only a small part of the long-term retirement income picture.

The Effect of Inflation on Purchasing Power, Part 2

This table takes that **$100,000** and puts it in a **CD at 5%**, and inflation continues at 3.5%.

	Bank Total	Purchasing Power	
Start	$100,000	$100,000	When your investment has a low rate of return, the effects of inflation are more apparent.
	+ 2%	- 3.5%	
End of Year 1	$105,000	$101,325	

With the CD, your real returns aren't negative, as they are with a savings account. However, you didn't end up with the kind of yield you expected, either! Instead of gaining $5,000, you only ended up adding $1,325 in "real" money to your wealth.

You can see how yield from cash products can be slowed by inflation, and that doesn't even take into account the state and federal income taxes that you probably have to pay on your earnings, which will further erode the "real" value of your cash products. It is easy to see why investments that have the ability to outpace inflation can be a more profitable way to invest: You have much more left after accounting for inflation and taxes.

Cash investments do have their place, however. They can provide liquid funds that allow you to provide for emergencies. During times of economic upheaval, you can acquire a degree of peace of mind from having some of your investment portfolio in cash. However, in many cases, cash should not represent the bulk of your retirement investments. While having a money market checking account, or some other interest-bearing checking account, can be beneficial in terms of allowing you to earn a yield on money you use regularly, and CD laddering (see below) can be a great safety net, it is important to recognize that cash is only a small part of the long-term retirement income picture.

As of October 2, 2014 according to BankRate.com the best 1 year CD rate was .26 percent and the best 5 year was .84 percent

INCREASE YOUR CASH YIELD:
ALTERNATIVE CDS

Alternative CDs offer an interesting opportunity to see higher returns on cash. These are certificates of deposit that come with different rules that can result in higher yields.

(Chart 3.2)

Here are some of the higher yielding CDs that you might not have heard of:

1. **Bump-up CDs:** At some banks, if you get the right CD, you can "bump up" your interest rate if there is an increase on the CD yield. For instance, if the bank begins offering the same CD for 3 percent, and you've been getting 2.5 percent, you might have the option to renew automatically at 3 percent. Make sure you read the fine print, though. Some banks will let you bump up partway through the term, penalty-free, and others require you to wait until the CD matures to get the bump-up.

2. **Callable CDs:** These interesting CDs allow the bank to close the CD after a certain period of protection. To lure

savers into these products, callable CDs often have higher interest rates. Before you agree, make sure you know the length of the protection term.

3. **Brokerage CDs:** If you want to be able to sell your CD on the secondary market, you might consider a brokerage CD. You generally receive higher rates of returns on these CDs, since you have more banks to choose from. Additionally, you can recoup your deposit without the interest rate penalty when you sell on the secondary market before the CD matures. Be careful, though. A brokerage CD may not be FDIC insured[5], and sometimes they have a market value adjustment. In a rising rate environment, the surrender charges can be very high.

4. **Alternative rate CDs:** These are five- to seven-year CDs that are FDIC insured. Sometimes they have a fixed rate minimum such as 1 percent, but also offer an indexed account, like the S&P index, so they could yield a higher rate. They usually require you to take the interest earnings every year which cannot be reinvested back into the CD. This can be an excellent investment for someone who does not want to take the risk of a loss but wants a chance for gain while always staying FDIC insured.

5. **CD Laddering:** This is a way to always have liquid funds but to get a higher rate than money market funds. For example, you have $100,000, so you buy a one-year CD every month for $10,000 until you have 12 CDs with one coming due every month, and you always have $10,000 of liquid funds every month, but you receive a much

---

5Redeeming a brokered CD prior to maturity may result in a loss of principal due to fluctuations in the interest rate, lack of liquidity, or transaction costs. There is no FDIC insurance coverage for any principal losses that may be incurred.

higher rate on all of your funds. Currently, local money market funds are at 0.20 percent and a one-year CD is at 1 percent, so by using this strategy you would get five times the earnings and all insured by FDIC.

Cash or bank-insured products can be a reasonably safe addition to your investment portfolio and a good place to keep an emergency fund. Cash is especially comforting to those with low risk tolerance. However, it is important to carefully consider your cash investment options so that you can maximize your returns, and you should beware the insidious and wealth-draining effects of inflation.

HOW SAFE IS YOUR MONEY IN A BANK?

Our government decided to make 10 banks too big to fail, which, in plain language, means there wouldn't be enough in FDIC funds to cover your FDIC savings deposits if one of these banks were to fail. Currently, these 10 banks control in excess of 77 percent of *all* bank assets.

Isn't the FDIC designed to protect your savings in case of bank default? Well, if your bank is too big to fail, the Federal Reserve System (FED) just prints more money. Who pays for it? You do! Well, in reality, your children and grandchildren are the ones who will be paying your bill.

In my opinion, our government caused the banking crisis of 2008, just as it did the savings and loan crisis in the 80s and early 90s, but it always has a partner and this partner is known as the big banks, usually the largest contributors to politicians' campaigns.

Why isn't Congress or the President held accountable when their actions affect the economy or why isn't their fat pension put in jeopardy the way our Social Security funds have been? It's because we let them get away with it.

In my opinion, the repeal of the Glass-Steagall Act in 1999 created the banking crisis of 2008. I am not the only one who believes this, and it is based on facts, not propaganda techniques that you hear every night on local TV stations! Read the information below and gain knowledge that most Americans have no clue about. Remember, what you don't know can hurt you.

> The oldest propaganda technique is to repeat a lie emphatically and often until it is taken for the truth. Something like this is going on now with regard to banks and the financial crisis. The big bank boosters and analysts who should know better are repeating the falsehood that the repeal of Glass-Steagall had nothing to do with the panic of 2008.
>
> In fact, the financial crisis might not have happened at all but for the 1999 repeal of the Glass-Steagall law that separated commercial and investment banking for seven decades. If there is any hope of avoiding another meltdown, it's critical to understand why the Glass-Steagall repeal helped to cause the crisis and without a return to something like Glass-Steagall, another catastrophe, a greater one, is just a matter of time.

It is very difficult for ordinary Americans to get a handle on just how large these financial institutions are; for example, the big six US Banks banks (Goldman Sachs, Morgan Stanley, J. P. Morgan Chase, Citigroup, Bank of America, and Wells Fargo) now possess assets equivalent to approximately 60 percent of America's gross national product.

JAMES RICKARDS

"REPEAL OF GLASS-STEAGALL CAUSED THE FINANCIAL CRISIS"

James G. Rickards is an American lawyer, economist, and investment banker. Also a writer and regular commentator on finance, Rickards has been advising clients of an impending financial collapse. Go online, read this article and gain some knowledge. It is power, and over 50 percent of Americans do not know these facts. Don't believe me?

Just ask your neighbor what the Glass-Steagall Act was and see what they say.

You should also check out Malcolm Berko, a syndicated writer who can be reached at mjberko@yahoo.com. He wrote an article dated June 24, 2011 titled "Glass-Steagall Act's Repeal Contributed to Financial Crisis," and here is the closing paragraph of his response to a reader's question, but you must read his article and educate yourself, because we always end up paying for the stupid things our politicians do.

And what these commentators are telling you
is that it was the repeal of the Glass-Steagall Act that

contributed enormously to our financial crisis, not the act itself. Allowing these Wall Street banks to continue feeding their greed is destroying our democracy, our economy, our retirement plans, and our freedoms.

As of **August 27, 2014 the United States was over $17.685 trillion in deb**t according to <ins>http://www.usdebtclock.org/</ins>, and you and I are on the hook to pay off this debt! The only ones who can stop this madness are our politicians and they won't as long as stupid voters put them back into office. We can decide to vote only for those who will use financial restraint in spending and save our country from a total collapse.

We have the best politicians money can buy, and they are all bought and paid for, and while this reckless spending goes on, where was the AARP? Where were our news reporters, ABC, NBC, CBS? Where was either political party?

Are we really this stupid? Apparently we are, since more and more economists are realizing that the next big bubble could well be the government bubble, due to overspending, and underfunding issues like Social Security, Medicare, and government pensions are heading for a crash. There is no accountability in our government or among politicians since they will continue to get their pensions when our Social Security is reduced or stopped.

Insanity is defined as **"Doing the same thing over and over and expecting a different outcome."** This sounds like Americans voting for the same politicians over and over, expecting they will do the right thing. Wake up, America, and stop voting for incumbents; **they are the problem.**

CHAPTER 4

BONDS

The concept behind bonds is simple: You lend money to some organization, and that organization pays you interest on your investment until the bond matures sometime in the future and you get back your original investment. Most bonds pay you a fixed rate of interest during the term of the bond, which means you receive an interest payment at regular intervals (monthly, quarterly, semiannually, or annually).

When the bond matures, the organization repays the face value of the bond, returning your principal to you. It is worth noting that the longer the term of the bond, the higher the rate of return in general. If you are willing to lend your money out for a longer period of time, restricting your access to it and accepting only interest payments, then you are likely to earn a higher rate of return over time.

The main risk you have with bond investment is that the organization may default on its obligations, leaving you with only the interest that has been paid to you up to that point. Bonds are just like CDs, offering a fixed interest rate for a certain period until maturity, but the big difference is that bonds are not FDIC insured.

Bonds, generally, earn a better rate than cash. Adding bonds to your portfolio can result in regular income from the interest payments and can also help you protect your assets by reducing the chance that you will have to tap into your core capital to make ends meet. The point of earning a yield is to try to avoid spending your principal. Inflation, taxes, and the fact that you have to withdraw money regularly can eat into your returns. The table below illustrates a hypothetical comparison between cash and bonds, and your potential gains over the course of 10 years if you start with $100,000.

TABLE 1: HYPOTHETICAL YIELD OF CASH VERSUS BONDS[6]

Starting with $100,000 assumes a generous cash investment gain of 3 percent and a bond gain of 6 percent annually; however, this table does not take into account inflation and taxes, which will erode the value of your gains. Also not considered is the fact that you withdraw money regularly and cash and bond yields fluctuate with market conditions and do not remain steady, but once you purchase a bond, the rate is fixed until maturity of the bond or called if the bond has a call feature.

This table is intended for illustrative purposes only.

You can see that there is a difference of more than $40,000 over the course of 10 years, and that's just with the simplest of calculations. You can also see how having that extra money would be helpful as you combat inflation and withdraw your money. With the cash column, it is easy to see how spending all of your interest could easily result in digging into your core capital once inflation and taxes take their toll. Adding in some bonds can help provide a higher yield.

6The table is designed to illustrate mathematical compounding principles and is not indicative of the performance of any specific investment.

(Table 4.1)

END OF YEAR	AMOUNT IN CASH (ROUNDED TO NEAREST DOLLAR)	AMOUNT IN BONDS (ROUNDED TO NEAREST DOLLAR)
1	$103,000	$106,00
2	$106,090	$112,360
3	$109,273	$119,102
4	$112,551	$126,248
5	$115,927	$133,823
6	$119,405	$141,852
7	$122,987	$150,363
8	$126,677	$159,385
9	$130,477	$168,948
10	$134,391	$179,085

Although they are not FDIC-insured, bonds are still considered investments on the conservative end, presenting a lower risk to your principal. Bonds can also reduce the likelihood that you will have to begin using your core capital to make ends meet.

There are four main entities that can sell bonds to you:

FEDERAL GOVERNMENT

In order to fund its programs and processes, the federal government borrows from a number of sources, including individuals. You lend money to the government when you buy US Treasury securities. You receive a fixed rate of interest, and you get the principal back at the maturity date. Treasury bonds are very versatile, and it is possible to choose maturities ranging from one year to 30 years.

You can purchase federal bonds through a broker, or you can do it yourself using Treasury Direct, available at www.treasurydirect.gov. You can set up your own account and manage your US Treasury purchases. When you use electronic certificates, without asking for a paper certificate, you can begin investing in US Treasury bonds with as little as $25.

US Treasury bonds are backed by what is generally considered to be the most stable taxpayer base in the world. Because these bonds are often considered to have the lowest amount of risk and you can get them just about anywhere, it is little surprise that they offer some of the lowest yields. As of August 4, 2014, a 30-year Treasury bond was yielding 3.30 percent, and that is still enough to beat inflation

If you are looking for capital preservation, Treasury investments are among the best you can choose. The last high point was on January 17, 2000. The 30-year Treasury bond was yielding 6.7090 percent, and during times of economic turmoil, many investors turn to these investments in order to maintain their capital. You will see the yields drop as demand increases. When the economic climate is good, US Treasury bonds offer higher yields in order to attract investors[7]. Wouldn't you like to own some of those Treasury Bonds today?

If you are concerned about US Treasury bonds yielding enough to beat future inflation, especially if you worry about hyperinflation, you can turn to I-bonds or TIPS. Both of these US Treasury products are inflation protected, meaning that the yield grows along with inflation, and it is one way to protect your core capital from the ravages of inflation.

---

7 Treasuries can fluctuate and if redeemed prior to maturity, may be worth more or less than the original amount invested.

However, there are restrictions on the amounts individuals can purchase and limits on the amount of your portfolio that is inflation protected. Nevertheless, having a portion of your portfolio in inflation-protected securities can provide a solid capital base.

At one point our government was printing monthly $85 billion, and that will be reduced down to $25 billion as of August 2014, but there will still be a day of reckoning for the American tax payer, but who knows when? Just look at Japan and its 20-year recession and we are heading down the same path like a freight train out of control.

In my opinion, the QE strategy is a recipe for long-term disaster and the proof is that we are following in the footsteps of Japan since we are in our 13th year of a long-term bear market or recession, and contrary to the opinion of many, we have not recovered! Time will tell if I am right or if quantitative easing (QE) is the answer. Of course, it has never worked anywhere in the world so far, making it a dangerous strategy to rely on. Just take a look at the following actual headline: **"Japan launches QE 8 as 20-year slump drags on" by Ambrose Evans-Pritchard, The Telegraph, Wednesday, September 19, 2012.**

This headline is important because our federal government is following the same path as Japan. Doesn't it seem a little crazy to think you can just print money you don't have and everything will magically work out and debt will just disappear? How's it working for Japan? How is it working for us?

MUNICIPAL OR STATE GOVERNMENT BONDS

Cities and states also need to raise capital to meet their expenses. Many municipal bonds are free of federal taxes and free of state taxes to purchasers who reside in the same state where the bonds were issued[8]. Federal bonds are not free of taxes, but many city and state bonds come with tax advantages. It is important to carefully consider the implications. While generally considered to have little risk, municipal and state bonds are thought to be riskier than federal bonds.

Before you invest in these types of bonds, in order to take advantage of tax savings, it is important to consider your situation. As a general rule, tax-free bonds offer the most benefit to those who pay 25 percent or more of their income in federal taxes. In some cases, tax-free bonds pay a lower rate of income, which means that the tax savings are the primary reason for investing in them. If you are below the 25 percent tax bracket, chances are that you can do better with higher-yield bonds, even if you have to pay taxes on the gains. A financial professional or tax professional can help you assess your situation.

With the recent collapse and bankruptcy of Detroit, can Michigan be far behind? What about California? At this point, you need to be very careful about which municipalities you invest in and their ability to keep paying on their bonds. Always consult with your CPA or tax advisor before investing in tax-free bonds because they just might not be tax-free to you based on your income and/or depending on the type of tax-free bond. Buyer beware and ask first.

This could be the next big bubble to burst. What if the federal government has to bail out city and state governments by printing even more money we do not have? Stay tuned ...

8Income may be subject to state and local taxes and, in some cases, the alternative minimum tax.

FOREIGN GOVERNMENT BONDS

In this world of increased globalization, it is possible for you to invest in foreign bonds. You can purchase bonds to help fund the operations of other countries and even regions or towns. These bonds vary in risk with emerging market bonds often viewed as carrying a higher chance of default. With the higher risk, though, comes the chance of higher returns.

Many foreign bonds come with higher yields than domestic bonds. In some countries, including China, India, Brazil, and some Eastern European countries, it is possible to find bonds with very high yields. While China has reached a point where it is almost considered safe to purchase Chinese bonds, there are still risks associated with foreign bonds.

Another consideration with foreign bonds is the fluctuation that occurs in the currency market since foreign currencies change relative to the value of the US dollar, which can affect how much you end up with overall when the bond reaches maturity. Be sure to consider the exchange rate of any foreign bonds you might have approach maturity. At this point, there isn't a country in the world that is on solid economic ground. It is true we are in the best financial shape, but we are still heading the wrong way since the US debt is over 105 percent of GDP and the debt of Japan—the world leader, in its 20th year of recession—is over 230 percent of GDP. **How much longer can our countries go until this theory is proven not to work?**

You can't spend and borrow your way to prosperity, and anyone who says you can is an idiot and history has proven this time and time again.

Our federal government, including both political parties, just doesn't get it. The US government has been going into debt every year since Lyndon Johnson was president, and we just keep digging a deeper hole. Do we really want a 20-year recession like that of Japan? The people we keep electing to office are putting us on that path and we just keep putting them back into office; who is the idiot?

CORPORATE BONDS

The first three types of organization that offer bonds are all government entities. It is also possible for companies to issue bonds. Corporations often need to raise capital to fund their operations, and bonds are a way to do so at a relatively low cost. Corporate bonds work the same way as other bonds: You receive regular interest payments and get the principal back upon maturity.

Be aware that many corporate bonds also often come with a call feature, which gives the company the right to pay back the face value of the bond after a certain number of years. For example, you may get a corporate bond from IBM for 10 years, but IBM may have the right to call that bond in seven years. This means that after seven years, IBM has the right to pay you off and return your original investment.

You still get your principal back, and any interest you have received to that point, but you won't get as much as you had anticipated since IBM is paying you back early in order to save money. It's the same reasoning you use if you pay off an auto loan or a mortgage early. If a corporation pays off the bond early without the call option, you normally get a small premium.

Until the financial crisis of 2008, corporate bonds were generally considered to be very low-risk investments. However, some doubt has been shed on them. In the grand scheme of things, corporate bonds can be a viable alternative, although there is always the risk that default or bankruptcy could erode the value of your investments. But the result of the recent turmoil has had a positive effect on corporate bonds, at least from an investor standpoint: Companies are having to pay more in interest as a result of the higher perceived risk of corporate bonds.

BOND RATINGS

When it comes to selecting a bond, one of the biggest issues of concern is determining whether or not you are investing in a higher quality bond. The higher the quality of the bond, the more reliable the borrower is expected to be in repaying the loan. This is known as credit worthiness, and investing in bonds with higher credit worthiness means that you are more likely to get all of your money back. Ratings agencies evaluate bonds offered by different organizations. These ratings agencies evaluate different bond issuers, comparing them to one another and to their own past performance and expected performance.

While many bond ratings agencies exist, the two that are considered the most credible are Moody's and Standard & Poor's. These ratings agencies do not actually insure or guarantee the bonds they rate. Rather, they evaluate the issuer's ability to repay the debt holder. The highest possible rating is AAA.

US Treasury bonds are rated AAA, and so are some other government bonds from well-established countries. Some municipal bonds are also highly rated. The recent financial crisis has forced ratings agencies to take into account different shadings with the AAA rating, and some countries are being relegated to the lower end of AAA due to increased government debt, without actually losing that highest rating. Britain and the United States are good examples of countries that have been reduced to the bottom of the AAA pile. Greece received a true downgrade recently. So, even though these are sovereign countries, their debt is still rated and assigned to a category.

TABLE 2.2: HIERARCHY OF INVESTMENT-GRADE AND NON-INVESTMENT-GRADE BONDS

(Chart 4.2)

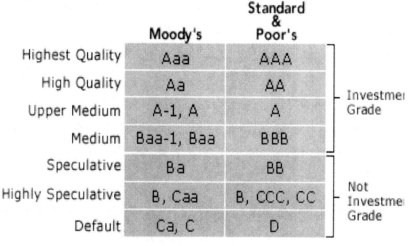

	Moody's	Standard & Poor's	
Highest Quality	Aaa	AAA	Investment Grade
High Quality	Aa	AA	
Upper Medium	A-1, A	A	
Medium	Baa-1, Baa	BBB	
Speculative	Ba	BB	Not Investment Grade
Highly Speculative	B, Caa	B, CCC, CC	
Default	Ca, C	D	

Image obtained from fidelity.com

When looking at bonds, most conservatives choose those labeled "investment grade." These bonds run from AAA at the top to BBB at the lower end of the investment grade. It is important to note that bond ratings can change, and they do not eliminate the inherent market risk that exists with any investment. Additionally, it is vital to realize that even though AAA is the highest credit rating a bond issuer can be assigned, it does not guarantee that the issuer will repay the principal or pay the interest agreed upon.

AA bonds are usually those offered by large corporations and are considered almost as safe as AAA bonds. However, it is important to note that the lower a bond is on the hierarchy, the less safe it is considered. In addition, as with all investments, the safer something is rated, the lower the return it typically offers. What that means is that even though you are more likely to get your principal back with an AAA or AA rated company or country bond, you will not see spectacular returns.

Another important point to keep in mind is that ratings agencies have flaws in their methodologies. We saw with CDOs and CMOs (the derivatives you heard so much about during the financial crisis of 2008) that the AAA bond rating can be given, even if the underlying assets are less than investment grade. Another concern is that corporations pay ratings agencies for their ratings, and that can compromise the objectivity of the ratings. The fact that the methodologies used by ratings agencies have flaws, and the fact that ratings agencies do not insure the bonds they rate, should be considerations when investing in bonds. That's a reason not to rely entirely on ratings, even though ratings can be helpful in making investment decisions.

In order to boost returns, some will choose noninvestment-grade bonds. These bonds offer higher rates of returns because investors are taking on higher risk. Most investors looking for growth in their portfolios will do their best to stick with bonds that have at least a BB or B rating. Just because a company has a BB rating doesn't mean it's not worth looking into. Some companies with household names actually have ratings of BB. Emerging market countries with ratings of CCC and lower often provide interesting chances for higher bond returns. You just have to be able to stomach the risk that comes with the higher possibility of default. Ratings can change after they have been issued, and ratings agencies regularly reevaluate the financial situations of different companies. See the definition of junk bonds below.

As companies see changes in profits, and in the amount of debt that they have, it is common for them to see differences in ratings. Even governments can see changes to their bond ratings. So, before investing in a bond, it is a good idea to consider a number of factors before making a decision. After all, as GM bond holders can tell you, a rating can change a great deal over the years, or even over a period of months or days.

DEFINITION OF JUNK BOND

Junk bond is a colloquial term for a high-yield or non-invest-ment-grade bond. Junk bonds are fixed-income instruments that carry a Standard & Poor's rating of BB or lower, or a rating of Ba or below by Moody's. Junk bonds are so called because of their higher default risk in relation to investment-grade bonds.

LEAVING BONDS TO YOUR HEIRS

It can be tempting to choose only short-term bonds in some cases, certain that you will outlive the bond maturity. You might not want to leave non-mature bonds to your heirs. However, while you might worry about any inconvenience you are causing, you must take care of your needs first. Your goal should be to ensure that you have enough core capital to keep earning adequate income during retirement. Your life expectancy may only be 10 more years, but you could conceivably live another 15 years, or even 20 years. Longer-term bonds that can continue to provide you with interest income can offer a good choice for you during retirement. At the same time, it is important to think about liquidity needs during retirement. If you need to access bond principal for some of your expenses, a mix of short-term bonds should also be included in order to help you avoid the penalties associated with redeeming a bond early.

There is a market for bonds, so even if you do pass on before the bond matures, your heirs can decide what to do with any bonds that are left. They can collect the interest, and the principal when it matures, or they can sell it on the open market. You can also sell your bond on the open market if you think that is a wiser decision, but if interest rates have risen since the initial purchase, the amount redeemed might be less than the original amount invested. While it's nice to consider the convenience of your heirs, it is essential to make the investment decisions that are best for your situation. If it is important to your estate plan, you should also note that some bonds have an estate feature that pays the full value of the bond at death.

ADDITIONAL RESOURCES

SIFMA "Investing in Bonds"

FINRA Bond Market Center

FINRA, http://www.finra.org/

In my opinion, contrary to that of many economists and so-called experts on TV and on the radio, "not all bonds are created equal." So-called junk bonds actually move more in line with equities or the stock market and do not move in the opposite direction to the interest rates of the day. Unfortunately, many so-called economists ignore facts, but not with their own money. This is more evidence that financial TV shows and radio shows, as well as some articles, are written in half-truths. Don't follow the flock like sheep.

Most of my clients are either retired or about to retire and they just do not like to lose their money. For them, we have several managed bond portfolios (fee-based accounts). One such portfolio has not had a loss in the last 18 years, and another one has not had a loss in the last 22 years, as of July 9, 2014. This includes all expenses and fees. So, just remember that not all bonds are created equal. We cannot guarantee future results on past earnings. The fact is that bonds have outperformed the S&P 500 index as well as the Dow Jones Industrial Average (DJIA) for the first 14 years of this century and there is nothing I see coming to change that for the next seven to 10 years. Things have changed in the investment world. Have you?

Beware of those who want you out of all bond exposure. It's true that what you don't know can hurt you, but it's even worse when advisors don't know. Usually, they just want to sell you an annuity. They don't really understand how things should be working in your portfolio. Now you do.

Check the numbers and the history before you cash out; sometimes, getting out of a 6 percent bond is not better than transferring your funds into an annuity at 3.5 to 5 percent, is it?

Over the last 14 years, many money-managed bond portfolios have actually outperformed the S&P 500 index (growth funds) or the DJIA Index (stability) by three to four times the net return and two to three times the net return of fixed indexed annuities (guaranteed income), but none of these compare to an actively managed bond portfolio when it comes to investment net return.

Look at the numbers of high-yield performance in a rising rate environment:

(Table 4.3)

PERIOD	10 YR. TREASURY YIELD MOVE	HIGH YIELD BONDS	LEVERAGED LOANS	INVESTMENT GRADE BONDS
AUG 86 - SEPT 87	+267 bps	10.60%	N/A	1.96%
SEP 93 TO NOV 94	+263 bps	1.82%	13.38%	-3.78%
DEC 95 TO AUG 96	+153 bps	6.57%	6.11%	-0.52%
SEP 98 TO JAN 00	+225 bps	5.21%	6.08%	1.80%
MAY 05 - JUNE 06	+177 bps	32.71%	21.22%	9.79%
DEC 08 TO DEC 09	+163 bps	69.28%	47.14%	26.41%
OCT 10 - FEB 11	+127 bps	4.78%	5.46%	-3.08%

Sources: Bloomberg, Credit Suisse, and BofA Merrill Lynch; High Yield Bonds: BofA Merrill Lynch High Yield Master II Index; Leveraged Loans: Credit Suisse Leveraged Loan Index; Investment Grade Bonds: BofA Merrill Lynch US Corporate Master Index

This table isn't meant to sell you anything but rather to show that sometimes you are only hearing half of the story. Sometimes, that half is slanted to sell you something, or to persuade you to sell something so you can reinvest. Could it be that someone isn't making any money from what you currently own?

For those who want to learn more, we also offer the white paper "Investment Risk versus Investment Return." It is available on my website at www.AskTheFinancialDoctor.com. Below is a highlight of that white paper:

> The premise of this section is that most advisors and certainly most investors do not understand the dynamics between risk taken versus expected investment return. As stated, most investors are taking far too much risk in their portfolios for the expected return. It really boils down to whether you agree with the following statement: "Investors should take the least amount of risk to reach their investment goals."
>
> In other words, why would someone invest in something more risky if the potential return is the same as a lower-risk investment? No sane person would do so. What needs to be done next is to figure out how to measure the risk of an investment. It is not as simple as it sounds. It is not possible here to cover the many different ways the investment industry measures the risk of an investment. I've chosen to cover some of the main ways the investment industry measures risk and a few ways that it should but are not widely used.
>
> ("Investment Risk vs. Investment Return" by Roccy DeFrancesco, J.D., CWPP, CAPP, CMP, founder of Wealth Preservation Institute, co-founder of Asset Protection Society)

For a complete reading of this white paper, please go to www.pfgwm.com and click on Articles.

(Chart 4.4)

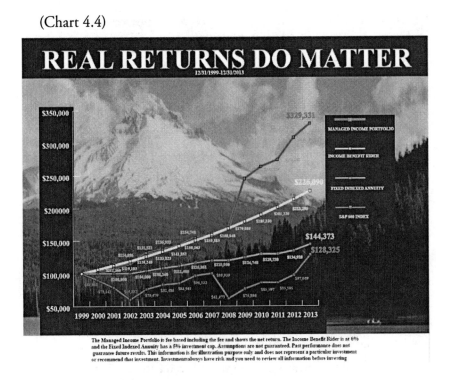

REAL RETURNS DO MATTER
12/31/1999-12/31/2013

The Managed Income Portfolio is fee based including the fee and shows the net return. The Income Benefit Rider is at 6% and the Fixed Indexed Annuity has a 5% investment cap. Assumptions are not guaranteed. Past performance does not guarantee future results. This information is for illustration purpose only and does not represent a particular investment or recommend that investment. Investments always have risk and you need to review all information before investing

The Top Line is a managed income portfolio that has a 2.75 percent fee associated with it and the line reflects the net return and shows values net of all fees.

The 2nd Line reflects a fixed indexed annuity with a guaranteed income benefit rate of 6 percent, so the value goes up every year by 6 percent.

The 3rd line reflects the Cash Value of that Fixed Indexed Annuity and includes the 1% annual fee for the 6 percent Income Benefit Rider.

The 4th line reflects the S & P 500 Index which is one of the lowest cost investments you can buy.

These numbers are not guarantees of future returns and only reflect what happened during the period from Dec. 31, 1999, to Dec. 31, 2013.

If, you look at the chart on the previous page 61 and the chart on page 111 of the S & P 500 it is very clear to see that our stock market changed with the new century and the start of Y2K our markets became world markets and not just the US economy.

Once and for all time understand that Bill Clinton did not leave office until January 20, 2001 and George Bush took over an economy that was clearly in trouble, then add 9/11 and war and the reality is, it all started under Bill Clinton, this is a FACT...look at the graphs.

The point here is the Democrat's have blamed Bush for an economy he inherited from Bill Clinton, but the press covered up the facts and the Republican's are too stupid to refute the facts , but these graphs clearly show the markets started down while Clinton was in office, so President Barrack O'bama needs to blame Bill Clinton as well as George Bush, of course unfortunately for Barrack O'bama he made it worse.

CHAPTER 5

STOCKS

For many, retirement is the time to liquidate stocks and buy bonds, or put money into cash investments or annuities. However, stocks can still be an important part of your retirement portfolio even though you may not see a lot of income from all of your stocks. If you plan to outlive your money, it is important to realize that some of your core capital is needed for growth potential. If you retire at age 65, there is a chance you could live for another 25 to 30 years, or even longer.

Medical technology is advancing to such a degree that it is likely you will live longer than you had expected. You need to be prepared with assets that grow in value and can keep pace with an ever-increasing cost of living. Growth investments are a vital part of the retirement investing portfolio, and stocks are some of the most popular and understandable growth investments available.

There is no question in my mind that investing in individual stocks is the fastest way to create wealth, but it also can be very risky. Proceed with care when investing in individual stocks.

Stocks provide a growth opportunity that no other investment can match with a relatively small investment and you can make trades for as little as $7.95 a trade. Stocks offer you significantly better inflation protection, as well as growth opportunities.

However, it is important to note that the growth opportunities provided by stocks come at the price of increased volatility. Bonds offer lower returns, but they have typically experienced lower volatility. It is important to assess your individual needs in order to determine how much volatility your portfolio can handle.

Recognizing the growth potential of stocks is an important part of retirement investing. You want investments with growth potential that work a little harder with your money so that if you were to live longer than you had expected, that portion of your core capital will have provided greater returns to ensure you live comfortably. In many cases, it is a good idea to periodically take the interest you earn from growth investments and shift it into your portfolio's income portion. However, if you can help it, you should avoid touching the core capital you are using for stock investments.

Stocks grow in value over time, and generally, they have done very well in the long term. It is important not to get caught up in the occasional bad years. It's hard to ignore the noise of the financial press and others panicking about what is happening in the stock market. However, moving your money around with the whims of day-to-day volatility is costly. You incur transaction fees, and unfortunately, while you are constantly shifting your holdings about in response to hysterical predictions, you might actually miss the perfect time to buy, which is when stocks are very low in price. While many consider stocks as a quick way to get rich, the truth is that for retirement investing, a long-term approach is sounder.

That means that, sometimes, you must be prepared to stay invested in the market through bad years, such as 2008, and you should be aware that, over time, stocks, generally, make money. After the crash of 2008, many quality stocks recovered in 18 to 24 months, while it took over five and a half years for the market and most mutual funds to get back to their highs. Of course, when we discuss managed portfolios, you will find that there are some very good alternatives to staying in the market and waiting for the rebound. Many of us feel that buying and holding is just not working. If you are retired or close to retiring, you just can't wait five or six years to recover.

PREFERRED SHARES (PREFERRED STOCK)

One of the more difficult investments to classify is the preferred share, also referred to as preferred stock. These shares are classified as equity on corporate balance sheets, but they have some similar features to bonds. In fact, Standard & Poor's ranks preferred shares in a similar manner to bonds. You earn a return on these shares, but there is no set maturity rate. Instead, you own them until you decide to sell them elsewhere, or until the issuing corporation calls them back. Sometimes preferred stock is converted to regular stock at a predetermined price.

Most preferred shares come with some sort of call feature. The conditions under which a preferred share can be recalled by the issuer are set forth when you purchase the preferred shares. While many preferred shares simply let you collect interest for as long as you like, or have a call feature that returns the original value of the share to you after five or ten years, there are variations in the way call features work. You might find that the share you bought for $30 can be called back a year later for $25. This means that you are granting the corporation the right to pay you less for the share than you paid for it. Normally, though, organizations that do this pay a high dividend to make up for it.

Preferred shares pay quarterly dividends and can provide a good source of regular income, in many cases. There are also adjustable-rate preferred shares that will keep pace with the market, paying out dividends that are based upon US Treasury bond rates. This means that as interest rates rise and fall, so does your income. However, it is possible to look for preferred shares with a minimum rate so that you are guaranteed a certain income. A minimum rate adjustable preferred share can help you hedge against falling interest rates while, at the same time, leave you open to earn more when interest rates rise.

Preferred shares also offer interesting opportunities to earn regular dividends. As long as you check the call feature, and you and your financial advisor agree that they can make a valuable addition to your portfolio, they can be integrated into your retirement portfolio as an income investment.

Perhaps the most famous of all purchases of preferred stock came when Warren Buffett declared the market crash of 2008 was over and invested $5 billion in Bank of America stock, recommending that investors get back into the markets. The fact was, however, that it was really Bank of America preferred stock he was buying. It had a guaranteed 6 percent interest rate and was convertible to regular stock at the market price of that stock at the time of conversion. Ultimately, what was his real risk with a bank that is too big to fail? Absolutely zero. Why can't you and I do that?

How would you like to invest in a stock with a guaranteed 6 percent interest rate and be able to sell it later since you had purchased it at a historically low common stock price? Can you say "guaranteed winner?"

It is a shame, and a scam on the American investor, to compete in a stacked deck against wealthy, politically connected billionaires like Warren Buffett. No ordinary person would have been offered that deal, and most honest people would say it was probably the largest insider trade of all time. Worst of all, no one went to jail or even was fined.

Was anybody home at the SEC? This goes on all the time in Washington DC, and if you don't believe me, you should read the book *Throw Them All Out* by Peter Schweizer.

You should also read his book *Extortion: How Politicians Extract Your Money, Buy Votes, and Line Their Own Pockets*. Published on October 22, 2013, this book describes a bombshell investigation revealing how Washington really works: Politicians extort money from us and use it to buy one another's votes.

You need to read these two books to see how corrupt both parties have become. The good news is we can band together to change this. You have to get mad enough to make a difference. Visit our website www.AsktheFinancialDoctor.com and sign one or more of our petitions to stop this activity in America now.

DIVIDEND INVESTING

While stocks are generally viewed as investments that provide growth, they can also offer income potential. There are stocks that pay dividends. Many companies designate a portion of their profits as dividends. Shareholders receive an extra cash payout monthly, quarterly, semiannually, or annually, in proportion to the number of shares that they own. Corporations can also issue special dividends at any time they feel they are warranted. While it is possible to issue store credit or additional shares to settle dividends, most organizations just pay cash.

If you decide to take advantage of dividend-paying stocks, you will receive a regular income in addition to the growth potential of a stock you own, and then sell it down the road. You are likely to see most dividends at between 2 and 4 percent. Some companies may pay less, or more, depending on how they feel they are doing. During times of economic trouble, though, you are likely to see your dividends drop.

Some companies reduce their payouts in order to keep more of the profits. However, there are a few companies that actually increase dividends, even in times of recession. These companies are either doing quite well, or they are increasing their payout in the hopes of luring investors and their capital. While dividend income can be a solid part of your investment portfolio, it is important to remember that it can fluctuate, and you might find your dividends cut just when you need them the most. Make sure that you have a properly balanced portfolio in order to make up for this.

DRIPS

If you aren't overly concerned about receiving regular income from your dividend-paying stocks, you can take advantage of dividend reinvestment programs (DRIPs). A DRIP automatically takes your dividend payment and reinvests it in company stock, usually without a transaction fee. Many DRIPs are administered by the companies themselves, so you buy in directly. However, there are some brokerages that can help you invest in DRIPs as well. When you take advantage of a DRIP, you are basically adding more stock for free. These additional shares add to your overall returns, usually at a greater rate than if you took the money and invested it in a cash vehicle.

For those who are in the years leading up to retirement, DRIPs can provide a helpful way to grow a portfolio. They can also be useful, for a time, in the growth portion of a retirement portfolio. Some online brokerages will waive DRIP transaction fees, but not all do. Make sure that your reinvestment truly is free.

Under current law, qualified dividends are taxed at a lower rate than interest from bonds or CDs. You should always check with your tax advisor or CPA. These laws can change from year to year.

CHOOSING STOCK INVESTMENTS

Before purchasing an individual stock, you must read two books by Harry S. Dent Jr.: *Spending Waves: The Scientific Key to Predicting Market Behavior for the Next 20 Years* and *The Demographic Cliff: How to Survive and Prosper during the Great Deflation of 2014–2019.*

One of the most difficult investment decisions can be which stock or stocks to buy. When deciding on stocks, it is often a good idea to consider the long-term potential of the company. Look at the management of the company, its financial situation, and its growth prospects. Solid companies will often provide smaller returns than riskier companies, but the returns are usually a little more consistent. For those with low risk tolerance, the stocks of solid companies can provide adequate growth, without causing undue risk, and minimize recovery time in adverse markets.

If you want a little more growth, you can consider stocks with small market capitalization, or stocks in sectors such as technology and green energy, which are expected to take off. You are taking a chance, though, and it can help reduce your risk of loss if you research where the companies get their funding, how the companies are run, and their potential for growth and likelihood of success[9].

Another way to help increase the chances of success with stock investing is to have a system. Your system can be anything from using a money manager or financial advisor to manage your stock investments to using dollar cost averaging or using preset systems and technical analysis. No system is foolproof, but using a system is a good way to reduce the emotion that goes into your investment decisions. This is vital, since emotion can get in the way of rational and profitable stock investing.

Buying when a stock is "hot" normally means that it is already near its peak. If you buy when everyone else is buying, chances are that you already missed the optimum time to buy. Likewise, panic selling when everyone else is selling is a sure-fire way to guarantee that you will violate the time-tested first rule of investing, which is to buy low and sell high. Before you sell out of concern for last month's stock market performance, take a look at your investment. If the fundamentals haven't changed, or they have changed very little (assuming they were solid in the first place), chances are that the investment will weather the current downturn.

9Investments in a specific industry or sector such as small cap may be subject to a higher degree of market risk than funds whose investments are more diversified.

There are known knowns; there are things we
know that we know. There are known unknowns. That
is to say, there are things that we now know we don't
know. But there are also unknown unknowns; there are
things we do not know we don't know. (–US Secretary
of Defense Donald Rumsfeld)

Before you buy an individual stock, ask yourself the following questions:

1. Do you personally use this company's products or service?
2. What is the future of this product or service?
3. What do the demographics tell you about consumers' long-term usage?
4. Does the company make a profit?
5. How much debt does this company have?
6. How much are you willing to lose before you sell?
7. How much profit are you willing to take before you sell?

Always keep account of the stock's purchase price and set a selling price. It is an investment, so have a plan and follow it. *The biggest reason people lose on stocks is that they have no plan or exit strategy.* "Should have, could have …" Ever heard of that?

There is no doubt that individual stocks offer the best opportunity for large gains, but they also have the highest risk. Just look at what happened to General Motors, Worldcom, Lehman Brothers, Enron, Washington Mutual, and EF Hutton.

How are you protected from this downside risk? You are not.

DOLLAR COST AVERAGING

One of the most effective ways for ordinary retirees—and anyone else, for that matter—to invest is to use dollar cost averaging[10]. With this method, you invest a certain amount of money in your account on a regular basis. You can arrange for automatic withdrawal, helping you make a habit of investing. The method creates a hassle-free way to make sure you can keep using stocks to grow your wealth.

Here is an example of how it works: Each month, you decide you have $200 to invest in stocks. You have the money automatically transferred to your investment account on the same day each month, and predesignated stocks or funds are chosen. If you are investing in one solid company (bonus points if it pays a dividend), shares might be $50 apiece this month. Your $200 buys four shares and adds it to your total holdings. If, next month, shares have dropped to $30 a share, you will purchase six and two-thirds shares. The month after that is a good one, rocketing shares up to $400 apiece. You automatically buy half a share. Of course, if you are interested in capitalizing on that insane increase—and an unlikely one in the real world—you can sell 10 of your shares and get $4,000. Whether the market is up or down, you continue to invest, which means that you buy more shares when the market is down and benefit more when the market cycles back higher a couple of years later.

For many, dollar cost averaging may not provide amazing returns, but it can help remove emotion from the equation. This is important if you want to protect yourself from some of the poor decision making that comes with overthinking your stock investments.

10Systematic investing does not assure a profit and does not protect against loss in declining markets. Since such a plan involves continuous investment in securities regardless of fluctuating prices, investors should consider their financial ability to continue purchases through periods of low price levels.

Another stock investing strategy is to forgo individual stocks altogether and invest in index funds. These funds provide diversification that can help offset negative effects if one of the individual stocks within the index collapses. Additionally, with index funds you benefit from the performance of an entire sector, or even the whole stock market, rather than relying on a single stock. We will look at index funds in Chapter 6.

There is no question that in volatile markets, investing through dollar cost averaging in a quality stock will pay off in time much better than just holding the stock.

In my opinion, buying and holding individual stocks is very high risk/high reward, so invest carefully.

Below are some examples of stock returns from 1999 to the week of June 22, 2014.

(Chart 5.1)

In this example of Microsoft stock, you can see that if you had purchased 1,000 shares (1) in the week of 12/27/1999 for $58.38 a share ($58,380), your value in June of 2014 (2) would be $41,480 or $41.48 a share. That's a loss of $16,900 over 13-plus years of investing in one stock.

However, if you had dollar cost averaged into the stock you would be way ahead.

My favorite is to buy on the dips, let's say that you purchased 200 shares at $30 per share for $6,000 in shares on the dips and that you had done that nine times for a total investment of $54,000, those shares would now be worth about $74,664. That is how you change lemons into lemonade.

(Chart 5.2)

Bank of America hit a high of $54.56 the week of November 20, 2006 and was at $15.49 the week of June 22, 2014. Only time will tell, but this would not have been a good investment for dollar cost averaging unless you always purchased only below the $10 per share price. Then you would have made a profit.

This is an example of a very long haul out of the bottom. For those who invested prior to 2008, it will continue to be a long time coming back.

This is one of the banks that is too big to fail?

Looking at this chart, you have to ask why the government didn't bail out the individual homeowners and let the banks fail. Could it be the banks contribute to political campaigns?

USING ONLINE BROKERS

Technology has made investing more accessible to more people. There are a number of online discount brokerages that can help you direct your own investment accounts over the Internet. These brokerages offer a number of investment options, but stocks and funds are among the most common. Some even allow you the chance to open retirement accounts for investment purposes. Before you invest, it is a good idea to compare online brokerages and determine which is most likely to fit your needs. Some investors use two brokerages, managing their portfolios differently, according to their goals with particular investments.

Online brokers normally charge lower transaction fees than traditional brokers. Transaction fees are usually at a flat, per-transaction rate, starting as low as $7.95 for some real-time trades and even going as low as $0.99, in some cases. Some brokers don't even require an account minimum, while others require between $1,000 and $5,000, or up to $20,000 to get started.

You can set up dollar cost averaging through online brokers, and you can usually even get transaction fees waived when you make use of DRIPs. Most online brokers will lower your account minimum or get rid of it altogether if you set up automatic deposits into your account, especially if you are investing in a retirement account or if you are using funds.

Many online brokers offer research tools that can help you investigate your investment options before you make a decision. It is vital that you do careful research since you will be making your own choices, and it can become costly when you use the consultant services offered by some online brokers. A financial planner or advisor can be of great help to you in such cases, providing you with guidance while letting you make the final decisions on your investments.

In addition, many online brokers offer day trading. Make no mistake, however. Day trading is a form of gambling, so invest only what you can afford to lose. Many people have gone bankrupt while thinking they can beat the market daily. It is very risky.

Television shows such as 60 Minutes and 20/20 have revealed the risks of day trading. There are plenty of reasons to be fearful. I have many clients to whom I have recommended opening up a Scottrade, TD Ameritrade, or Schwab account for their trading. They are not day traders, but they enjoy playing the market and they only risk what they can afford to lose. There is nothing wrong with this, if you are inclined to do so. America is all about the ability to make gains. If you use common sense and you do not risk any more than you can afford to lose, it is a personal choice worth considering.

At my firm, we decided not to be in the trading market for our clients or ourselves, so we do not invest that way, but for that 7 to 10 percent of do-it-yourself investors, trading can be very worthwhile.

There is no question in my mind that the fastest way to wealth creation is with stock investing, but it is also the fastest way to go broke. Know your risk equation.

The Kenny Rogers song "The Gambler" could also be about buying individual stocks:

> You've got to know when to hold 'em
>
> Know when to fold 'em
>
> Know when to walk away
>
> Know when to run

I have never heard of any online brokers who would share their actual results over time—for example, over a period of 10 years or 20 years—have you? They talk about low fees, but not about results. Why is that? Have you ever heard them say what their net return on their stock portfolio has been for the past 10 years? It's a mystery.

STOCK PICKING RESOURCES

I would recommend you read anything you can find by Malcolm Berko. You can read his column in your local paper or on the web. I have personally read his column for years and his philosophy is as close to my beliefs on investing as that of anyone whose articles I have read.

To address your financial questions to Malcolm Berko, e-mail him at mjberko@yahoo.com.

I believe if you don't know where we have been, you can't know where we are going.

Here are additional books to read to help fill in your knowledge on the subject:

1. Harry S. Dent Jr.
    a. *The Great Boom Ahead*
    b. *The Great Crash Ahead*
    c. *Economy & Markets Daily* is a free newsletter at www.hsdent.com
2. David Wiedemer, PhD, Robert A. Wiedemer, and Cindy Spitzer
    a. *AfterShock*
    b. *AfterShock Revised & Updated*

In addition, there are many newsletters on investing. Here are a few that I recommend you check out if you want to invest in individual stocks. They are not free, but they are excellent:

1. The Sovereign Society: www.sovereignsociety.com
2. The Money Map Press: www.moneymappress.com
3. Boom & Bust: www.hsdent.com

CHAPTER 6

FUNDS

There is no question that investing regularly in mutual funds in a volatile market and taking advantage of dollar cost averaging increases your opportunity for a good return. However, holding a large investment in a mutual fund can be disastrous in a declining market and could take 5 to 10 years to recover. That's because a mutual fund is a passive managed account and is not designed to move in and out of the markets.

Because stock picking can have such disastrous consequences, it is little surprise that funds have become a favorite way to invest for many people, especially those with a 401(k) plan, who are usually swamped with fund choices. Most plans have more than people know what to do with, and most individual investors have no clue which funds to invest into. We are going to try to simplify this by breaking things down; for example, most funds can be classified into three broad categories:

1. Mutual funds (including index funds)
2. Exchange-traded funds
3. Fund of funds

When you invest in a fund, you have instant diversification since you are investing in a group of stocks (or bonds or commodities or currencies) rather than just one. In the event that one investment does poorly, it is outweighed by several others that are doing well. You can choose funds based upon your goals, and you should look for funds that are more likely to help you accomplish your ideas of a prosperous retirement.

Make sure you check the track record of the fund for a minimum of 10 years and also verify how long the fund manager has been in charge. I have seen funds show a 20-year record, but if the fund manager has only been there for five years, what is the real track record? Always read the prospectus very carefully before investing in a mutual fund, and don't fall asleep! Even if it is very boring. you need to understand the objectives of the fund because they cannot change, no matter what is going on in the economy or market.

Also, look at the per-year results, especially 2008, the worst market in 78 years, and 2009, one of the best markets ever—how did your fund do? Is that a risk you are willing to take? How long did it take your fund to recover after 2008? It took the S&P 500 almost 5 years, and *if your advisor isn't showing you the best and worst numbers of the investment performance, you need to change advisors.*

LOOKING FOR LOW-FEE MUTUAL FUNDS

Mutual funds are essentially a group of individual investments bundled into one investment. You can choose to put together something like your own mutual fund, or you can have someone else manage the fund for you, determining which investments are most likely to help you reach your goals. *Cost is not as important as your net return. You need to understand this concept.*

Just remember the only people who talk about low fees have no results to talk about. If you don't ask them what their net return was, who is the fool?

A fee-based financial planner or advisor will be able to offer you a platform that charges a fee based on the size of your investment as opposed to a transactional fee common to most mutual fund purchases. Remember, low fees do not automatically mean higher returns. Avoiding big declines and having to recover from that dip in the market is far more important to your end results than a low fee. Isn't your goal to make money?

Another concern is that you may still have to pay taxes on any gains in some mutual funds, depending on the type of account they are in. Many retirees were surprised to find that, even with the down year of 2008, costs were still associated with the gains, some stocks made it in spite of the overall down performance of their funds, and to add insult to injury, some funds took five to six years to recover. I would rather pay taxes for a gain than have to write off a loss, wouldn't you?

Although mutual funds are great for dollar cost averaging in volatile markets, they often can be a disaster for lump sum investing. Get the facts on any mutual fund on how it will handle your money in bad markets, and how long its recovery time is. I know you have probably never heard this from your advisor, but you should have, and now you know what you don't know, but should know!

BASIC TYPES OF MUTUAL FUNDS

Most mutual funds fall into three main categories:

- Income mutual funds or bond funds
- Balanced mutual funds or growth and income
- Growth mutual funds or aggressive growth

INCOME MUTUAL FUNDS

You may wish to cultivate regular income with your mutual fund investment. If you want to get a regular monthly or quarterly check, an income fund may be the best choice for you. These are funds that invest in bonds or preferred shares. Some income mutual funds also include a healthy mix of dividend-paying stocks to boost some of the income potential. You can keep your core capital working on your behalf while you collect regular income.

You can also include DRIPs in your mutual funds, automatically reinvesting the returns. However, this means that you won't be receiving the regular income from the dividends. If you want the income, make sure that your financial advisor helps you make the appropriate choices that fit your goals.

Of course, when the markets see difficulty, your income may drop. While bonds pay a fixed rate of interest (and assuming the issuer doesn't default), if your income fund includes dividend-paying stocks, you can see a decrease in income if the company cuts the amount it pays as a dividend. Additionally, because income mutual funds are considered to be less risky, they usually offer lower returns than growth mutual funds. You run the risk of seeing inflation eroding the value of your returns.

BOND FUNDS

Some investors like to invest in a number of bonds at once. Bond funds are a way to do this. However, it is important to realize that when you purchase a portfolio of bonds in a mutual fund, you do not have as much control over which bonds you are investing in. Bond managers choose which bonds to purchase, depending on what they are trying to accomplish with the fund. Additionally, bond managers will buy and sell bonds depending on the trends they see in the markets.

If fund managers believe that interest rates are falling, they may decide to move into longer-maturity bonds to lock in the higher rate for a longer period of time. As of this writing, interest rates are rather low; many bond fund managers may decide to purchase shorter maturity bonds while they wait for better yields. In exchange for less control over the composition of the bond portfolio, you receive professional management, diversification, and reduced risk.

There are some bond funds, such as Government National Mortgage Association (GNMA) funds, that function a lot like checking accounts with a reasonably decent yield. Ginnie Mae (GNMA) funds feature mortgage-backed securities guaranteed by the US Treasury. This is a fairly liquid investment when you sign up with companies that allow you to write a limited number of checks from the account.

However, like any other fund, there are fees associated with this type of bond fund. In some cases, you can get better yields from online savings accounts or CDs. While bond funds like this can be tempting as emergency funds, they are usually better suited to long-term capital preservation, provided the returns can beat inflation. A properly set-up CD ladder can work better as an emergency fund in many cases.

Before investing in a bond fund, you should do research[11] to figure out which fund is most likely to meet your goals. There are funds that are designed for quick growth, investing in riskier bonds, and there are funds that invest only in tax-free bonds or only in convertible bonds. Research companies such as Wiesenberger or Morningstar can help you learn more about bond funds, and you should always read a fund's prospectus before sending any money. Financial planning professionals can also be of help when you are deciding which funds are most likely to help you accomplish your retirement income goals.

BALANCED MUTUAL FUNDS

You can get a balance of growth versus lower risk/volatility when you choose a balanced mutual fund. You get the benefit of some growth with the diversity of some bonds and some more solid value stocks added in to reduce volatility. You might even get a small amount of income with the bonds and some dividend-paying stocks.

DRIPs make a better choice for balanced funds than they do for income funds since they can boost the growth factor in a balanced fund, which isn't particularly designed to provide regular income. Balanced mutual funds are for those who are interested in beating inflation by a good margin but don't have the risk tolerance for growth mutual funds.

11Consider the investment objectives, risks, and charges and expenses of any mutual fund carefully before investing; the prospectus contains this and other information. Contact your financial advisor or the mutual fund directly to obtain a copy of the prospectus, which should be read carefully before investing.

Before choosing a mutual fund, it is a good idea to consider the possibilities and your needs. You might even find that a mix of the different types of mutual funds in your portfolio can meet your needs. You can purchase mutual funds through many brokerages, both online and offline. Additionally, there are companies that specialize in mutual funds, and many brokers offering retirement accounts can provide you with access to mutual fund investing. A financial advisor can help you sort out your goals and help you choose funds that are more likely to meet your needs.

GROWTH MUTUAL FUNDS

If you are looking to grow your capital and see higher returns, growth funds are likely to fit your requirements. These funds invest mainly in stocks. Many growth funds include quite a few small companies and companies expecting to see large amounts of growth in the next few years.

Growth funds historically have provided the greatest potential for higher absolute returns but, in exchange, do not provide dividend or interest income. Investors who do not have a need for current income, or who have longer time horizons, may wish to consider growth investments since they are better able to withstand the short-term fluctuations that typically accompany this asset class.

Realize, though, that while some mutual funds return high gains in isolated years, many of these types of returns are typically short-term in nature and, historically, do not reflect the long-term returns of stock investments. Additionally, a fund is unlikely to see such returns without a high amount of turnover in the fund, meaning that transaction fees can easily offset some of your gains. Even so, this aggressive type of mutual fund investing can help you grow your capital for further use.

There are risks associated with growth funds. The fact that the fund favors riskier stocks is an indication that there is a chance that it might lose value. With the potential to earn higher returns comes the increased chance of big losses. Some growth funds can lose a great deal in a single year, especially if a stock market crash is part of the equation.

And, of course, if you have a managed fund and the manager chooses a "hot" company stock that turns out to be a dud, that can impact your growth returns too. For me, the biggest problem with passive managed funds is their inability to go 100 percent to cash and get out of a very bad market decline. This is when the advisors say, "Hold on, it will come back," but they don't say that the recovery time is four to six years and you make nothing during the recovery time; would that bother you?

Most mutual funds are passive managed accounts, and their prospectus mandates they have to stay invested in the market at 80 to 90 percent of the account, unlike active managed portfolios that can go to 100 percent cash and get totally out of the market.

INDEX FUNDS

An index fund is actually a kind of mutual fund, but many people prefer to consider them separately. An index fund is a collection of all of the investments on a single index. An index is a grouping of investments, usually based on some unifying characteristic.

John Bogle, the founder of the Vanguard Group, offered the first index fund on December 31, 1975. He believed that ordinary investors could benefit from what was going on collectively in the market rather than having to pick and choose stocks, or have fund managers pick and choose for them. Other companies soon followed suit, and now there are a number of brokerages, insurance companies, and others that offer access to index fund investing. Because there is very little turnover in index funds, and because many fees beyond basic administration fees are rendered unnecessary, many index funds charge relatively low fees.

The issue of turnover does not get much scrutiny. Turnover can result in transaction fees and other expenses in more traditional mutual funds. Index funds generally experience less turnover than actively managed funds and that is because they are based on set groupings, so turnover happens only when an investment is taken off an index, which is infrequently. With mutual funds, investments are switched out when managers think that they are affecting the overall fund performance negatively. With index funds, managers are still present, but they select investments in such a way that the weightings and composition of the fund reflect the index the fund is designed to mirror.

It is possible to take advantage of a wide variety of index funds. There are index funds that focus on Asian investments, global indexes, index funds based on the Russell small-cap index, index funds based on clean energy indexes, and even funds that are based on the Wilshire 5000 Total Market index[12]. It is possible to find

12Funds that have a higher concentration of investments in a specific industry or sector may be subject to a higher degree of market risk and fluctuations than funds whose investments are more diversified. International investing may also be subject to additional risks not present in domestic funds, such as higher volatility, currency fluctuations, and differences in auditing and financial standards.

index funds full of growth stocks and funds full of value stocks. You can also find index funds based on bonds.

Index funds are most effective as long-term investments since they are based on entire segments of the market. As long as the market does well, the investor does well. There is no need to try to beat the market, which is extremely difficult to do, even if you have a professional fund manager. With index funds, you can keep pace with the market, less a small fee. That's usually enough to provide you with what you need, even after you subtract losses due to inflation and taxes. You can also, of course, increase your tax efficiency by using index funds in tax-advantaged retirement accounts.

The biggest problem is that index funds are not managed, and when the market is going down, you just ride it down—you have to manage them yourself.

EXCHANGE TRADED FUNDS (ETF)

Even newer than index funds are exchange traded funds. These are interesting investments that combine elements of mutual funds with stock trading. As are mutual funds, exchange traded funds are also composed of individual investments. However, unlike mutual funds, exchange traded funds (ETF) can be traded on the stock market like individual equities. ETFs are formed when an institution decides to put together a basket of investments. The shares are deposited with a holder that then issues creation units.

A creation unit usually has around 50,000 shares of various investments. These units are broken down further into the ETF shares, which can be sold just as stocks are on the exchange.

Exchange traded funds offer dividend investing opportunities, but unlike mutual funds, they don't offer the option to automatically reinvest the dividends. If you decide to reinvest the money, you may have to pay normal transaction fees.

In fact, when you buy and sell ETFs, your transaction fees will be whatever the broker charges for regular stock transactions. However, since they are funds, ETFs also include administrative fees on top of the transaction fees you accumulate for trading ETFs. Most ETFs, though, have very low fees, so you can keep more of your money rather than losing some of your gains to extra fees. There are also some ETF strategies that offer tax efficiency and these are strategies that you can discuss with a tax professional, investment professional, and/or a financial planner to determine the best strategy for ETF investing.

ETFs can be composed from just about anything, including stocks, bonds, commodities, and currencies. There are even real estate ETFs that allow you to add real estate to your investment portfolio without needing the capital to buy the physical property. Many investors also find that ETFs make it easier to purchase gold and currencies. This way, some of the risk associated with this type of investment can be reduced through instant diversity. Some investors like ETFs so much that they compose entire portfolios of such investments, creating diversity for a low cost. But before you invest, make sure you understand your situation and consult with a professional who can help you determine what is best for you.

If you have a higher risk tolerance, you can also consider exchange traded notes, which are debt instruments that come with a higher degree of risk but also with the chance of increased returns. Of course, these are risky, and should be approached with caution.

FUND OF FUNDS OR TARGET RETIREMENT FUNDS

Because of volatile markets, the fund of funds has become a very popular investment vehicle. You can diversify your funds into models comprising 12 to 16 categories of funds. The funds are rebalanced every month or every quarter to maintain the diversification of the portfolio.

These are generally part of conservative, moderate, or aggressive growth portfolios. Next to having a money manager, the fund of funds can provide an excellent way to get diversification for a low cost and minimal investment of time or money. It also provides you with some monthly management of your funds without paying a direct management fee. Many people invest their 401(k) or 403(b) portfolios in short-term strategies instead of going to all cash.

A number of fund companies offer retirement funds that are designed to keep you in a balanced portfolio until your retirement year, for example, in 2020 or 2025. Then, you transition into taking income for retirement. So far, I have been unimpressed with their results, but you should still check them out for yourself. Sometimes, they are one of the most conservative portfolios in a 401(k) plan that only offers a few choices. It could be your best or only option. However, usually, a money market account or a fixed income option is much better in a declining market.

Just remember that all mutual funds are *passive managed accounts.* They must stay invested as mandated by their fund prospectus and they must maintain that investment in the stock market at 80 to 90 percent. This is why most mutual funds took anywhere from four and a half years to seven or eight years to recover after 2008, and some have yet to do so. Has yours?

RECOVERY TIME FOR YOUR FUND INVESTMENT

Below are some graphic illustrations you need to note. We used some well-known funds. The graphs show actual results, how funds reacted to market declines, and their recovery:

1. VWNDX: Vanguard Windsor (no load)
2. FCNTX: Fidelity Contrafund (no load)
3. AMECX: Income Fund of America (American Funds)
4. FKINX: Franklin Income Fund
5. VTXVX: Vanguard Target Retirement 2015 (no load)

Why these funds? Because they are all rated with four stars by Morningstar and they are included in the majority of 401(k) plans or in many investors' portfolios.

These pages will show a clear problem with passive managed accounts that you need to know about if you have a large investment in one of them. However, if you are investing in your 401(k), these could be excellent investment opportunities for the long term if you don't leave large amounts exposed. You need to really understand these graphs and what their recovery time does to your real rate of return (RR). After all, this is your money.

(Chart 6.1)

#1 WWNDX Vanguard Windsor a No Load Fund

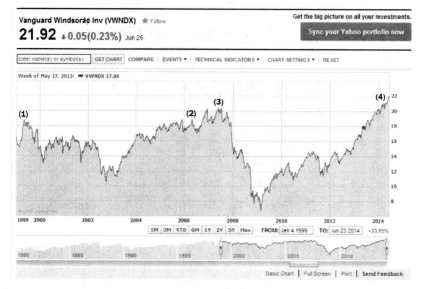

Vanguard Windsor is a large value fund and rated Four Stars by Morningstar.

When you own a mutual fund, you need to be aware of the volatility, especially if you are retired.

As you can clearly see above, (1) the week of 5/10/1999, the fund was at $18.65 and then went down and did not recover until (2) the week of 10/2/2006. This fund was in recovery for seven years and five months.

Then the fund went up to another high of $20.40 on 7/9/2007 (3) only to again crash until (4) 2/17/2014 when it recovered at $20.45, and that was another six years and seven months of playing catch-up.

My point is that if you have large amounts invested in a mutual fund, you need to consider a managed account that can reposition your funds daily. Otherwise, you could ride the roller coaster as will see in our examples.

(Chart 6.2)

2 FCNTX Fidelity Contrafund

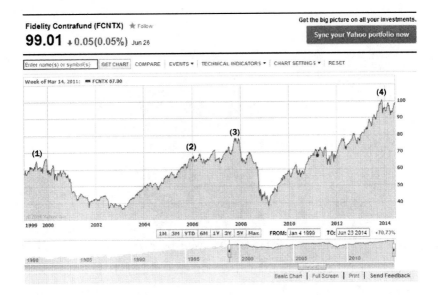

Fidelity Contrafund is a large cap growth fund and rated with four stars by Morningstar. As you can see:

(1) This fund hit a high of $66.51 on 11/29/1999, and the the account did not recover until the start of 2006 (2), a six year recovery period.

Then it went up to a new high on 10/22/2007 (3), only to go back down and not return to those numbers until 1/14/2013 (4), a recovery time of five years and three months.

(Chart 6.3)

3 AMECX American Funds Inc. Fund of America

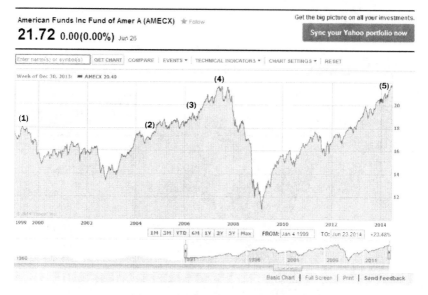

American Funds is a fund family used by many brokers that has become a favorite fund in many investors portfolios, individually and in 401(k) Plans.

(1) In the week of 5/10/1999, the fund hit a high of $18.01, then the fund proceeded to decline. The fund did not get back to that value (2) until the week of 11/1/2004 at $18.07, and that's five years and five months of recovery and playing catch-up. (3) Then the fund moved up to a value of $21.56 for three years until the the week of 11/1/2007 (4) only to crash and not recover until the week of 5/26/2014 (5), which is another six years and six months of recovery and playing catch-up.

Can you imagine spending 11 years and 11 months playing catch-up over a 15-year period of investing?

If you had drawn your retirement income from this fund, you would be in deep trouble.

(Chart 6.4)

4 FKINX Franklin Income Fund

Frankin Income Fund is another fund that many brokers like to use for their clients, but seldom tell them the whole story.

So let's look at the numbers: (1) In March 1998 this fund hit a high of $2.57 and then declined and did not get back to that value until October 2006 $2.62 (2), which is eight years and seven months in recovery and playing catch-up.

This fund then went up for seven months until May 2007 (3) and it hit a value of $2.81. Then the bottom fell out and it crashed.

The fund has still not recovered (4) as of August 2014, which totals seven years and three months and still playing catch-up. Would you be happy if you owned this fund?

Knowledge is power. You need to see these charts before you ever purchase a mutual fund.

After the down markets of 2000 through 2003, many fund companies came out with Target Funds as an answer to the volatile markets.

One such fund is the Vanguard Target Retirement 2015 fund, a Four-Star MorningStar Fund. This fund was designed for people who will retire in 2015, when they need to start using their funds for Retirement Income.

(Chart 6.4)

5 VTXVX Vanguard Target Retirement 2015

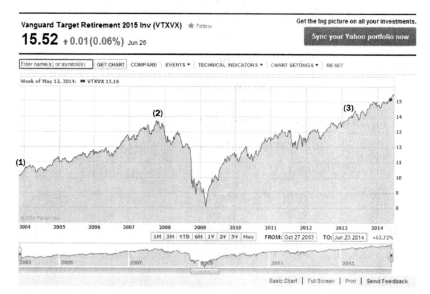

This fund was started the week of 10/27/2003 (1) and went up to $13.73 the week of 10/8/2007 (2). However, the fund then crashed and did not get back to $13.75 until on 2/18/2013 (3).

That's five years and four months of recovery and playing catch-up.

So over 50 percent of the fund's life has been spent in playing catch-up or not making any money.

The real story will be coming in 2015, especially for those investors that are in this fund.

MONEY MANAGERS

Money managers run actively managed portfolios and usually are paid a flat fee or a percentage of the assets, so if you make money, the manager makes money, and if you lose money, you should fire the money manager. However, if everyone lost money and your money manager lost less than the markets, you might want to keep them.

We all hear all the time that **past results do not guarantee future returns**, and that is true. However, is it still important to see how your mutual fund advisor or money manager performed in **good and bad times**?

Common sense would answer yes, if your money manager only performs well in a recovery period and didn't preserve your principle in the first place, you need to change money managers. Avoiding a large decline is more important than performing in recovery; it is critical to your investing performance and real rate of return.

Sometimes, it can help to hire a money manager to advise you on making the best use of your assets while limiting your liabilities.

Fortunately, choosing a money manager is simple if you take the time and really look at that firm's investment objective. If that objective fits your needs and risk tolerance, that manager could be a good fit for some of your funds. The next step is to do your due diligence on the manager's credentials, determine the firm's qualifications, and evaluate its track record and regulatory history. If your objectives are aligned and the history looks good, you might want to see how it goes with that money manager.

In general, money managers trade stocks, bonds, and cash to meet their objectives. There are several money managers who have preservation of capital as their number-one objective. One of the advantages of a money manager is the ability to go to all cash and get out of the market, whereas mutual funds, usually, can only go to 10 percent cash. (To find out, check the fund prospectus.) Also, with a mutual fund, or when investing in individual stocks and bonds on your own, you have to make the choice to buy or sell and pay the transaction fee.

Money managers, on the other hand, charge a fee for a percentage of assets, so there are no trading costs. Additionally, the money manager makes more if you make more and makes less if you make less, providing an incentive to avoid churning your account by running up commissions selling and buying stocks or bonds.

One concern relates to accounts with little activity, which could be called reverse churning—in other words, getting a fee for not actually managing the funds. A fee-based platform can actually be more expensive over the long term in such cases and this is why it is so important that you do research and consider your individual needs and situation when choosing a money manager. Look at *perfor-*

mance, which means your *net return* on investment after paying fees. Low fees do not guarantee or lead to higher returns and that is a fact!

Some well-known money management firms are Fisher Investments and/or Becker Capital Management, but check their numbers out and make sure you would feel comfortable with this type of investment management.

There are money managers that have preservation of principal as their primary concern, if you are retired or close to retirement, you need to have your serious money in a preservation of principal portfolio.

Consider the risk versus reward; for example, what did the fund do in 2008 during the downturn, and what was the return in 2009? Are you willing to accept that amount of volatility?

Three questions to ask your money manager:

1. What was your net return in 2008?
2. How long is your recovery from a bad year?
3. Do you ever go 100 percent out of the market?

FEE-BASED ADVISOR

You can hire a registered investment advisory firm that invests money for a fee, sometimes using a third party money manager and sometimes managing it's own model portfolios. Advisors who work for these firms are called Investment Advisor Representative (IAR), and they are paid a portion of the fee that the client pays. If you make money, they make more money, and if you lose, they get less. Most importantly, if they do not meet expectations, you can, and should, fire them and take your investments with you.

IARs will buy and sell and manage the risk you want to take in your portfolio; just make sure your advisor makes investments based on your risk guidelines rather than their own. This is the purest form of investing. You do not pay commissions or expenses; instead, you just pay an asset fee related to the value of the account. It's very easy to tell what your return is since the reporting is based on net return, including the fees paid. Unlike mutual fund fees, the fees are out in the open.

The key point here is: You know exactly your cost and net return on your investment.

If the risk was exactly the same, which investment below would you pick?

1. You pay a fee of 2 to 3 percent to make a net return of 9 percent
2. You would you feel better if you only paid a 1 percent fee to make a return of 4 percent

As comedian Ron White says, "You can't fix stupid." This is not rocket science; this is your money. Look at the numbers below:

- $100,000 invested at a 3 percent fee or $3,000 cost, and at the end of the year with a 9 percent net return = $109,000 in your hand
- $100,000 invested at a 1 percent fee or $1,000 cost, and at the end of the year with a 4 percent net return = $104,000 in your hand

Is $9,000.00 not more than $ 4,000.00? If you picked number two, you are brainwashed by one of the biggest lies in investing!

You have got to understand that the most important thing to know about investing is your net return; did you make money or not?

Do not base your investing decision only on cost, but on your net return!

Please don't leave this page until you understand that it's not the fee you pay, it's the net return you receive that matters most!

For more, read Appendix A, "The Four Principles of Risk-Intelligent Investing."

CHAPTER 7

WHAT YOU DON'T KNOW CAN HURT YOU

We have discussed a lot of things, and we have tried to stick to the formula of *Investing Simplified*. However, at this point, we need to discuss the biggest misconception and outright deception in all of investing.

THE BIG DECEPTION BETWEEN AVERAGE ANNUAL RETURN AND REAL RATE OF RETURN

Average annual return (AAR) supposedly means how much you have made on your investment for a period of time. In reality, this is the *biggest lie* of all on Wall Street. What's even worse is it's a lie mandated by law.

The fact is that it means nothing and it is mandated by law by the SEC and FINRA when returns of mutual funds or securities investments, including managed accounts, are quoted to the public.

Of course, they have to say that past results are no indication of future returns, but how could they be when the AAR (Average Annual Return) is a lie to begin with?

Average Annual Return

Year 1	Year 2
$100	$80
-20% = - $20	+ 25% = + $20
$80	$100

What is your Average Annual Return? **According to the SEC and FINRA, when you start with a $100, you end up in two years with $100!**

Year 1   -20 percent

<u>Year 2 +25 percent</u>

         + 5percent

         Divide by 2 years = 2.5 percent Average Annual Return

Let's review this:

You started with $100 and you ended up with a $100 and your AAR was 2.5 percent?

Your Real Rate of Return (RR) is zero.

This is truly investing simplified. Everyone should be able to understand that the AAR method is not an accurate way to account for your return on your investments, and yet this is what has been used since the 1930s; has anyone said, let's update this every 80 years or so?

The following is a little more complicated, but you need to understand that losses in the early years can really affect your real rate of return as well. The facts are that when you have large losses in your investment portfolio, the AAR does not take into consideration the time needed to recover and here is a simple example:

BOTH PORTFOLIOS HAVE AN AVERAGE ANNUAL RETURN OF 5 PERCENT

(Table 7.1)

	PORTFOLIO A	PORTFOLIO B
STARTING VALUE	$100,000	$100,000
YEAR 1 RETURN	-35% = $65,000	+5% = $105,000
YEAR 2 RETURN	+35% = $87,750	+5% = $110,250
YEAR 3 RETURN	+15% = $100,912.5	=5% = $115,7625
AVERAGE ANNUAL RETURN	AAR = +5% (-35+35+15) = +15 DIVIDED BY 3 = +5%	AAR = +5% (-5+5+5) = +15 DIVIDED BY 3 = +5%

This is why you need to question the AAR everytime you hear it! Always verify the actual annual rate yourself because AAR means nothing.

The above are examples of AAR versus RR and this is not difficult to understand but can get very complicated in a hurry if you do not understand some basics of math when we discuss longer periods of time. Let's start with the Rule of 72, which clearly shows why AAR is not the best way to measure your real earnings on investments.

The rule of 72 is an easy way to show, using compounding interest, how long it takes to double your investment. For example, if you invested $100,000 and earned 7.2 percent every year, it would take you 10 years to get $200,000. You take the number 72 and divide it by 7.2 (The Interest Rate) = 10 years to double.

However, the big misconception is that there is no investment that earns the same rate every year; investments are not guaranteed and have fluctuating rates of return and they are not the same every year. This will help.

RULE OF 72

One of the basic tools you can use to help plan for the future is the rule of 72. This rule of thumb states that if you divide your expected return into 72, the answer will tell you how long it will take your investment to double if you do nothing with it. For example, if you expect to earn 7 percent on a mutual fund, you would perform the following calculation: Divide 72 by 7 = 10.29 years or 10 years and almost 4 months for your money to double if you just let it sit there and earn interest. So, if you invest $10,000 of your retirement assets at 7 percent, it will take more than 10 years for your money to double to $20,000, and that's pretty easy to figure out.

The higher the rate of return, the less time it takes for your money to double. A growth investment in a high risk ETF, at 15 percent per year, could conceivably double in 4.8 years, yielding that extra $10,000 faster. On the other end, a bond investment with a return of 4 percent would take 18 years to double, helping you reach your goal of $20,000 at a much later date.

You can see from this example that putting your money in a traditional savings account at 0.75 percent would mean your money would take 96 years to double. However, this rule does not take into account the fact that there will be down years as well, nor does it consider taxes and inflation, and that your rate of return will not always be that steady: it is more of a sketch of the possibilities or a ballpark number.

The following table shows the Rule of 72 in action, with an investment of $100,000 earning 7.2 percent over those 10 years:

Rule of 72 showing 7.2 percent over 10 years
(Table 7.2)

YEAR	STARTING AMOUNT	AMOUNT EARNED @7.2%	YEAR END AMOUNT
1	$100,000	$7,200.00	$107,200.00
2	$107,200	$7,718.40	$114,918.40
3	$114,918.40	$8,274.125	$123,192.525
4	$123,192.525	$8,869.862	$132,062.387
5	$132,062.387	$9,508.492	$141,570.779
6	$141,570.779	$10,193.096	$151,763.875
7	$151,763.875	$10,926.999	$162,690.874
8	$162,690.874	$11,713.743	$174,404.617
9	$174,404.617	$12,557.133	$186,961.750
10	$186,961.750	$13,461.246	$200,422.996

You can clearly see the Rule of 72 shows a real compounded interest rate of return and shows that your investment doubled and what was the AAR? This is simply 7.2 percent since that is what it paid every year (10 x 7.2 = 72)

Now, what is your simple interest rate of return? It's 10.04 percent. Take the gain of $100,422.996, divide by 10, and you get $10,042.2996 per year; then divide that by 100,000 and you get the simple interest rate return of 10.04 percent.

Now let's look at a typical fund that shows the same 7.2 percent AAR but comes up with different results:

(AAR) Average Annual Return of 7.2 percent Exposed:
(Table 7.3)

YEAR	STARTING AMOUNT	AMOUNT EARNED	YEAR END AMOUNT
1	$100,000	@10% = $10,000	$110,000
2	$110,000	@-20% = $22,000 LOSS	$88,000
3	$88,000	@25% = $22,000	$110,000
4	$110,000	@10% = $11,000	$121,000
5	$121,000	@-10% = $12,100 LOSS	$108,900
6	$108,900	@35% = $38,115	$147,015
7	$147,015	@20% = $29,403	$176,418
8	$176,418	@-10% = $17,641.08 LOSS	$158,776.20
9	$158,777.20	@-3% = $4,763.286 LOSS	$154,012.914
10	$154,012.914	@15% = $23,101.938	$177,114.852

The AAR is 7.2 percent, really, just add up the positive years and subtract the negative years to get 72 percent, and then divide by 10 years to get 7.2 percent, and according to the Financial Services Industry, that is your Average Annual Rate of Return. However, the simple interest is 7.71 percent, and you find this by dividing your gain of $77,114.852 by 10 to get $7,711.4852, and then divide that by $100,000 to get 7.71 percent.

However, the **RR is 5.9** percent because you earn interest on your interest or real compounding rate of return. See table below:

5.9 percent (RR) Compounding Interest Table = 7.2 percent AAR
(Table 7.4)

YEAR	YEAR INVESTMENT	TOTAL INVESTMENT	YEAR INTEREST	TOTAL INTEREST	BALANCE
1	$100,000	$100,000	$5,900	$5,900	$105,900
2	$0	$100,000	$6,248.10	$12,148.10	$112,148.10
3	$0	$100,000	$6,616.74	$18,764.84	$118,764.84
4	$0	$100,000	$7,7007.13	$25,771.96	$125,771.96
5	$0	$100,000	$7,420.55	$33,192.51	$133,192.51
6	$0	$100,000	$7,858.36	$41,050.87	$141,050.87
7	$0	$100,000	$8,322.00	$49,372.87	$149,373.87
8	$0	$100,000	$8,813.00	$58,185.87	$158,185.87
9	$0	$100,000	$9,332.97	$67,518.83	$167,518.83
10	$0	$100,000	$9,883.61	$77,402.44	$177,402.44

We used 5.9 percent interest every year, so the 7.20 percent Average Annual Return was actually a 5.9 percent Real Rate of return, and this proves: **What you don't know can hurt you.**

When your advisor tells you that your investment has had an AAR of a certain percent you need to ask, **"What is the Real Rate of Return?"** your advisor will probably look at you and say, "What do you mean?" Then you can explain the difference and your advisor will know you know what investing is really all about: your *real rate of return.*

The **RR** takes into consideration what it takes to come back from a loss, while the **AAR** does not. Any time your portfolio has a year with a loss in the numbers, the **AAR** will be inaccurate and will show a higher number than you actually earned.

The question is whether you want to feel good or you want to know the **RR** from your investments. This is why I have always tried to run the numbers for the last 12 months because they are the most accurate, but I have fought for years with reporting companies to point out to them that their numbers were wrong and they are overstated. Unfortunately, their response has been that they are required by law to show the **AAR**, so why change; one executive even told me it's too complicated and AAR is easy to figure out.

One of my reasons for writing this book is to get the powers that be, including the SEC and FINRA, to actually require honesty in reporting by eliminating the **AAR** and requiring companies to show the **RR** instead. Wouldn't you prefer the truth?

Negative returns exponentially affect your **RR** and here is a perfect example:

Consider investing $100,000 in the S&P 500 index, the lowest cost investment you could ever make, starting on 12/31/1999 and going up through 12/31/2013

The S&P hit 1527.46 the week of March 20, 2000 (1) and never returned for good until the week of March 4, 2013 (2), 13 years in recovery. Just imagine if that was your retirement fund and you had to take income out of it? In retirement, you cannot afford long recoveries in your portfolio.

The **AAR** for the S&P 500 index from 12/31/1999 through 12/31/2012 was 3.79 percent. However, if you had invested $100,000 at the end of 1999, it would have been worth only $97,069 on 12/31/2012. That works out to a negative return of -3 percent, or an annual **RR of - 0.25** percent.

(Chart 7.5)

This should be called funny math instead of Average Annual Return. Why haven't FINRA or the SEC addressed this? Has your advisor ever talked to you about this?

The Effect That a Loss Has on Your Recovery: (Table 7.6)

POTENTIAL PORTFOLIO INVESTMENT LOSS	GAIN REQUIRED TO GET BACK TO EVEN
-10%	+11%
-20%	+25%
-30%	+43%
-40%	+67%
-50%	+100%
-60%	+150%

The overall effect of a down year can be devastating to your financial success. My purpose in providing you with this information is to make you angry; you should be furious when you discover that you have been lied to all of your life about the returns you have received on your investments. Hopefully this will create an outrage in you and motivate you to help me change this, but you must take action if you want this changed. We should have the right in America to be told the truth and in this case, we can handle the truth, can't we?

We have set up a blog and a petition on my website: www.AskTheFinancialDoctor.com.

Our petition is to the SEC—and we are not talking football, but the Securities Exchange Commission—that is there to protect us, and we are talking about your money and mine. We need the *truth*, and we deserve it. That's why we will be asking the SEC and FINRA to mandate a law that investment companies, broker dealers, registered investment advisors, mutual funds, money managers, and any other types of investment vehicles and services **must clearly state the Real Rate of Return and totally get rid of the Average Annual Rate of Return** because it means nothing and should be replaced by a rate of return that will actually tell people something useful about their investment performance, like the truth!

All investments with a track record should be required to disclose the volatility or the highest high and the lowest low they have ever had. Many funds do this now but still do not discuss recovery time and how long it took to get back to positive returns.

Morningstar has been a leader in providing this information, but unfortunately, most investors are not aware that this information is available. It is time that all investments should have to show their actual recovery history, shouldn't they?

Do you think this is important to know?

Do you think this might change your mind on what you want to invest in?

Understanding the difference should save you thousands of dollars in your investing future.

CHAPTER 8

ANNUITIES: HALF-TRUTHS AND MISCONCEPTIONS

Here's a fact: In the 44 years I have been licensed for annuities and the 43 years I have been licensed for selling and servicing securities, I have never met or heard of anyone who claimed to have become rich by investing in annuities or life insurance, have you?

On the other hand, I have met countless investors and clients who said that their life insurance and annuities gave them peace of mind about their future, helping them to protect themselves from the unknown.

In my opinion, annuities and life insurance are not investments, because they help protect people from the unknown and provide peace of mind; a better term for them is *insurance or guaranteed insurance contracts, since they are guaranteed by the insurance company issuing the contract.*

Anyone who has ever contributed to Social Security owns an annuity, by law!

When you start working, the government requires that your employer takes out of your paycheck 6.2 percent, and that is matched by your employer at 6.2 percent. Those funds are paid to the government to provide you an income payment at retirement. This is not an option! If you want to work, you have to pay into Social Security. At retirement, a lifetime income benefit is paid to you, and if you are single, it stops at your death. There is no refund. The paycheck deduction for Social Security is required by law and you must pay into a retirement account that will be paid out to you at retirement.

Unfortunately, for all of us, the government has raped and misused our Social Security funds for over 50 years, and now there are no funds available. If an insurance company were to misuse our annuity funds like the government has, the insurance company executives would be heading to prison and their assets would be seized for restitution. Isn't it comforting to know that we hold our private insurance companies to a higher standard than our politicians and government? Why don't those in Congress who have been there for more than one term have any accountability for the misuse of these funds?

We need to change that. You can go to www.AskTheFinancialDotor.com and sign our petition to require that all federal politicians, Social Security employees, and government employees, including the IRS have their pensions reduced by the same percentage by which our Social Security is reduced. For example, if the government reduces our Social Security by 20 percent, then all politicians and all federal government employees, including and especially the Social Security Administration, must get the same reduction in their Government pension. Do you think this might motivate them to watch our money a little more? Why isn't anyone accountable anymore?

Returning to annuities, "All annuities are bad" is a quote from Clark Howard's radio show in the past; however, he recently has changed his tune and now he says that some income benefit annuities are okay. It sounds as if he has finally done some research. I would be happy to debate Clark Howard or Suze Orman on national TV or on radio, as long as we could limit the discussion to historical evidence and not just their feelings about annuities, particularly the lifetime income benefit and death benefit that many annuities have.

You can go on YouTube and see Suze Orman's comments and also read her many statements on annuities; however, I do agree with both of them that annuities are not investments, with the exception of the Variable Annuity (VA) or the Variable Life (VL), since the SEC and FINRA have declared them securities, and therefore investments under the law.

Some Facts:

There is no question that for those who owned a Fixed Indexed Annuity with a guaranteed income benefit from 12/31/1999 to June 27, 2014, the income benefit has outperformed the S&P 500 index and the DJIA index—and the results are not even close.

Also, for annuity owners fixed or variable, who passed away during the market declines and had a death benefit, their heirs actually received a lot more than they would have if their funds had only been in the market. This is a fact!

In my opinion, the investment world changed at the turn of the century and many of our old investment theories such as the "Buy and Hold" and the call to be diversified, have just not worked as well since then. I think it is better to protect yourself either from market volatility or from running out of income in retirement.

Let's take a look at an actual fixed indexed annuity and how it actually performed from 12/31/1999 to 12/31/2013.

The graph below shows, on the top line, what happened to an actual Fixed Indexed Annuity (FIA) with a **6 percent Guaranteed Income Benefit**. The cash value is on the middle line.

There is no question this annuity outperformed the S&P Index during this period since the cash value never incurred a loss, while the S&P had eight up years and five down years. **The problem for the S&P was recovery time and the annuity never had a recovery time; this is as simple as it gets.**

This graph awaits a debate with Clark Howard or Suze Orman, since figures don't lie, but liars figure. I am not calling them both liars—I would prefer to say they are both misinformed and uneducated on the facts about annuities and the real volatility of the market and how devastating that can really be to retirement planning:

(Chart 8.1)

LIFETIME INCOME BENEFIT (RIDER)

It has been said that a picture is worth a thousand words—or should we say, thousands of dollars in this example. Let's look at a $100,000 investment in a fixed indexed annuity with a lifetime income benefit (rider) that grows at 6 percent per year for retirement income versus the same amount invested in the S&P 500 index that has no fees or expenses, making it the lowest cost investment you could have made. So, do low fees really mean a better return? **See for yourself.**

During the period illustrated from **12/31/1999 through 12/31/2013**, the chart above assumes a $100,000 initial premium, or investment, with no withdrawals in a **fixed indexed annuity that has *no fees or expenses*,** *except* there is a **Guaranteed Income Benefit Rider 1 percent fee that is charged against the cash value**, and the crediting method of accumulation is based on a 5 percent annual point to point following the S&P 500 index. Why are the numbers better than the S&P numbers? The annuity eliminates all the down years and has no negative returns..

Obviously, annuities are not for everyone, but in the right situation they can greatly influence your future, and once you really understand how annuities work and what their purpose is in various financial planning situations, you just might change your mind. Usually, when people learn the facts and don't let their emotions control them, they can come to a logical conclusion.

If you are concerned about having a guaranteed lifetime income benefit and not having to worry about losing your principal moving up and down, the fixed indexed annuity will unquestionably do that, but as an investment, the cash value had a return of 3.41 percent and the annuity never had a loss in any year and that is insuring your peace of mind.

Now that you have seen an actual annuity in action, let's get into the nuts and bolts of annuities and I will try to take a very complicated situation and simplify it for you. In the Glossary of Terms I will include definitions of an annnuity and its various types, but at this point we will be discussing the use of an *annuity* in your investment portfolio and who can sell you which annuity product.

> **Annuities (fixed, indexed, or immediate):** These are issued by insurance companies, and you have to be a licensed agent in the state in which you are selling the annuity. All requirements and regulations are mandated by the state insurance department of the State.

> **Variable annuities:** This a security mandated by law that requires a securities license in addition to a state insurance license. The state insurance department sets down regulations and requirements and the state securities department, along with FINRA, can add additional requirements and regulations.

> **Fee-based annuities:** Requires an additional license to receive fees (RIA or IAR) but also requires a state insurance license, and if the agent is licensed through a broker dealer, must follow regulations and rules of FINRA. Registered Investment Advisors (RIA) and Investment Advisory Representatives (IAR) who are not regulated by FINRA are regulated by either the state securities department or by the SEC. Wow, is

that confusing enough for a Philadelphia lawyer, let alone the public. Who's on first?

WHAT IS AN ANNUITY DESIGNED TO DO?

An annuity is designed for two main functions:

1. To defer income tax on your earnings
2. To provide an income you cannot outlive for a predetermined time, either immediately or at a later time, and it can be guaranteed for life by the insurance company issuing the contract.

An annuity can be a way to accumulate earnings, and you can control when you pay income tax on the earnings; however, understand that annuities in general are not investments and whether it is a fixed annuity or an indexed annuity, the earnings do not compete against an actively managed portfolio, but the annuity is guaranteed by the insurance company not to lose principal if you hold the contract until it is out of surrender fees. This is called peace of mind, but remember that an annuity is not an investment.

Variable annuities and variable life insurance are securities and they are investments, and their values can fluctuate and are not guaranteed. In some cases there are guaranteed death benefits or guaranteed income benefits that are guaranteed by the issuing insurance company. According to regulators, these annuities are investments and should only be sold by securities licensed individuals.

Fee-based annuities, in my opinion, are the only annuities that are true investment products and can have investment-like returns. When you purchase a fee-based annuity, you pay a set fee—for example $20 per month (tax deferral fee)—and then you pay whatever the fees are for the investment you have chosen. You can cash out with no surrender charges and this type of annuity does not, generally, offer a lifetime income benefit. You should only buy this type of annuity to control the taxation on your earnings.

WHO ARE YOU DEALING WITH?

Is the agent or advisor licensed to discuss investments as well as annuities?

You need to know. If you are going to be sold a product or solution for your needs, you need to understand the difference.

Do advisors (or agents) represent several insurance companies or just one? If they represent one company, you know what they are going to present to you, so shouldn't you ask for options?

Are they licensed to sell variable annuities, fixed annuities, or fee-based annuities? You need to ask.

Because annuities are offered through insurance companies, you want to have an idea of which companies are more likely to be reliable. Because they deal in investments and asset protection, insurance companies are rated. Standard & Poor offers ratings similar to bond ratings, with AAA, AA, and A representing companies that have the highest chance of retaining their value and being able to support their guarantees.

Another ratings company associated with insurance companies is A. M. Best. The top grades from A. M. Best are A++, A+, A, A-, B++ and B+. It is important to realize that a rating of "secure" doesn't mean that a company can't fail. Ratings apply only to a company's financial stability and claims-paying ability, and not to the safety or to the performance of the variable accounts, and variable accounts will fluctuate in value.

Some companies that do not have the highest rating can be quite reliable, but ratings do give you an idea of whether a company is likely to stand the test of time. Ratings are a useful guideline, but you shouldn't just rely on the ratings, because the states, not the federal government, regulate insurance companies and every company has to meet state requirements to do business in a state. If you have a concern, check with your state insurance department, which oversees insurance companies inyour state.

CHANGING MARKET CONDITIONS

With the recent stock market troubles, it is little surprise that annuities, and especially Fixed Indexed Annuities (**FIA**), are gaining in popularity right now; the promise of guaranteed income is one that is quite alluring, especially in times of market turmoil.

I do not consider FIAs or Equity Indexed Annuities (**EIA**) to be the in same category of investment as a money-managed account or even a mutual fund or stock portfolio investment and why is that? My answer may surprise you.

If you were to purchase a **FIA**, you would never have a loss in your principal, provided you held the contract to maturity, or to death, or to the point when you start taking income. Granted, **FIAs** do not lose principal, but what earnings they provide the investor is the big question. I have yet to see a **FIA** product over a 10- to 20-year period have higher returns than traditional investments. It might be better than a CD or the S&P or the DJIA index, and many mutual funds for the first 13 years of this century; however, it performs well below the managed money accounts I know of.

This is why knowledge is power. There is a reason the **FIA** is not called an investment: It doesn't carry the risk or the reward of a traditional investment money managed portfolios do. On the other hand, the VA is a security, but it's very expensive as an investment and has performed very badly because the market has as well.

However, when you add the guaranteed lifetime income benefit, and a death benefit, the VA just may be one of the best income protection investments ever designed to protect the investor from declining markets; this is why **FIAs** have followed suit and started providing these benefits as well.

Remember that at retirement, most people are not concerned about how much they have, but how long their income will last, and a lifetime income benefit is for life and you cannot outlive it.

Some financial advisors love annuities and others categorically refuse to recommend them to clients. It is important that you get as much information on your options as possible before deciding whether an annuity would work well in your situation or not.

All annuities sold in a state have to be approved and supervised by the state insurance department. Does your state only allow annuities to be sold because it gets revenue when one is sold? State insurance departments are there to protect state citizens, so why would they allow bad annuities to be sold in their state?

As in any industry, there are good annuity salespeople (insurance agents) and there are bad ones who sell the wrong product to the wrong person; it is as simple as that.

This is not the fault of state insurance departments and in fact, they do have the power to fine or cancel the licenses of any annuity or life insurance salesperson who is not working in the consumers' best interest or who is in violation of state regulations or state law—and this is done all the time. Ultimately, there is no question that many insurance departments and state regulators need more staff to do a better job, but it's not for lack of trying.

Contact your own state insurance department and it can provide you with tons of information—after all they work for you—to protect your interests. You can check out the insurance agents as well to see if they have been fined or sanctioned by your state insurance department, and advisors who are securities licensed can be checked out at brokercheck.finra.org/. You need to check both sites and verify the agent or advisor you are working with.

As of July 1, 2014, the Colorado Insurance Division has expanded the list of terms that it said should not be used in life insurance and annuity advsrtisements, due to the potential for misleading consumers. These terms are "certificate of deposit" or CD, "safe," and "secure." The Colorado advertising regulations essentially follow the version of the model developed in 2000 by the National Association of Insurance Commissioners (NAIC).

To date, 13 states have adopted that version as it relates to the form and content of advertisements, including the NAIC Model's list of (generally) prohibited terms. The 13 states are: Alabama, Arkansas, Colorado,

Illinois, Louisiana, Missouri, Nebraska, New Hampshire, New Jersey, Rhode Island, Virginia, West Virginia, and Wisconsin.

On our website www.AskTheFinancialDoctor.com we will be petitioning the state insurance departments on something we call **"Stop AAR reporting"** to require life insurance companies to provide actual results of life insurance policies and annuities in plain language. In addition, if hypothetical figures are given, the insurance companies must clearly state that they are doing so and if related to past results of the stock market, they must use real numbers, *not* AAR numbers. Currently, insurance companies show AAR numbers, and by now we all know that AAR means nothing but *false hype, and is misleading.*

On our site we will also be petitioning the state insurance departments on something we call **"Full Disclosure of Service,"** and it is something you are spending dollars on every day. Almost every premium you pay for life insurance, annuities, long-term care, Medicare, and medical and disability insurance policies, usually a portion of that premium goes to pay for the servicing of your policy—anywhere from .25 percent to 15 percent or higher. However, you have no control over who you work with, so shouldn't this be disclosed to you? This is something that, in my opinion, has gone on way too long and I have never heard anyone from any insurance department say this needs to be changed.

Insurance companies are receiving billions in fees from policies that have no advisor or agent assigned to them to provide the personal service you were told you would get for the rest of your life; how's that working for you? Insurance is sold, not purchased, and insurance companines build in fees to retain agents to sell and service their products, but what happens when the agent leaves?

In my opinion, everyone who buys a policy that has any ongoing service fees should have the right to have them assigned to their personal agent who helps them. If an insurance company has their own sales force, it should be fuly disclosed at purchase time who and what the servicing requirements are. For example, you purchased a long-term-care policy from an advisor with Merrill Lynch or Bank of America and you decide to move all your investments and insurance policies to another advisor, but you find out you cannot move the service of your long-term-care policy and the service fees still go to Merrill Lynch even though you want nothing to do with them. Should you have the right to move that to an advisor you want to work with and shouldn't that advisor, if licensed in that state, be able to receive the service fees for advising you?

In other words, there should be freedom for the policyholders (aka you and me, the consumers), who are paying the premiums, to decide which agent gets to service their policy and that should include who receives the ongoing fees.

Go to my website at www.AskTheFinancialDoctor.com and look for the petitions to state insurance commissioners. Join in the fight.

I can not leave this section without a comment on Life Insurance and how it is being sold as an investment. If you are very wealthy it makes sense and if you are wealthy and young it makes a lot of sense, but if you are 55 and older and worth less than 5 million, it does not, and the reason why is, it is Life Insurance and there is a cost for the Death benefit and the the numbers in most cases do not work out, if you challenge and verify the history!

I will do a Free Analysis for any purchaser of this book that wants me to review any and all proposals they get for Life Insurance as an Investment. Why you ask? Because most of them are misrepresentations of the product. I will give you a second opinion for FREE, just email me at info@AsktheFinancialDoctor.com

What you Don't Know can Hurt you!

CHAPTER 9

OTHER INVESTMENTS

There are a number of other investment opportunities available that can help you grow your wealth and set up income streams. These investments vary in riskiness and several other factors. You should be careful when deciding where to fit some of these into your retirement portfolio.

They can add an element of lower volatility/risk/diversification, or an element of growth, depending on the investment, but some can also tie up large amounts of capital, causing a liquidity problem. Others can devastate your portfolio if you rely too much on them and the market crashes. Some of these other investments include real estate, commodities, currencies, and person-to-person lending.

REAL ESTATE

There is no doubt in my mind that next to individual stocks, real estate investing is the second fastest way to create wealth. With the real estate market in turmoil right now, and property values down, many people think that now is a good time to get into real estate. If you like the idea of investing in real estate, you can use it in a number of useful ways.

First, you can buy a property and hold on to it, hoping that it appreciates in value enough to make up for the interest and taxes you have paid on it, and then sell when it has appreciated enough. Second, you can buy investment property and rent it out, earning a regular income from the rental payments that others make to you.

Owning real estate has its advantages. Depending on your situation, you not only earn a return on your investment, but you can also save money on taxes by deducting property taxes, property insurance, and mortgage interest paid. This can save you money, allowing you to keep more of what's yours and, in turn, put it to work for you in another investment for even more of a return. You should speak with a tax professional about increasing your tax efficiency when it comes to your property.

You need to be careful when buying property, though, because market crashes do happen, as we saw recently, and real estate doesn't always appreciate. In addition, the outlay of money to purchase real estate can be substantial. Even if real estate is profitable as a long-term investment, it will tie up some of your core capital for a long time. You should carefully consider whether you could afford to have a large chunk of your nest egg tied up in property, especially if there's a chance that the market could crash just before you need to sell.

There is no debating that the purchase of a home is absolutely the single best long-term investment you can make, because you always need a roof over your head. However, you have to be smart and do your homework before you purchase. You don't want to find out too late that your house was built on swampland or next to an airport. As with any investment, you need to find out as much as possible about it before you purchase.

Remember the Latin warning "Caveat emptor" (Let the buyer beware). What you purchase is "as is," or subject to all defects, including market conditions and demographics.

In my opinion we are in for another Real estate Crash and property values will go down another 10 to 20 percent or more. I also believe the lowest Real Estate price's in my lifetime are coming, since we still have in excess of 12 million homeowners underwater or in deep trouble and have not been foreclosed to prevent another Real Estate crash, but it is coming.

Let's take a look at real estate with a twist.

REITS

It is actually possible to invest in real estate without owning property when you use real estate investment trusts (REITs). Investing in a REIT can provide your retirement portfolio with real estate holdings without the large amount of capital required to purchase physical property. A real estate investment trust is basically a company that owns a number of income-generating properties[13].

This can include commercial real estate, residential real estate, storage facilities, warehouses, and nearly any other type of property you can think of. Additionally, many REITs include investments in other real estate related businesses, such as mortgage companies and mortgage insurance providers.

When you invest in a REIT, you enjoy certain benefits of diversity. Some REITs are exchange-traded and can be bought and sold just like

---

13Investing in REITs is subject to a number of risks including possible declines in the value of real estate, risks related to economic conditions, possible lack of availability of mortgage funds, overbuilding, extended vacancies of properties, and dependency upon the skills of the management.

individual equities, with transaction fees that are similar. However, many REITs are nontraded or private. Many of these REITs offered through broker dealers may have limited liquidity.

Although generally considered to be illiquid investments, REITs still provide greater liquidity[14] than a direct investment in actual property, and they have good potential for growth since they include different aspects of real estate. This makes it fairly simple to get involved with real estate investing if you have the risk tolerance and if a qualified financial professional thinks that it might be a good move for you.

Most nontraded REITs will either liquidate the funds in cash or allow you to roll over to a new REIT. They might also become an individual exchange traded fund (stock) that you can buy or sell whenever you want.

Make sure you read the prospectus to see how long a REIT is expected to last. We do not recommend putting more than 10 to 20 percent of your investable assets into a REIT, and there are limitations in some states that only allow 10 percent or less to be invested in REITs.

REITS are generally long-term investments, so plan accordingly. There are many good ones available and some not so good, so get all the facts before investing.

14A nontraded REIT is not suitable for all investors. An investor must meet certain income, net worth, and other suitability standards. REITs are generally long-term, illiquid investments that are not suitable for all investors. Share redemption is limited, and there generally is no active trading market for shares.

ALTERNATIVE ASSET CLASSES

In addition to the above possibilities, there are alternative asset classes that can be considered for investing. Some of these are a little more difficult to invest in, and many of them have limited liquidity, meaning that you will have to find specific buyers who are willing to pay a good price. Most investments in these alternative asset classes require a long-term commitment. In some cases, being able to liquidate these assets requires luck. If you're investing for retirement, you should focus on more liquid assets that are a mix between income and growth.

However, if after considering your goals and consulting with a knowledgeable financial advisor, you feel that you can benefit from alternative asset classes, you might look into the following:

- Collectibles (sports cards, coins, stamps, etc.)
- Businesses
- Domain names
- Websites
- Art

As you can tell, most of these alternative investments are almost completely subjective in value and they are wholly dependent on the market and what people perceive their value to be. This makes them risky and possibly illiquid, if they go out of favor. Still, some of them offer tangible assets that you can hold in your hands. Insuring these types of assets can provide another layer of protection in the event a catastrophe strikes and the items are stolen, lost, or destroyed. In the end, you simply need to have a handle on the potential risks and rewards of these other asset classes. If they fit into your financial and retirement goals, then investing in them could be a good idea for you.

PRECIOUS METALS

Most financial planners recommend investing only 3 to 5 percent of your investable assets in gold and or silver. However, in the last 13 years, they have been two of the best investments you could make and moving that to 10 percent would have provided large returns to your overall portfolio.

Currently, neither the USA nor Europe, nor any major country, is on the gold standard, and I doubt that will change. I still think if you want to purchase physical gold or silver for a long period—say, 10 to 30 years—you will come out very well, but I really think you can make more buying these metals on the dips and selling them on the highs. There are many places you can go to learn about gold and silver investing. At my firm, we say an investment of 3 to 5 percent of your portfolio will work.

Again, just remember: "Caveat emptor." This is crucial when making this type of investment. Buyer beware—and be aware.

CHAPTER 10

RETIREMENT PLANS

As we go to press the US Government is currently reviewing the fee's on 401K plans and determining if they are too high and need to be mandated by the government. How about the government take a look at Net Returns instead? As usual the Federal government just doesn't get it and how could they, all they do is spend and lose money, so why should they allow private companies to make money for their investors and share in that growth? The fact is, the last people that should be looking at any expense is a group that has put our country over 17.6 Trillion in debt. There are facts here that they don't want to hear, but net rate of return is what matters, if you have a low fee and lose what are they going to do, make the companies put a guarantee on their 401K plans? The Government needs to get as far away from controlling investments as possible, since they have ruined EVERYTHING THEY HAVE TOUCHED!

The major problem with retirement plans is the number of options you have to invest in.

You are far better off with more options, such as you get with a personal choice retirement account (PCRA). If your employer is not offering this to you, you need to ask for it. Generally, there is no cost to employers, so they have no financial reason to deny your request.

Take this book to your employer, who is welcome to call me or e-mail me and I will be glad to help get one for you. The company retirement plan has to allow for a PCRA, but that is usually an easy fix.

Most 401(k)s, or company-sponsored retirement plans, have no managed opportunity for their employees and no strategy for volatile markets. Instead, you just buy a fund and hold on, even if it takes five to seven years to catch up. There is a better way and you need to inform your employer about it. After all, this is your retirement you are saving for.

After you get a general idea of what you would like your asset allocation to be and how much money you think you might need to retire, it's time to figure out where to put that money. The very first place you should put your money is in a tax-advantaged retirement plan. These plans provide you with the ability to grow your wealth while at the same time helping you either defer taxes on your earnings or avoid taxes on your earnings altogether.

It is best to put money into qualified, tax-advantaged plans before you put money into other investment vehicles. Speak with a tax professional or financial advisor to see how many plans you can open. You can usually have more than one type of tax-advantaged plan, and when possible, you should concentrate first on putting as much money as you can in as many investment vehicles that offer tax breaks. Only after you have maxed out funding within your tax-advantaged plans should you put money intended for retirement into other investment vehicles.

Many companies offer retirement plans known as deferred compensation. These are plans in which a portion of the salary is deferred, or paid out at a later date. These types of plans include profit sharing, pension, stock options, and more. Deferred compensation allows you to delay paying taxes on your earnings until you actually receive them. With a qualified deferred compensation plan, your money grows tax deferred, and your distributions are usually eligible for rollover into an IRA.

Your employer also gets a tax deduction for contributing money to the plan, but employers cannot discriminate among their employees, and their contributions to the plan are limited.

If you have a nonqualified deferred compensation plan, the employer doesn't get the tax deduction until benefits are paid to you, but the employer can pick and choose among employees, and contributions are not limited. As an employee, you are taxed according to when you have the right to receive benefits, no matter when the benefits are actually paid. It is a good idea to fully consider your employer's retirement plan and understand how it works so that there are no unpleasant surprises down the road.

COMPANY MATCH

If you are working for a company that offers a matching contributions program for your contributions, you should take full advantage of it. While some companies have done away with matching contributions due to the economic climate, some companies still offer this method of providing you with free money. Basically, your employer will agree to match your retirement account contribution up to a certain amount. That number is usually a match of between 3 and 5 percent up to a certain dollar amount. If the company maxes out the contribution amount at $400 per paycheck, that is how much you should try to contribute each time.

The match amounts to free money that goes into your account and begins working for you. Be careful, though. In many cases, there is a period in which you have to wait before the money is truly yours. This is known as being vested. The vesting requirement encourages company loyalty for a certain number of years. It prevents you from working for the company and getting the match for a couple of years and then taking the retirement account—with the free money—elsewhere. It is also important to note that unvested company match funds are not usually eligible for borrowing in the event that you take a loan out against your retirement plan.

(Chart 10.1)

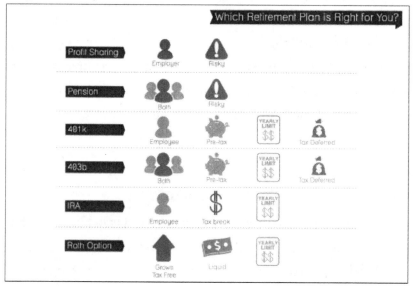

PROFIT SHARING

In a profit-sharing plan, the employer is the only contributor. The employer puts a portion of the company's profits into retirement plans for employees, and they grow from there. Companies that offer profit sharing sometimes offer it in conjunction with other retirement plans. However, most often these plans are offered by small businesses, start-ups, and others that may not have the means for large and sweeping retirement plans for their employees.

With profit sharing, the amount you receive each year is dependent on the profitability of the company, and so it will fluctuate. In many cases, it is best if you open your own retirement account with a brokerage in order to put a little more in, rather than relying on an irregular contribution. The key to building a solid nest egg is a degree of consistency in your contributions.

PENSION

Some organizations still offer pensions. Most of these are government organizations, usually on the state or federal level, but a few private companies still do so. Pension plans can include contributions from both the employer and the employee. The idea is to provide a set amount of regular income to employees. Much of the time, employees receive a percentage of their ending salary, each month, from the pension. Some pensions become more generous the longer the employee has worked for the company.

Pensions that allow employees as well as employers to contribute can result in rather generous payouts during retirement. Pensions come with rigid guidelines for employers, and they can also be quite expensive even though employers receive a tax benefit. It is little surprise that pensions are becoming quite scarce these days. You also need to be aware that when a company files for bankruptcy protection, it can change the structure of your pension and even lower your payout if it's overfunded. Relying entirely on a pension for your retirement income is usually a bad idea.

401(K)

This type of qualified retirement account is probably the most well known. Many companies accelerated the process of phasing out pensions during the last 25 years, and replaced these pensions with the 401(k). This meant that companies could offer you the chance to invest and improve your fortunes. In return, companies got plans that were less expensive, shifting more of the responsibility and risk to employees. Indeed, with Social Security funds shrinking and pensions disappearing rather quickly, it is quite likely that you will find yourself required to accept responsibility for an increasing portion of your own retirement, and the 401(K) is the most popular method for growing your nest egg.

Money that you put into a 401(k) is taken out of your paycheck "pretax." Perhaps you receive $2,500 on the first and the fifteenth of every month. You also like to take advantage of the 401(k) retirement plan, having the amount of your contribution deducted automatically. If you put $800 a month into your retirement accounts, that would work out to $400 every time you get paid. Your money comes out before taxes, so it's really as if you are getting $2,100 every other week. This lowers your income, and it can even help you stay in a lower marginal tax bracket, reducing the amount of taxes you owe right now.

Another advantage associated with the 401(k) is the fact that earnings grow tax deferred. This means that you do not have to pay taxes on the gains you enjoy from the retirement plan. You will eventually have to pay taxes on the money, which is why it is called "tax deferred." However, until you start taking distributions from your retirement plan, you will not have to pay taxes on any earnings. Once you do start withdrawing money, you will have to report any gains from your 401(k) so that it can be taxed as income.

Until you start withdrawing, your money can sit in the account, working for you and earning income. The fact that taxes are delayed means that you have that money compounding now, helping you build wealth more quickly. Rather than giving some of it to the government and having a smaller principal available to you, you can compound your money in the 401(k) for decades to accelerate your earnings.

Unfortunately, there are limits to how much money you can contribute to a retirement plan in a year. Once you hit that limit, you cannot contribute again for the year. It is likely that contribution limits will rise in the future since they have been rising periodically in order to keep up with inflation.

There is no percentage limit to the income that you make when it comes to contributing to your 401(k) plan. It is actually based on a dollar amount. Most companies and their employees believe the contribution is based on a percentage of salary, but it is not! For 2014, the limit on a 401(k) the maximum contribution is $17,500, plus a catch-up provision for individuals 50 years of age and up who can contribute an additional $5,500 or a total of $23,000. The catch-up contributions are also eligible for employer matching contributions. Today's 401(k) contributions no longer use a percentage of salary or earnings, but most plans still use that terminology even though it's outdated. It's especially confusing because the employer's matching contribution is based on a percentage of salary—for example, up to

3 percent—while the contribution itself is a flat dollar amount. You should be aware of that, even though it doesn't make a lot of sense.

403(B) RETIREMENT PLAN

If you work for a public education organization (primary, secondary, or higher education), an eligible nonprofit, cooperative hospital organization, or you are a self-employed minister, you are likely eligible for a 403(b) retirement plan if your employer offers it. This type of plan is basically the equivalent of a 401(k), allowing you to contribute money prior to taxes being taken out. This lowers your tax liability and allows the money in your account to grow tax deferred until you begin withdrawing it. A 403(b) is not subject to all of the regulatory requirements of a 401(k), but on a practical level, it operates in much the same way.

CONTRIBUTION LIMITS

Generally, contributions to an employee's 403(b) account are limited to the lesser of the limit on annual additions, or the elective deferral limit.

> Limit on Annual Additions: The limit on annual additions (the combination of all employer contributions and employee elective deferrals to all 403(b) accounts), generally, is the lesser of $51,000 for 2013, or 100 percent of includable compensation for the employee's most recent year of service. Generally, includible compensation is the amount of taxable wages and benefits the employee received in the employee's most recent full year of service.

Limit on Elective Deferrals: The limit on elective deferrals—the most an employee can contribute to a 403(b) account by means of a salary reduction agreement—is, as of 2014, $17,500.

Catch-Ups for Employees with 15 Years of Service: If permitted by the 403(b) plan, an employee who has at least 15 years of service with a public school system, hospital, home health service agency, health and welfare service agency, church, or convention or association of churches (or associated organization), has a 403(b) elective deferral limit that is increased by the lesser of:

1. $3,000
2. $15,000, reduced by the amount of additional elective deferrals made in prior years because of this rule
3. $5,000 times the number of the employee's years of service in the organization, minus the total elective deferrals made for earlier years

In 2013, an employee who qualified for the 15-year rule could have an elective deferral limit as high as $20,500.

Catch-Ups for Employees Age 50 or Over: As of 2014, if permitted by the 403(b) plan, employees who are age 50 or over at the end of the calendar year can also make catch-up contributions of $5,500 beyond the basic limit on elective deferrals.

If Both Catch-up Provisions Apply: While the age-50 catch-up is subject to an annual limit, the 15-year catch-up is subject to a use test, lifetime limit, and an annual limit. When both catch-up opportunities are available, the law requires deferrals exceeding the standard limit ($17,500 in 2014) to be first applied to the 15-year catch-up (to the extent permitted), and then to the age-50 catch-up.

Example: Assume Pat, age 50, has worked as a teacher in XYZ School District for 15 years, is eligible for the 15 years of service catch-up and has eligible compensation of $70,000 for 2014. The maximum employee and employer contributions to the XYZ 403(b) plan, for 2014, for Pat, would be $56,000:

- Pat may have elective deferrals to the 403(b) plan, totaling $20,500 ($17,500 plus $3,000 for 15 years of service catch-up).
- Her employer contributes $30,500, bringing the total employee and employer contributions to $51,000, the annual additions limit.
- Pat may also defer an additional $5,500, age-50, catch-up contribution for 2014.

Now assume that Pat only deferred $22,000 of her salary under the 403(b) plan. The plan provides both the 15-year and age-50 catch-up deferral opportunities. Under the use test, Pat is eligible for a 15-year catch-up of $3,000. Of the total $22,000 deferred for 2014, the maximum standard deferral of $17,500 is first applied, followed by application of the 15-year, catch-up deferral of $3,000, and finally application of the remaining $1,500 to the age-50, catch-up deferral.

EMPLOYEES WHO ALSO PARTICIPATE IN ANOTHER PLAN:

Employees must combine contributions made to their 403(b) accounts with contributions made to all other plans in which they participate (other than 457 plans): qualified plans, SEPs, and SIMPLE IRAs of all corporations, partnerships and sole proprietorships in which they have more than a 50 percent control. The employee's total elective deferrals to all of these plans combined cannot exceed the annual deferral limit ($17,500 in 2014).

ADDITIONAL IRS RESOURCES:

- 403(b) Plan Basics, Home page (http://www.irs.gov/publications/p571/ch01.html)
- Publication 571, Tax-Sheltered Annuity Plans (403(B) Plans) for Employees of Public Schools and Certain Tax-Exempt Organizations
- Publication 4482, 403(b) Tax-Sheltered Annuities for Participants

TRADITIONAL IRA

Another popular retirement plan is the traditional individual retirement account (IRA). All those who work and report income on their taxes are eligible to open an IRA. Traditional IRA contributions are tax deductible. You can lower your taxable income by contributing to an IRA. As with the 401(k), you get the tax advantage immediately.

There is a limit to how much you can contribute annually to an IRA and to a Roth IRA. For 2014, the limit is $5,500. If you are age 50 or over, you can make a catch-up contribution of $1,000, with a total of $6,500 per year. It is important to note that the IRA comes with a requirement for you to take minimum distributions once you reach the age of 70½ years old. Once you reach the required age to begin making regular withdrawals, failure to do so can result in the confiscation of half the value of the mandatory withdrawal as a penalty by the IRS.

There is a phase-out for the deductibility of your IRA contribution. For 2014, if you are covered by a company retirement plan for a single person or head of household, this phase-out starts at $60,000 and goes up to $70,000, at which point your IRA is no longer deductible. For a married/joint filer, it starts at $96,000 and goes up to $116,000, at which point it is no longer deductible. If you are not covered by a company retirement plan, but your spouse is covered, the phase-out ranges from $181,000 to $191,000. If you file married-separate, your phase-out range is $0 to $10,000.

Traditional IRAs can be quite useful to those who expect to have a lower income when they retire. If you think that you will be in a lower tax bracket after retirement, you can take advantage of the tax break and use the tax deduction to lower your income so that you do not have to pay as much in taxes now. Then, when you start living off your retirement account money, since withdrawals are taxed at the marginal income rate, you will be paying taxes on a lower income.

ROTH IRA

The IRA has had a Roth option for a number of years. More recently, an option for the Roth 401(k) and the Roth 403(b) has become available as well. The Roth option basically changes the way taxes are figured. Instead of taking the money out of the paycheck before taxes are figured, your contributions are made with after-tax dollars. This means that you pay taxes on your income, and then the money for the Roth contribution is deducted from your paycheck.

The real advantage comes from the fact that money in a Roth retirement account grows tax-free. Since you have already paid taxes before the money was put into your retirement account, you never have to pay taxes on your earnings. Another advantage of the Roth IRA option is that you can always withdraw your contributions at any time, unlike a regular IRA. However, earnings on those contributions should remain in the Roth until at least age 59½, or federal income taxes will apply to withdrawals, as well as a 10 percent federal penalty (unless an exception applies).

The contribution limits to Roth accounts remain the same for their respective types of plans. A Roth 401(k) or 403(b) has the same limit as a regular 401(k) or 403(b), and the Roth IRA has the same limit as the regular IRA. The difference comes in with income limits. When the Roth IRA was introduced, the ability to contribute was phased out as income grew. That means the amount single individuals can contribute begins to phase out when their adjusted gross income reaches $114,000. Single individuals can no longer contribute to a Roth IRA when their income reaches $129,000. For married couples, the income phase-out begins at $181,000, and contributions are stopped when the couple's income reaches $191,000.

In the case of the Roth 401(k), however, that income limit has been removed. You can contribute to a Roth 401(k) no matter how much money you make. As more people become aware of the Roth 401(k), it is likely that it will increase in popularity, and more companies will offer it as an employer-sponsored retirement plan option.

SELF-EMPLOYED RETIREMENT ACCOUNT OPTIONS

If you are self-employed, you will still want to set money aside in tax-advantaged accounts. There are plenty of options, even for those who are not working for "the man." You should explore the possibilities, and perhaps even open more than one type of account. Of course, any time you are earning money and filing a tax return, you are eligible for an IRA or a Roth IRA. Many self-employed people use these vehicles to invest money in a tax-advantaged account.

Self-Employed 401(k) Plans

Self-employed folks can also set up and fund their own 401(k) profit-sharing plan, which allows for the same type of contributions mentioned above. Using this type of plan, which is easily set up at any major brokerage firm, you can also make an additional contribution that is a percentage of net profit (this is the profit-sharing component of the plan).

For individuals who declare about $75,000 net profit from self-employment, the total pretax amount they can contribute to this type of plan is about $31,000, as of 2014. If they are age 50 or older, they can contribute about $36,500. For self-employed folks who are age 50 or older and made a profit of $180,000 or more in 2014, the maximum pretax contribution to this type of retirement plan for the self-employed is $56,500.

SEP IRA

The simplified employee pension (SEP) IRA is very similar to a traditional IRA. However, the contribution limits are higher. You can set up an SEP IRA anytime before the due date of your tax return (April 15, or October 15 if you file for an extension) and contribute. As of 2014, you can contribute up to $52,000 to a SEP IRA. However, the $52,000 is very clearly an "up-to-the-limit" situation since you can only contribute 25 percent of up to $260,000 in compensation.

The formulas for figuring this out can be found on the IRS website, or you can consult a knowledgeable tax professional to help you figure out your compensation. When you make use of a SEP IRA, you are considering yourself an employee, and if you contribute to your SEP, you have to contribute to SEPs for other employees you may have as well.

The catch-up contribution provisions do not apply to SEP IRAs. They still apply to old salary reduction simplified employee pensions (SARSEPs) in effect before 1997. No new SARSEPs were allowed after 1996. SEP contributions can be made up to the due date of the tax return, including extensions. For example, a 2013 SEP contribution can be made up to April 15, 2014—or up to October 15, 2014 if you have a valid extension to October 15, 2014.

SIMPLE Plan

Another form of IRA, the savings incentive match plan for employees (SIMPLE), can allow you to contribute up to $12,000 a year for your retirement. If you are 50 or over, you can add a catch-up provision of $2,500 for a total 2014 contribution of $14,500. A SIMPLE plan comes in a Roth version as well. It is a deferred compensation plan that you can offer to your employees, as well as yourself, since you are an employee.

If you have a side business that is not needed for your living expenses, you can actually contribute up to 100 percent of the net profit. For example, if you have a website affiliate business, and your net profits are $12,000 a year, you can contribute the entire amount to the SIMPLE plan. A SIMPLE plan can be a good way to put small amounts of income from a side business to good use. You can contribute up to $12,000 in 2014 to a SIMPLE IRA, which is significantly more than with a regular Roth IRA. Many people who have side income in addition to a regular full-time or part-time job find that the SIMPLE IRA is a good choice, and an excellent way to grow a nest egg.

Keogh Plan

In 1962 the legislation creating the Keogh plan was crafted, and in 1981 it was expanded. The Keogh plan is the original retirement investment vehicle for the self-employed. There are two different types of Keogh plans: a defined contribution plan and a defined benefit plan. You have to decide which you will be using when you open the plan.

The contribution plan is based on a percentage of your compensation. The money purchase version of the defined contribution plan establishes a set amount of money to be contributed each year the business earns a profit, while the profit-sharing version provides for discretionary contributions out of the company's profits.

The defined benefit Keogh plan offers a fixed retirement benefit that can be a set amount each year or can represent a percentage of salary. A formula is used to establish this benefit. For older owner-employees, the defined benefit Keogh plan is an attractive option since it allows them to contribute 80 percent or even 100 percent of their "compensation" to the plan, and it offers a fixed payout during retirement.

Defined Benefit Plan

The defined benefit plan is now usually only used by highly compensated self-employed business people. It is the plan with which you can shelter the highest amount of income from current taxation, and it works especially well if you are age 50 or older. To avoid unnecessary expenses and taxes, you should consult a specialist.

Many self-employed business owners find that one of these specialized plans—in addition to an old 401(k) from a job or a traditional or Roth IRA—can provide a number of benefits. The idea is to increase the amount of money you invest, while at the same time increasing your tax efficiency as a home business owner.

CATCH-UP CONTRIBUTIONS

One of the biggest issues many seniors face today is attempting to meet their nest egg goals for retirement. If you wish you could put a little bit extra aside each year to help you build your core capital for use during retirement, you are in luck. Those who are age 50 and older can make "catch-up" contributions to their retirement plans.

For a traditional or Roth IRA, the catch-up contribution is an extra $1,000 each year. For the 401(k), you can contribute $23,000 ($5,500 extra), and for the SIMPLE plan you can contribute up to $14,500 ($2,500 extra). These catch-up contributions can allow you to make use of the time after you turn age 50 to increase your principal. If you plan to retire when you are age 60, those extra 10 years can mean between $10,000 and $55,000 of additional contributions, depending on the plan you use.

If you combine different plans (a SIMPLE, an IRA and a 401(k)), you could even see $90,000 extra in catch-up contributions over the course of 10 years. With proper planning now, using catch-up contributions can help you increase your nest egg significantly. If you were planning to retire at 55, you might consider running the numbers and seeing whether it is worth waiting another five years and making catch-up contributions.

BORROWING FROM YOUR
RETIREMENT PLANS

Sometimes situations arise in which you might feel you must borrow from your retirement plan. There are certain exceptions with some IRAs that allow you to withdraw money penalty-free prior to the age of 59½. This includes certain qualifying education expenses as well as the construction or purchase of a first home. Note that you cannot borrow against your IRA.

Taking a loan from your 401(k) means you are borrowing against your retirement account and you normally have five years to pay it back with interest. The good news is that you are essentially paying interest to yourself. The bad news is that you have taken a chunk of principal out of your account, and it is no longer helping to earn compounding returns. This can seriously impair your ability to grow wealth in your retirement plan. Borrowing against your retirement account is a decision that requires a great deal of thought and should not be taken lightly.

While borrowing from your retirement account is better than taking out a high-interest loan, you still have to weigh the pros and cons. If you are earning 8 or 9 percent on your retirement plan, but a loan would cost you 6 percent, it doesn't make sense to take out the principal. If your only options are high-interest loans, such as those in the range of 15 percent, it might make some sense to borrow against your retirement account if you are in dire straits. Be warned, though: If you don't pay back the loan in the prescribed amount of time, you will be assessed taxes and penalties.

Taxes for early withdrawals from your retirement plans are figured at regular income rates. Penalties for early withdrawal, which are assessed on top of taxes, often run about 10 percent of the amount that you take out. Your early withdrawal could add to your income, bumping you up to another tax bracket and further compounding your financial problems. If you switch jobs, or have some other reason for getting rid of your current retirement plan, don't just cash it in and withdraw the money. Instead, set up a rollover so that the money moves into another retirement account. That way, you can avoid the taxes and penalties that come with early withdrawal. However, if you have a loan, it will need to be paid in full. Otherwise, it will be a taxable event.

When in doubt, talk to your financial planner or tax advisor or to whoever is helping you with the plan before you take out a loan on your retirement plan.

Ask your advisors if they are familiar with Ed Slott, CPA, or David Royer, and if they are not, you need to get another advisor. They are without question the top two retirement planning specialists in the country and have been for many years.

If your advisor, or insurance agent, is not familiar with them, your advisor likely does not keep current on laws and regulations for retirement plans—and you need to change your advisor.

Any mistake regarding the beneficiary options on your retirement plans can actually disinherit or cause unnecessary taxation for your heirs.

Read the following books to learn more about IRAs, Roths, and 401(k) plans than most advisors know:

- Top 10 IRA Mistakes: How to Avoid IRS Tax Traps by David F. Royer
- Fund Your Future: A Tax-Smart Savings Plan in Your 20s and 30s by Ed Slott, CPA, "America's IRA expert"

CHAPTER 11

DESIGNING YOUR INVESTMENT PORTFOLIO

O nce you have a basic idea of how different investments work, and the ways they can be used to benefit you in retirement, it will be time to start putting together an investment portfolio. You can think of your portfolio as being divided into three sections: cash, income, and growth.

Below is some basic information you should know about, but this is for educational purposes *only* and is *not* a recommendation for investment.

THE CASH PORTION

The cash portion is more of a safety net, providing you with a certain degree of capital preservation. It is best to try to find cash investments that keep pace with inflation, as a bare minimum. It is also a good idea to choose cash investments that are relatively liquid so that you can access them in case of emergency. A preservation managed portfolio is recommended for most ages with the majority of these funds. You must minimize your risk.

THE INCOME PORTION

The income portion of your portfolio represents the portion of your core capital that provides you with immediate cash flow. This is money that you can use right now to cover expenses and make living more comfortable if you are retired. If you are still working, you will need to build up the potential guaranteed income you will need in retirement.

THE GROWTH PORTION

The growth portion of your retirement portfolio is designed to get your money working harder for you. The capital you use in the growth section of your portfolio should be providing you with the means to avoid outliving your money.

A financial advisor can help you determine a likely allocation, but this provides you with a basic look at the priorities in dividing your retirement portfolio. It also serves as a reminder that you will need to rebalance your investment portfolio as you transition into retirement and change the primary focus of your investments. The types of investments that fall into each category will vary as well, depending on your needs.

Before you figure out actual asset allocations for your retirement investing portfolio, you must decide how much money you need to live on. One of the best ways you can do this is to consider how much you need to bring in each month. If you decide that you need $4,000 each month to live comfortably and do what you would like to do, then it is necessary to look at all of your possible income sources.

If you receive $1,500 a month from Social Security (which might be reduced later) or other income sources, you need to come up with the other $2,500 from your investments, combining withdrawals from retirement accounts and other investment accounts that you might have. If you have a pension (a disappearing retirement tool), you can factor that into your calculations. You can also include regular income that you might receive from a business that you own, or rental property, or from a website that you operate. Look at all of your income streams, and figure out how much your investments need to make for you. Ideally, you can live off these income streams while leaving your core capital mostly intact.

The $2,500 per month that you need from your investments in order to make up the difference from Social Security Benefits and other income, comes to $30,000 per year. Let's say that you can get a 5 percent return on the income portion of your investment portfolio, so that means that you will need $600,000 in the income portion of your portfolio. Thus, $600,000.00 at 5 percent gives you $30,000 per year.

Another option, of course, is to tap into your principal, though this will reduce your ability to earn returns over time and you will have less core capital to earn interest for you in the future. However, it can still be a viable option, as long as you don't withdraw too much of your principal. If you are careful about only withdrawing a small portion of your capital along with the interest you earn, there is a good chance that your money can still outlive you. A financial professional can help you estimate, using a number of variables, how long your money might last if you tap into your principal. Normally, such items as taxes, inflation, estimated rate of return, and increased health-care costs, can all be included in models that help you see how long your money might last.

If passing a large estate on to your heirs is not vital to you, it becomes less important to avoid using your principal. Of course, a huge market crash or some medical catastrophe could wipe out a large portion of your nest egg, and if you have used up your core capital, all of the calculations in the world won't stop you from outliving your money. It's a delicate balance and, unfortunately, there is no surefire way to guarantee that your money will last. If you stick to the 80/20 rule, though, the odds will be in your favor.

UNDERSTANDING RISK TOLERANCE

As you build your investment portfolio, both before and after retirement, it is important to understand risk tolerance. Your risk tolerance will make a big difference in the types of investments you make, and in the asset allocation of your portfolio. Your ability to handle risk, on the financial and emotional levels, will shape how you invest. A good financial advisor can help you understand your risk tolerance, and help you create a plan based upon what you can handle.

Risk tolerance is your ability to handle the volatility of the markets. If you have a high risk tolerance, it means that the prospect of larger losses would not be devastating to you. If your risk tolerance is lower, it means that you cannot afford very many losses, and that you are likely to need to focus more on investments that are less volatile. While you will not see returns that are as high, you won't have the large fluctuations in value that frequently accompany riskier investments.

To get a better picture of your overall risk tolerance, you need to consider it from both a financial and emotional perspective.

FINANCIAL RISK TOLERANCE

Your financial risk tolerance is fairly straightforward. It defines how much risk you can handle from a purely financial standpoint. It is a rather objective measure of the potential losses that your assets are capable of handling. You run the numbers and see what is possible. Can you afford to have money tied up in an illiquid investment for five to seven years? What will happen to your overall wealth if an up-and-coming alternative energy company doesn't make it and you lose a large stake?

When calculating financial risk tolerance, you look at your income streams and your overall nest egg and figure out whether, according to the sheer numbers, you have enough money to take a few risks. If something will financially devastate you in the event that it goes bad, you probably do not have the financial risk tolerance for that move. If your assets can absorb the loss, then you are probably okay to move forward.

Think of it this way. If you had $250,000 invested and you woke up tomorrow and it was worth only $200,000, what would you do? You don't want to spend your golden years working at the golden arches of McDonald's, do you?

EMOTIONAL RISK TOLERANCE

As you might imagine, emotional risk tolerance is entirely subjective. Your emotional risk tolerance deals with your visceral responses to what is happening with your investments. You might have the money to absorb an investment loss, but anxiety over possible losses may prevent you from being able to deal with your portfolio as losses mount.

Venture capitalists can usually ride out the market, even when it is in a tailspin, and emotionally handle it when investments don't go as expected. Others, though, feel their health and well-being is affected by such volatility. Understanding your emotional risk tolerance and how it fits into your financial risk tolerance is important. Being able to remain calm and evaluate your investments without giving in to fear and panic is vital if you want a successful retirement.

INVESTING AND DRIVING THE FREEWAY

Risk-averse investors are the types who drive 50 to 60 miles an hour on the freeway. They are the CD buyers who cannot stand risk or losing any money. No risk brings no rewards, so you can grow broke safely, thanks to taxes and inflation.

Moderate investors drive at 60 to 65 miles per hour; they want a little bigger boost while keeping a limit on risk and they are willing to invest in asset classes such as bonds and mature stocks with low volatility or a managed portfolio designed for preservation of principle.

Growth investors drive 65 to 75 miles per hour; they want to get where they are going faster and will take a little more risk to get there more quickly. They might invest in some growth stocks, but they still have a cap on the risk they take.

Aggressive investors go 75 miles per hour and up, investing in the fast lane. They are willing to take the very largest risk in order to get a very big and very fast reward. They might speculate in stocks and/ or real estate or bet big in alternative asset classes.

(Chart 11.1)

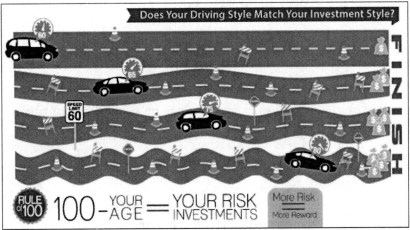

THE ONE HUNDRED YEARS METHOD OF ASSET ALLOCATION OR RULE OF 100

Another method for determining proper asset allocation is done with a stock/bond mix. You subtract your age from 100, which becomes the percentage of your portfolio that should be devoted to stocks. For example, in this type of allocation, if you were 30 years old, you would put 70 percent of your portfolio in stocks, and 30 percent in bonds. As you age, you adjust your asset allocation; retirees who are 65 years old would consider shifting their asset allocation so that only 35 percent of their portfolio is in stocks and 65 percent is in bonds or fixed income. You can use the 10-5-3 Rule (see below) in conjunction with this as well, just to see possible investment returns in this type of asset allocation.

How often you rebalance this type of investment portfolio depends on your risk tolerance and your goals; remember, though, that rebalancing may involve tax consequences. Make sure you understand the consequences associated with rebalancing your investment portfolio; many choose to rebalance every 10 years before retirement, and then every five years after retiring. What you do depends on your needs, goals, and the advice you get from a trusted financial planner.

Any type of asset allocation method will probably require tweaking to fit your needs and your style, but you can get an idea of the possibilities when you take into account varying scenarios. A financial planner can help you assess your options by using different rules of thumb for portfolio building, helping you create a plan that is more likely to result in your money outliving you.

PUTTING TOGETHER AN INVESTMENT PORTFOLIO

When you are ready to put together your retirement investing portfolio, you need to consider your risk tolerance and your goals for your money. Decide how much you need to retire, based on what you want to do. Then, build your portfolio around your goals, paying attention to your risk tolerance and what you can afford. When you set up your portfolio with consideration for the three categories of (1) cash, (2) income, and (3) growth, as we discussed earlier in this chapter, it helps to review which investments are considered income investments, and which are considered growth investments. Here is a quick refresher:

1. **Income Investments:** Bonds either corporate or government, dividend-paying stocks, preferred stocks, some real estate, or rental property (could be residential or commercial property), some annuities, and some managed funds, spread the risk.

2. **Growth Investments:** Stocks (especially small caps, some technology, and start-ups), some REITs, and some growth managed funds, spread the risk.

There will always be a degree of overlap in some asset classes, depending on how risky the investment is. In many cases, growth investments are thought to be riskier, since they often carry a greater risk of loss, and experience more volatility. Most people find that their level of risk tolerance can handle stocks, divided between established and solid, well-known companies with modest returns and a few small-cap companies and start-ups with potential for growth, which means higher returns.

There are those who like to actively trade with a portion of the money set aside for growth investing. If you have the financial risk tolerance for this type of investing, and you enjoy it emotionally, this can be a way to quickly experience growth. It can even be a satisfying hobby during your retirement years—but be careful. Active trading can also be a fast way to lose a chunk of your core capital. It works best when only a tiny portion of your investment portfolio is devoted to the riskiest and most volatile investments.

Most of my clients will have the majority of their investment dollars in a preservation of principal managed portfolio that is always 100 percent liquid. Depending on their needs, they may use 20 to 30 percent to have some guaranteed income. They may also place 10 to 15 percent in a managed portfolio designed for growth if needed for the future.

THE 10-5-3 RULE OF ASSET ALLOCATION

One method of determining asset allocation is the 10-5-3 Rule, which assumes that over time, stocks will earn 10 percent returns, bonds will earn 5 percent, and cash will earn 3 percent annually. Due to market fluctuations and changing financial conditions, your investments will return less than this in some years and more than this in other years.

In the year or so leading up to the financial crash of 2008, cash was actually returning around 5 percent for some investments; however, right now, cash investments are generally returning less than 3 percent so, like most rules of thumb, this method of asset allocation is meant to be a general guide to the results you can expect. It is also important to note that because this rule is more likely to hold true over a period of 15 to 20 years, you should think of it as a long-term planning tool only.

You could use the 10-5-3 rule in conjunction with the rule of 72 that helps you figure the time it take for your money to double:

- Cash: 72/3 = 24 years
- Bonds: 72/5 = 14.4 years
- Stocks: 72/10 = 7.2 years

The 10-5-3 rule helps you to determine what you need to do in order to grow your investment portfolio over a period of 30 years to your target amount. If you start at age 30 and put money into a portfolio with the expectation of beginning to use it at age 60, your money will double four times for stocks, twice for bonds and once for cash. You can roughly estimate how much you need to start with by working backward.

Note, though, that you may not have to put all of the money in at once. The 10-5-3 rule assumes you put in a lump sum and then do nothing with it. You will likely set up a plan so that you regularly invest money on a schedule (possibly using dollar cost averaging), allowing you to make up for the fact that you do not have a large lump sum right now. Clearly, the earlier you start, the better off you will be; the 10-5-3 rule offers a starting place, and a rough look at how you can begin.

When you are ready to retire, the 10-5-3 rule can also help. Let's say you have a retirement portfolio of $800,000 and you have 5 percent or $40,000 in cash and 65 percent or $520,000 for your income needs and 30 percent or $240,000 in growth like stocks or equities. We have divided it up according to the three categories of (1) cash, (2) income, and (3) growth just like we have been discussing earlier in this chapter. The money in the growth portion. 30 percent or $240,000, could, after 7.2 years, be at $480,000, barring any large drops in the value of your investments. If you are living on the income portion of your portfolio, and you are able to avoid touching your growth portion for another 7.2 years (for a total of 14.4 years), you might end up with as much as $960,000, to offset inflation or additional medical expenses at retirement.

Of course, how you change your allocation as you age is a big part of how your money grows. If you start taking distributions from your retirement portfolio at age 60, and you live off the income portion, at the end of the first 7.2 years, you can move the interest earnings from your growth investments into income investments. This will leave the core $240,000 in the growth portion of your portfolio to continue working for you, while you shift the interest earnings into the income portion, creating a larger base for your income core capital. Of course, the cash portion (which won't double to $80,000 until you are age 84, remains available for emergencies.

Remember that the 10-5-3 rule is not hard and fast; it is merely a guideline. It does not account for taxes, inflation, and down cycles in the market. It also doesn't include some other investments that might be of interest to you, such as commodities, currencies, and real estate. A financial professional and/or a tax professional can help you work through your needs with regard to asset allocation and rebalancing your retirement investment portfolio as you progress through life, as well as tweaking the 10-5-3 rule to include additional investments that you might be considering.

SPECIAL CONSIDERATIONS FOR YOUR INVESTMENT PORTFOLIO

When designing your investment portfolio, there are some different considerations that can improve the overall performance of your retirement investments. Check out appendix A.

DIVERSIFICATION

One of the most important aspects of putting together a portfolio is proper diversification if you are still working. You need to have diversity across asset classes and diversity across sectors. The idea behind this is that investments move differently in relation to each other. Bonds and stocks often move in opposite directions to each other, since investors gravitate toward stocks (and higher returns) in times of economic optimism. In times of economic uncertainty, many investors choose bonds because of their lower risk and their capital preservation objectives. Therefore, if you have diversity in your investment portfolio, you have bonds to help limit your overall portfolio losses from stocks.

The US dollar often moves inversely to commodities such as oil and gold, so if you are long on the dollar, it helps to have some commodities, just in case you are wrong and the dollar weakens instead of strengthening. A qualified financial advisor can help you figure out how much diversification you need, depending on your goals and risk tolerance, and help you avoid the pitfalls associated with diluting your gains from too *much* diversification.

It can also help to have diversity in terms of your individual investments. When you invest in individual stocks, it can be helpful to consider different sectors. If all of your stocks are in technology companies, and that sector tanks, your portfolio will take a substantial hit. If, however, you have some blue chips as well as tech stocks, you might be able to limit some of your losses as the blue chips return solid performances—or, at least, perform less poorly than the tech sector. The same is true of bonds and other asset classes. Having too much exposure to one type of investment can lead to the downfall of your investment portfolio if you are not careful.

This principle also applies to mutual funds. Many retirees have at least three or four mutual funds in their portfolios and if it were up to me, they would have no mutual funds and only managed portfolios for their serious money. If you need or desire tax-free income, a tax-free bond mutual fund is one of the best ways to do this, as long as you realize it will need to be for the long term since the fund will move with interest rates.

When you own mutual funds, you will find that some of these funds have several overlapping investments; always double-check your funds to make sure that they are not invested in all of the same sectors or stocks. You can imagine what happens if you have three mutual funds that are invested heavily in one sector. This consideration applies to index funds as well. Consider investing in different types of indexes in order to provide a little diversity in your portfolio. What is the recovery time in bad markets?

It is a good idea to check into the investments in your employer-sponsored retirement plan. In many cases, especially if your account is not self-directed, you might find that you have a disproportionate amount of company stock. This is not something that many think about until it is too late and the company has gone under, rendering the stock worthless and wiping out the value in the investment portfolio. Check into your company's plan, and make sure that you aren't exposed to this undue risk. If your company does not offer self-directed plans, you might consider opening an investment account at an independent brokerage—either online or offline—and creating some diversity in that way.

Don't forget diversity in foreign investments. While you might be tempted to consider only domestic investments, there are a number of enticing opportunities abroad. You can invest in foreign equities, indexes, or bonds, as well as a range of other investments. Just like domestic investments, though, foreign investments have differing levels of risk. Developed nations are considered less risky, so investments in Western Europe and Japan would be relatively safe, but they also offer lower returns.

Emerging markets such as China, India, Eastern Europe, the Middle East, and Latin America can provide a great deal of growth potential, but volatility can lead to large losses. Adding a few foreign investments[15] to your retirement portfolio, while paying attention to asset allocation and risk tolerance, can provide a much-needed bit of diversity. You need to understand the risk and reward of doing so.

It could help your overall portfolio continue to grow if domestic investments are struggling while foreign investments are soaring. Some investors prefer just to invest in the global stock index for foreign diversity and leave it at that. For those with low risk tolerance, or those who are uncertain of the research associated with foreign investments, this can be a practical solution.

SOCIALLY RESPONSIBLE INVESTING

In recent years, many investors have become increasingly concerned with ensuring that their investments correspond to their value system. This has given rise to the concept of socially responsible investing. With socially responsible investing, you choose companies with practices that align with your moral and social values. This can mean avoiding companies that do business in a country with a history of human rights abuses, or choosing to invest in green energy companies rather than energy companies that specialize in pollution-causing fossil fuels.[16]

You might invest in companies that encourage environmentally sustainable practices, or companies that offer living wages and generous benefits to their employees. In many cases, socially respon-

---

15International investing involves special risks due to specific factors such as increased volatility, currency fluctuations, and differences in auditing and other financial standards.
16Sector investing includes specific risks, including greater concentration in an industry, lower overall diversification, regulatory changes that might impact the sector, and other risks that can affect your returns. Additionally, fluctuations can result in losses.

sible investing applies to those who invest according to their religious convictions. For Muslims, this might mean avoiding usurious companies and practices. For Jews, it could mean investing in kosher enterprises. For some Christians, it might mean avoiding companies that support scientific research based on the use of stem cells.

Many devout religious investors of all persuasions actively avoid vice investments in such items as tobacco, alcohol, gambling, and even certain media. For those who do not want to comb through individual records of companies, it is possible to find indexes and funds that are built around socially responsible investments. Index funds and ETFs include clean energy and other socially responsible enterprises, and there are specific funds and indexes aimed at different religious sensibilities.

CREATING AN ALL-FUND PORTFOLIO

One popular portfolio building technique is the all-fund portfolio. Because there are a number of mutual funds, index funds, and ETFs to choose from, it is possible to build a diverse investment portfolio out of nothing but funds. There are stock funds, bond funds, commodity funds, currency funds, and real estate funds. With all of these options, it is little surprise that many are turning to this type of portfolio.

There are different tax advantages associated with some funds, and index funds and ETFs generally have low fees. Another consideration is that investing in funds takes a lot of the hard work out of investing, since you do not have to individually pick stocks and gauge their performance all the time. If you are careful about the funds you choose, it is possible to create a retirement investment portfolio that is easier to live with. It is also possible to use funds for a more growth-oriented portfolio by investing in riskier ETFs or indexes.

It is worth noting that you can use asset allocation methods with all-fund retirement portfolios. If you are using the 100-years method, you can allocate using bond funds and stock funds. There are also cash funds that can be used for that portion of your portfolio. And, of course, if you are concerned about adding a little more growth, you can add foreign funds, currency funds, commodity funds, and even alternative investment funds to your portfolio. It is not surprising that with the number of options available today, many investors are interested in using funds to create diverse retirement portfolios.

As discussed earlier, I do not recommend having a portfolio of mutual funds. The information I have provided on mutual funds is for educational purposes only.

"SET IT AND FORGET IT" AND AGE-BASED FUNDS

Other recent trends in portfolio design include "set it and forget it" funds and age-based retirement funds. Not only are these funds generally more expensive than other comparable funds, but these types of funds should be viewed with caution. While index funds and some ETFs may not need as much active management as other investments, due to their nature, it is a good idea to review what investments are present in any fund, as well as evaluate how well the fund is doing overall, and whether or not it is helping you meet your retirement goals.

One of the dangers of giving in to set-it-and-forget-it funds and age-based funds is the potential for a false sense of security. You might assume that everything will be properly taken care of. While some of these investments will probably perform well in your portfolio, they should not be an excuse for not periodically viewing how things are progressing, and making any changes that are necessary.

Once you have designed a portfolio, you will need to monitor it and change it as your life cycle changes. As you will see in the next chapter, we will share ideas on managing a portfolio with the help of an advisor.

In my opinion, the absolutely best option is to have the majority of your assets in a managed portfolio that manages your risk based on your risk tolerance. Anything else is bound to become a train wreck.

CHAPTER 12

HOW MUCH MONEY DO YOU NEED TO RETIRE?

The question people most often ask me is, "How much do I need to retire?" This question has been addressed to a lesser degree earlier in this book; however, we haven't really taken a look at some of the numbers. The amount you need to retire will be personal to you. No one number can suffice for everyone. You will need to determine your own retirement needs based on the following factors:

1. Current income
2. Your expenses; live on 90 percent of your income and you will be a survivor
3. Your fixed and variable income come from different sources
4. How much debt you have
5. What you plan to do: travel, volunteer, play golf, take classes, etc.
6. Your life expectancy
7. Expectation of long-term-care needs

The answers to these questions can help you determine how much money you need to retire. If you do not have your home paid off, you will need much more than someone who has no mortgage to worry about. The same is especially true of other types of debt. If you retire before you have paid off your debt, a large portion of your income is likely to go toward meeting your obligations, meaning that you will need more money in order to retire comfortably.

Other expenses, such as utilities and insurance premiums, will figure into your calculations, but they can be averaged, based on what you pay now. You can also find reasonable estimates of the costs associated with traveling, learning a hobby, and even the possibility of long-term care.

Figuring your life expectancy might be a little more difficult, especially since you are likely to outlive the average of 78.74 years, according to the most recent figures from the Centers for Disease Control and Prevention, in *National Vital Statistics Report of 10-10-2012*. You may also need to consider long-term-care expenses and other health-related costs as you age and you may need to devote a portion of your retirement portfolio to purchasing a long-term-care policy.

In addition to coming up with estimates for your monthly expenses, you will also have to consider inflation and taxes. Some retirees find that they have put enough money aside—and that it has grown enough—that when they retire, they could actually be in a higher tax bracket with their withdrawals. This can present a new problem.

Others decide to live more simply. This requires less money, so their distributions are smaller and they stay in the same tax bracket or even move into a lower bracket. Others choose to shelter their money through estate planning. Some retirement plans, though, require that you take a minimum distribution starting at age 70½, and this may present its own problems.

When trying to figure out how much money you need to retire, you can look at it in terms of monthly income as well as in terms of a total nest egg. Below are tables that calculate how much money you need to accumulate in order to meet various needs.

WHAT YOU WILL NEED TO RETIRE
Table 8.1: Capital Required for Annual Inflation-Adjusted Income

This table assumes a life expectancy of 81 years of age, a little longer than that of the average American woman lives, and assumes an inflation rate of 3 percent per year and 5 percent annual returns. The table helps you see the required nest egg for different annual income needs and the figures are hypothetical, since actual inflation and returns fluctuate. Additionally, the table does not take into account any taxes you might be required to pay[17]. (Table 12.1)

AGE AT RETIREMENT	YEARS TO LIFE EXPECTANCY	$36,000 PER YER	$48,000 PER YEAR	$60,000 PER YEAR	$96,000 PER YEAR	$120,000 PER YEAR
50	31	$842,000	$1,121,000	$1,402,000	$2.25 MILLION	$2.8 MILLION
55	26	$737,000	$983,000	$1,230,000	$1.97 MILLION	$2.46 MILLION
60	21	$623,000	$830,000	$1,038,000	$1.66 MILLION	$2.08 MILLION
65	16	$496,000	$663,000	$828,000	$1.33 MILLION	$1.66 MILLION
70	11	$357,000	$475,000	$595,000	$768,000	$1.19 MILLION

17This illustration is completely hypothetical and is intended to show how the mathematical principles of compounding can affect potential monthly income withdrawals. It should not in any way be considered to be investment advice, implied or otherwise. It also does not construe a projection of overall portfolio performance and is not intended to represent the performance of any specific individual investment. Please consult a qualified financial professional to ensure that your investment objectives, needs, and financial situation are properly understood prior to undertaking any investment program or strategy.

As you can see, your needs can have a big impact on how much of a nest egg you need. If you retire at age 60, and you need $48,000 per year, your nest egg will have to be $830,000. On the other hand, if you wait another 5 years, retiring at age 65, you only need $663,000 to live on your nest egg with no other income streams. Of course, if you end up living 10 years beyond your life expectancy, to age 91, you will require $1,363,200 in your portfolio to generate an income of $48,000 per year for 41 years.

If you can build up a regular income stream of $12,000 per year prior to retirement, that changes things a great deal and you would only need $36,000 per year to make your $48,000. That makes a huge difference and can even make it possible for you to retire earlier. Doing part-time work for part of your retirement can also affect your calculations, allowing you to put less into a nest egg.

While the chart above isn't foolproof, since you could live beyond 81 years of age, it does give you a ballpark number to work with. If you are 15 years away from retirement, it tells you what you need to do to hit the $1 million goal if you tighten the belt quite a bit. Making the necessary adjustments to retire in 10 years might be more difficult; you could stretch out the time you need to reach your goal by working longer, or by making a lifestyle downgrade during the first years of your retirement while working part-time. Of course, if you cultivate additional income streams, you won't need to rely entirely on returns from your retirement portfolio.

One of the most important things to remember as you consider how much you need to retire is that you really need to take care of your own needs first. If it is a choice between paying for your child's college or putting money away for retirement, you should put that money away for retirement. As many personal finance experts have observed, there are attractive loans for college education. There are no loans for retirement. It may sound selfish, but if you want to meet your retirement goals, it is vital that you set aside the necessary funds.

STRETCHING YOUR RETIREMENT SAVINGS

When you retire depends on how much money you can generate each month, and how much of that money you are likely to spend. Another consideration is market cycles. Specifically, you should prepare for possible crashes. During recessions, many people realize that their returns are not beating inflation and, sometimes, are even negative. This means that you are tapping into your principal in order to meet your needs. You can stretch your retirement funds by following a few strategies.

When it comes to building your nest egg, it clearly helps to start as early as possible. If your goal is to have $1 million in your investment portfolio when you retire, you will need to develop a disciplined saving strategy in order to hit your retirement goals. Also, a million dollars today is not what a million used to be.

Here is an illustration created with the help of Dinkytown.net:

Monthly Savings Needed to Save $1 Million by Retirement [18]

This hypothetical illustration assumes a return of 8 percent with a monthly compounding effect, and it also assumes that you have nothing set aside for retirement right now.

18This illustration is completely hypothetical and is intended to present how the mathematical principles of compounding affect the amounts needed now to fund future retirement targets. It should not in any way be considered to be investment advice, implied or otherwise. It also does not construe a projection of overall portfolio performance, and is not intended to represent the performance of any specific individual investment. Please consult a qualified financial professional to ensure that your investment objectives, needs, and financial situation are properly understood prior to undertaking any investment program or strategy.

As you can see, the earlier you start the better, in terms of retirement savings.

(Chart 12.2)

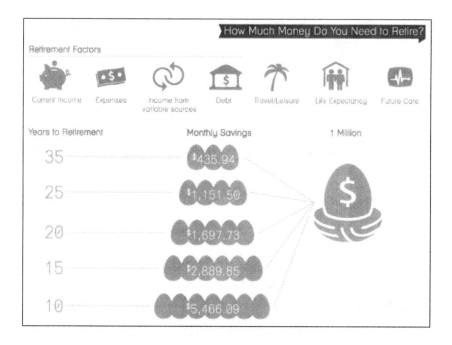

The following is an example of a retired client who started with $1,000,000 and needed income based on 4 percent withdrawals, using a 3 percent inflation adjustment:

Please be sure to read the disclosures that explain all fees and charges associated with the chart below. This chart is provided for educational information since past results do not guarantee future returns.

(Chart 12.3)

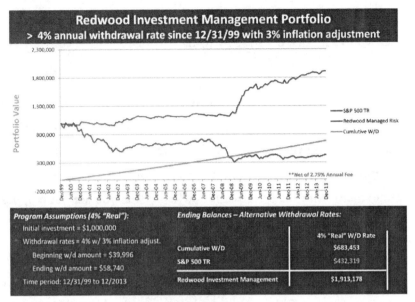

The above example started on 12/31/1999, the start of the worst stock market decade in 80 years.

SO HOW MUCH DO YOU NEED TO RETIRE?

The point is, you need to plan to succeed for retirement and then when you retire, have a strategy to have your funds last longer than you do.

If you have not been able to invest or save enough, you might need to postpone retirement for some time longer than you expected in order to build up your nest egg or keep from using your core capital. You might consider a part-time job, or some type of temporary employment just to keep the cash flowing so that you are not tapping into your funds.

Work longer: If you are coming up short of what you might need to enjoy a comfortable retirement, think about taking up a new career or staying in your old job. There is always part-time work. Unlike the federal government, you will not be allowed to just print money you do not have, so you will have to find options to earn money or cut your expenses. Below are some additional things you can do to help yourself in retirement:

- **Cultivate alternative income streams:** Instead of relying on a large nest egg, you can reduce your reliance on your retirement portfolio by cultivating income streams. This can be done through a side business, by making investments outside your retirement portfolio that pay dividends or offer regular interest, or by looking for online opportunities to make residual income. If you have some sort of creative talent, you can earn alternative income from the royalties related to your efforts. There are a number of ways you can create income streams that diversify the sources of your cash flow.

- **Cut costs:** Tough economic times often force us into making the decision to cut back on unnecessary items. You can stretch your retirement funds by cutting back on your spending when times are tough. Yes, retirement should be a time of enjoyment, but if you are reaching into your core capital to support a daily game of golf, or indulge in several nights out each month, or take elaborate trips, it might be time to reconsider the rate at which you are going through your money. Another consideration includes recurring expenses, such as subscriptions and insurance on an extra car, or on a motorcycle, or some other toy. Many times, we don't realize how much such things cost us beyond their original purchase value. Eliminating these items can save a great deal of money on a regular basis. Consider where you can cut back and reduce your expenses. When the difficulties are past, and your retirement portfolio is recovering, you can consider reintroducing some of the luxuries. Until then, it is important to make sure that you understand the difference between your needs and your wants, and be prepared to sell the boat or quit taking the class if things start to look dire.

- **Reconsider the financial help you give others:** It's a nice idea to support your children and grandchildren, but sometimes you might need to cut back on your charity. Evaluate your giving habits and make sure that if your own survival and financial situation is being threatened, you must pull back a bit. You need to remember that you are trying to make your money outlive you, and it might be necessary in times of economic turmoil to reduce how much you provide to others. This, of course, means that you have to be careful not to cultivate financial dependency on you in those around you.

- **Consider downsizing your home:** Instead of keeping a larger home, which is more expensive to heat and cool and power and might still have a mortgage remaining, many retirees sell and downgrade to something smaller. A lifestyle downgrade in terms of living quarters and things owned can free up more money for other items.

- **Rent your home:** In some cases, it is actually more cost effective to rent a smaller home in an adult active community, with all expenses (including yard work and snow removal) included, than it is to own a home and pay for its upkeep. What works best for you depends on your goals and your situation, but some find that these sorts of lifestyle changes free up more of their monthly income from the retirement portfolio for more pleasant pursuits such as travel and hobbies. How you decide to live your life can greatly influence how much money you need in order to retire.

There is a topic that very few financial advisors want to talk about, which is that most people need less money as they get older because they stop driving and traveling and buying clothes. The main exception is long-term care, which we will discuss later.

Most people somewhere around 75 to 80 start slowing down, usually from health reasons, but traveling isn't as much fun and long plane rides just don't work out well. There are exceptions to every rule, but most of my clients in retirement, usually after 80, are not spending anywhere close to what they had planned for.

CHAPTER 13

COMMON RETIREMENT
CONCERNS

What to Do with a 401(k) or Retirement Plan from Work? One of the main issues you face as you get older is what to do with your retirement plan once you retire. There are many estate-planning reasons to get out of your old 401(k) or 403(b), especially since most do not offer stretch options or contingent beneficiaries, as are available with a self-directed IRA. If you are too young to start taking distributions, you will need to decide where to keep that money until you can take them. If you're ready to begin taking distributions now, it's important to decide whether to withdraw all of the funds at once as a one-time payment, or to withdraw money on a regular basis, receiving periodic payments to cover your expenses.

It's often wise to transfer the money from your old retirement plans into a self-directed IRA. This can provide you with more control over your retirement portfolio, and it can even be arranged so that you withdraw a regular amount once you reach the age of 59½. Using an IRA to control your retirement investing portfolio can be a good way to help your money grow tax deferred.

You can roll over your IRAs to a Roth IRA. Be sure to check with a financial advisor or tax professional, though, to make sure you understand the tax implications of a rollover. Once the money is rolled over and the appropriate tax measures are observed, your investments will grow tax-free.

When you build a retirement portfolio out of your IRA, consider different places to keep different investments. With a traditional IRA, the money grows tax deferred, but you haven't paid tax on the income yet and that means that when you withdraw funds, they are taxed at your regular federal rate up to 35 percent as of this writing, not including potential state and local taxes. If you keep long-term investments in an IRA, you could be paying more taxes than necessary.

With the long-term capital gains tax still topping out at 15 percent (although it is likely to go a little bit higher), you'll want to consider keeping your long-term investments somewhere else. Short-term gains, such as those generated by many mutual funds and by fixed-income investments, can be kept in a regular IRA, allowing you to defer paying taxes on the gains until you actually make withdrawals.

You can see where a Roth IRA could come in handy. If you can roll your assets into a Roth IRA, they grow tax-free from that point on. Since you already paid taxes on the income, this means you won't have to pay any income tax on qualifying withdrawals in the future. Consult with a tax professional or knowledgeable financial advisor to review your options and decide which will work best in your situation.

PROFIT SHARING AND 401(K) PLANS

Many retirement plans from work can be rolled into an IRA. You can set up an IRA account, and then provide the account number to the payroll folks at your company. When you retire, the balance of your profit sharing or 401(k) plan can be transferred to your IRA account. Now you have complete control over your money, and you can set up a balanced portfolio that includes income investments, growth investments, and cash.

Before you do this, you might want to consult with a financial advisor. If it appears that your company retirement plan has taken a hit due to market conditions, it could be necessary to wait a little longer for the balance to recover a bit.

PENSIONS

Many people are disappointed when they find out that their pensions are not available in a lump sum. You might actually have to decide between options for regular payments (usually monthly):

1. Monthly income over the course of your lifetime, leaving your spouse with no continuing payments should you die
2. Largely reduced income over your lifetime so that your spouse continues to get the same payment when you die
3. Somewhat reduced income over your lifetime so that your spouse gets half of your monthly income if you die first

This can seem like a somewhat depressing choice at first. Many people choose option 2 in order to avoid creating a situation in which a beloved spouse is put into an undesirable financial situation. Even option 3 seems less harsh than option 1. The emotional pressure can be intense, however, in considering options 2 or 3, you should also take into account two scenarios: death and divorce.

You might outlive your spouse, in which case you have forfeited the higher income you could have had—or what happens if you divorce and you are still taking reduced payments from your pension?

There is another option that allows you to take option 1 and use life insurance to cover the potential loss of income; however, you need to have good health, and the numbers need to be checked out very carefully. Take option 1 for your pension payout, you will have a larger monthly income, out of which you can pay an insurance policy premium. Figure out how much life insurance is needed to support your spouse if you were to die.

You can use your monthly pension income and other income to help cover the premium, and if your spouse were to die first, you still receive the larger payments from your pension, and you have a few options:

1. If there is a cash value, you can close the policy and take the cash, since your spouse will not need support when you pass.
2. You can switch the policy beneficiary to your heirs and continue to pay on the policy.
3. You can quit paying on the policy and take a smaller policy that is paid up.

This strategy might not work for everyone; however, if the insurance is reasonably affordable, and your higher pension income could easily cover the premium, it might not be a bad idea. You keep more of your money, and you keep your options open.

LIFE INSURANCE AND IRA DISTRIBUTIONS

The technique of using life insurance to help shield your loved ones can also be used if you are planning to leave your IRA to your heirs. Once you reach the age of 70½, you are required to take minimum distributions from your IRA. You reduce your tax liability this way, minimizing the income tax you pay on your distributions. However, as the IRA balance continues to grow, your estate could become large enough that it becomes subject to the estate tax, in addition to income tax.

If you don't care if your estate is partially destroyed by taxes, and prefer to save the money now for yourself, this isn't much of a problem. On the other hand, if you want to shield your IRA from double taxation for your heirs, you can use a life insurance policy.

You take extra money out of your IRA each year, and pay the taxes on it. For instance, if you take out an extra $9,000 annually, and you are in the 35 percent tax bracket, you would pay $3,150 in taxes and that would leave $5,850. You could put that into a life insurance policy that is owned outside the estate, with your heirs and beneficiaries.

You still live off the minimum distributions, and the extra money keeps your estate down (and hopefully exempt from the estate tax), and your heirs get money tax-free from the life insurance policy. It's an interesting strategy, which you can discuss with your financial advisor. Check and double-check the numbers.

PAY OFF THE MORTGAGE?

If you can pay off your mortgage before retirement, this is ideal. It leaves you without an obligation on your home. You get more equity from it if you decide to sell, and you are eligible for more if it becomes necessary to borrow against the equity in your home. However, if you still have a mortgage payment when you retire, you need to carefully consider your options.

Many retirees consider taking a large chunk of their retirement portfolio to pay off the mortgage at once, but this reduces the amount of capital you have available to earn interest. If you have a mortgage at 6 percent, and you are earning a return of 9 percent on your investment portfolio, you can do better if you continue paying off your mortgage under the current terms while investing your portfolio's principal.

REFINANCE

Another interesting option is to refinance your mortgage just before you retire. Some retirees find it helpful to get a cash-out refinance while they still have a job and can get a better interest rate. As of this writing, mortgage interest rates are quite low and some retirees can get a nice, low rate with a relatively low payment, and then cash out. The money can be added to an investment portfolio, creating a large amount of core capital that is likely to return more than 5 percent over the years.

For example, if you have a home that is worth $200,000, and you have most of it paid off with only $30,000 owed on it as you approach retirement, you could refinance the loan for $165,000, keeping $35,000 cash for yourself (minus loan fees). Your payments would be fairly low, and you could add a nice chunk of money to your retirement portfolio which, if invested wisely, could exceed the interest you are paying. It is also worth noting that fees and interest on regular mortgage and refinance loans are much lower than most reverse mortgage fees.[19]

It is important to be careful when employing such strategies; you will need to make sure that you have enough monthly retirement income to make the payments because if you default on any loan collateralized with home equity, you can lose your house to foreclosure. Also, if you are in an environment of moderately high mortgage rates and fairly low returns, this plan could backfire horribly, since your returns would not be making up for the interest you are paying.

I do not recommend the above for younger people, but carefully consider your goals, and how you feel about money and if this works for you. I prefer, and most people prefer, to have as little debt as possible and make a plan to pay off all of their debt—including the mortgage—by the time they retire.

This leaves your assets obligation free, and makes it possible for you to live comfortably on a lower income.

THE EFFECT OF DEBT PAYMENTS ON RETIREMENT INCOME

When you are debt-free, you have less need for a high income. If you retire, and you are still making a mortgage payment of $1,000

---

19 It is crucial to remember that equity loans, lines of credit, reverse mortgages, and other methods of borrowing against unrealized equity in a home are collateralized by the deed to your property. In the event of default, your home may be seized by the lender and foreclosed to pay the outstanding debt, leaving little to no money for the original homeowner. These strategies should only be considered after proper evaluation of income needs and ensuring that you will be able to maintain the debt payments.

a month, and you have credit card payments that add up to $350 a month, and you have a car loan for $400 a month, that's $1,750 per month. You wouldn't need as much to retire comfortably if you weren't making debt payments of $1,750 per month.

Instead of all that debt, you could have the same money available to learn a new skill or travel. Figure out how much debt you have and what you can pay off before you retire. Even mortgage debt, though it is considered "good" debt, can limit you in retirement. Carefully consider your options and consult with a financial professional who can help you evaluate your situation and make a plan.

SELL THE HOUSE AND RENT

Another consideration is what happens as you age and are unable to continue upkeep on your home. If you have built up a great deal of equity in your home, you can use that to your advantage by selling. A large amount of capital, properly invested, could create income enough to overcome the costs of paying rent. Plus, as long as you have lived in your home for two of the last five years (using it as a principal residence), you don't have to pay capital gains taxes if your profit is less than $250,000 for a single tax filer or $500,000 for a couple married and filing jointly.

Table 13.1: Extra Income from Selling Your Home

This table is for illustrative purposes only and assumes that a mortgage has been paid in full and doesn't take into account inflation or state or local taxes. Actual returns, costs, rental rates, and home prices fluctuate according to market forces.

(Table 13.1)

SALE PRICE OF HOUSE	$250,000
COSTS RELATED TO SALE	-$15,000
AMOUNT RECEIVED	$235,000
AMOUNT INVESTED	$235,000
RATE OF RETURN	8%
ANNUAL INCOME FROM INTEREST	$18,000
ANNUAL FEDERAL TAXES ON INVESTMENT GAINS (25% RATE)	-$4,700
RENTAL COST EACH YEAR ($900 A MONTH)	-$10,800
EXTRA YEARLY INCOME	$3,300

If you choose your rental wisely, you won't have to pay maintenance costs, nor will you have to take care of the yard or snow removal. Utilities will probably still need to be paid, but it is unlikely that they would cost more than what you paid before, and they are already budgeted into your monthly expenses.

This means that you have a little extra that you can choose to reinvest, save up for a specific goal, or spend on little luxuries throughout the year. Depending on your situation, you can see how selling your home can be a good financial move in your retirement. Take into account your abilities, your costs, and the availability of acceptable and comfortable rentals in your price range.

LONG-TERM CARE
AND REVERSE MORTGAGES

For information on these, see appendix E for Long-Term Care and appendix F for Reverse Mortgages.

INCOME TAXES

Even during retirement you will have taxes to pay, and how much you pay depends on your income. The kind of retirement account you have will also affect how much you pay in taxes. In a tax-deferred account, you pay taxes when you take withdrawals, and your withdrawals count as income, which is taxed at whatever tax bracket you are in.

Many retirees make an effort to arrange their finances so that they can live on less after retirement. This allows them to move into a lower tax bracket. If you have an account that grows tax-free, your distributions from that account will not be subject to income tax. This is why a Roth IRA is so attractive to many. If you think that you will be in a higher tax bracket when you retire, a Roth IRA can be a great tool, since you will not have to pay taxes on the withdrawals. That means you can make them grow as big as you want. You will have to pay income tax on your other withdrawals, though.

OFFSETTING CAPITAL GAINS TAXES

In some cases, you may have to pay capital gains taxes. Fortunately, there are ways to offset these gains. If you have any losing investments, you can sell these to reduce some of what you owe in capital gains taxes. This is especially helpful when it comes to short-term capital gains, which are usually higher than long-term gains.

You can also reduce your taxable income by $1,500 (or $3,000 if you are married and filing jointly) through your investment losses. If you have $15,000 in losses, and $10,000 in capital gains, you can offset your gains and still have $5,000 left over. If you are married and filing jointly, $3,000 of what's left after offsetting your capital gains can be used to reduce your taxable income.

This can be quite useful if you are just barely into a higher tax bracket. A little bit can push you back down into a lower bracket. In our example, this leaves $2,000 that you can carry into another year. This is known as banking your losses. However, the $3,000 restriction still applies, so banking too many losses can start to become a problem. You also have to sell and clear your investments before the end of the year. Just having it on paper isn't good enough.

Be aware of the wash sale rule if you decide to sell losers. In order to use them for tax purposes, the IRS requires that you buy something substantially identical within 30 days of selling for a loss. You should also be aware of transaction costs associated with selling your losing stocks. Sometimes, those can start to add up. Before deciding to employ this strategy, it is a good idea to plan out your moves, and possibly consult a trusted financial professional for advice.

HELPING YOUR HEIRS AND DONATING TO CHARITY

It is not unusual for retirees to want to help their heirs while they are alive. This leads many to help pay for college for their grandchildren, or provide gifts for their adult children. After you have made adequate provision for yourself, and you are on track to meet your goals, it is acceptable to help others with their expenses.

HELPING GRANDCHILDREN WITH COLLEGE

Many retirees want to help their grandchildren with college. Happily, there are plenty of options these days for helping your grandchildren with colleg,

ZERO-COUPON OPTIONS

Zero-coupon bonds reinvest interest rather than paying it out at regular intervals. This way, money continues to grow. There are actual funds that combine zero-coupon treasury bonds with growth stocks. These funds ensure that you get your principal from the bonds back, along with the interest, but also contain the power of growth stocks. This way, especially if you have at least 10 years until your grandchild goes to college, you can help build up a good college fund.

THE 529 PLAN

One of the vehicles designed specifically for growing money to pay for college expenses is the 529 plan. This is a special tax-advantaged plan that allows you to invest in underlying investment portfolios that can be similar to CDs, mutual funds, bonds, or stocks. Contributions are not tax deductible, but like the Roth IRA, they grow tax-free and the withdrawals are tax-free for qualified education expenses.[20] The person who opened the account is considered the asset holder, and you can transfer beneficiaries as you like. Many 529 plans are administered by states, so it is important to carefully read the terms of the plan to see whether there are restrictions on using the money at out-of-state schools. Also, you need to decide which

---

20Withdrawals used for expenses other than qualified education expenditures may be subject to federal, state, and penalty taxes.

investments you will include, so be careful to check the administrative fees and other costs associated with funds that you include in a 529 plan. Contribution limits are set by the state, and usually fall between $100,000 and $350,000. There is no income limit associated with contributing to a 529 plan, and no restrictions on the beneficiary withdrawing money for qualified education expenses.

COVERDELL EDUCATIONAL SAVINGS ACCOUNT (ESA)

ESA's tax benefits were made permanent with the American Taxpayer Relief Act of 2012 (ATRA). Although it has been around since 1998—when it was called the Education IRA—the ESA has long been overshadowed by the 529 plan. Those receiving contributions must be under the age of 18. At the age of 30, if the assets haven't been used, or a new beneficiary has been named, the beneficiary gets the money in the account but has to pay taxes and penalties on the assets. If your child is young enough—not yet 18 years old— and your income is low enough—the income phase-out is $95,000 to $110,000 for a single taxpayer and $190,000 to $220,000 for a married couple filing jointly—you can contribute up to $2,000 per year to a Coverdell ESA for that child.

PREPAID TUITION

You can also prepay your grandchild's tuition. Many state university systems and private schools offer various plans for prepaid tuition. Basically, you lock in today's tuition for your grandchild to attend a school. When you do this through a state program, your beneficiary can usually attend any public higher education institution in the state. In the case of private schools, your prepaid tuition is normally only good at that one university. You can either enter a contract with the plan, or you can purchase units of tuition at current prices. Either way, the main snag is that prepaid tuition does not guarantee that your grandchild will be accepted to the school. Make sure you check the refund policy, as well as the transferability of the prepaid tuition purchase.

MONEY GIFTS

Another way you can help those still living is to give them money as a gift. Many retirees make annual gifts to their adult children or to their grandchildren (or both). This can also help them lower what they owe in estate taxes when you pass, because giving them gifts will reduce how much you have in your estate. If you have enough money to spread around to your relatives who might appreciate it, you should consider the tax rules of gift giving.

First of all, it is important to note that gift taxes are paid by the giver, and not the recipient. You should also understand that there is a $5.25 million lifetime exclusion. That means everyone can contribute up to $5.25 million in gifts to others without having to pay a gift tax. You can even avoid having your money gifts count toward this lifetime limit if you plan carefully. If you keep your gift to $14,000 or less to each person in a year, it doesn't count toward the lifetime gift limit. If you are married, your spouse can also give $14,000, making your total joint ability for gift giving $28,000 per year, per person.

You can give as many gifts to as many people as you want, as long as the total does not exceed the limit in any calendar year. This also means that the recipient has to cash the check by December 31, or the exclusion applies in the next year. It is important to make sure of this, since if you give any one person gifts exceeding the limit, you have to file a gift tax return, and the money will count toward your $5.25 million lifetime exclusion limit (married couples have a $10.5 million lifetime exclusion).

If you want to use the money gift to help a grandchild with college, you can contribute five years' worth of gifts at once to a state-sponsored 529 plan. You won't get a federal tax deduction (no gift is deductible on your income taxes), but some states will give you a state deduction for contributing to the 529.

Ultimately, the money gift is a really good way to help your heirs avoid estate taxes. It reduces the total value of your estate, allowing your heirs to get the money tax-free without having to worry about estate taxes. In addition, you get to experience the intangible benefits of being around to watch your family enjoy your largesse.

DONATING TO CHARITY

Many retirees like to do good for others on top of doing good for themselves and their families. For many, retirement offers the chance to donate their time and money to causes that they believe in. You can donate your time and talents to charity and get a great deal of fulfillment from that. You can also deduct many of the expenses related to your charitable works; mileage, supplies, and other expenses all come with tax advantages. Just make sure that you consult with a tax professional before taking these deductions.

You can also donate money to charity, you can itemize your donations on Schedule A of your Form 1040, which can help reduce your taxable income. You can also donate stock to charity, and if you donate a winning stock, you can do so and avoid paying capital gains tax. On top of that, you can deduct the full value of the stock on your income taxes; that means that if you bought 100 shares of something for $5 apiece, and now they are worth $15 apiece, in the eyes of the IRS you are donating $1,500 and not the $500 you paid.

You don't have to pay capital gains taxes on the $1,000 that the investment earned, either—you can see how this might be useful. The charity can keep the stock, using its dividend for income, or it can sell it. You are better off selling losing stocks, taking your deduction for the loss and then donating any money from the sale directly to the charity and taking that deduction; when you do this, you essentially get something of a double deduction. Double dipping isn't just for government employees; we can all take advantage of it.

IF YOU HAVE SAVED ENOUGH,

ENJOY YOUR RETIREMENT.

YOU'VE EARNED IT!

CHAPTER 14

HOW TO FIND AND WORK
WITH AN ADVISOR

The chapter your advisor hopes you never read.

One day a couple dropped by my office and asked if I could discuss their investment portfolio with them. At this time, I was with a well-known broker-dealer firm that is renowned for being honest and ethical.

I explained to the couple that I would need a week or so to review their portfolio and evaluate it, but first I needed to ask them some questions so I could know what their goals and objectives were for their portfolio. I asked them their dates of birth, annual earnings, retirement assets, their net worth, when they planned on retiring, and about any other assets they had. Their statement was kept at a large brokerage firm downtown, about 20 minutes from my office, so we scheduled a follow-up meeting for the next week.

After a week, they came back in and I proceeded to tell them that their advisor at the brokerage firm had done an excellent job with their investments and I couldn't have done any better. They were positioned, diversified, and well managed. They both looked shocked and the husband said to me, "I have been to several other offices with your broker-dealer, as well as a couple of independent financial planning firms in the area, and they all said our portfolio was in bad shape and that we should move our accounts to them so they could make changes. We knew our portfolio had performed well but the only reason we were looking for a new advisor was because our old advisor was retiring and we didn't feel comfortable with the person taking over at the brokerage firm since he wanted to change everything as well. We were looking for an honest advisor, and it seemed like we couldn't find one until we met you."

They transferred their account to me and remain my clients to this day. They were looking for someone who put their interests first. They knew the difference; do you? More importantly, does the advisor you are working with or talking with know the difference?

Don't get me wrong; I am not saying I am the only honest advisor in my area of town, because I believe that most advisors want to do the best thing for their clients. However, quotas and production requirements sometimes get in the way. This is a major problem in my industry, but unfortunately, there is no test for honesty or ethics. There is also the problem of which products or services the advisor can and cannot sell and be compensated for, which can sway the advisor's opinion and recommendations.

This is why I always recommend getting a second or third opinion. Just be sure to get the recommendation in writing. Maybe the reason an advisor wants you to get rid of your brokerage account is that he/she is not licensed to service the account and be compensated for it. The advisor might not know the difference, but you need to know the difference.

Advisors who recommend a change shouldn't have a problem putting it in writing, so you can ask your current advisor if you should be making any changes based on your current situation. You do not need to show your current advisor the new recommendation, but common sense should tell you if the changes make sense or not. Remember that new is not always better, so you need to listen and evaluate your situation and use your own common sense. Do what is in your own best interest, using logic instead of emotion.

There are two exceptions. First, if the new advisor, in reviewing your information, discovers that your current advisor has not made sure you have the proper beneficiaries or contingent beneficiaries to protect you and your family and your estate, you should move your accounts and not look back. Your old advisor deserves to lose your account. Always go with the advisor who wants to help you do things the right way and protect your assets for you and your heirs. Second, if your current advisor does not return your calls, get rid of that advisor now and do not look back.

Another example is an advisor who tells you that your current advisor is overcharging you and taking advantage of you, but who neglects to tell you that the net return or performance of your current advisor is actually better than the new advisor's portfolio, even though it costs more. The net return is always better. It's your money, not your advisor's. This type of approach is called planting the seed that your current advisor is bad, when in fact, that might not be the case. Think about it. If you could buy a Mercedes for the same price as a Volkswagen, which would you buy?

Shouldn't your investments be based on net performance, what you receive over and above cost, better known as profit? If you are not interested in profit, then why are you investing? This is an extremely competitive business, so use your common sense.

Does your advisor work with other professionals such as an attorney or a CPA or insurance agent or long-term care specialist? Think about it. Your attorney and your CPA are your safeguards as well as your back-up resources. You can get a second opinion from them. Who is checking the professional you are working with? Do you have any back-up support?

The absolutely best advice I can give you is to use this book as a guide to investing as well as estate planning, and work with a team of professionals and advisors who put your needs first, not with one jack-of-all-trades who is master of none. Your financial advisor should be a financial doctor who works with numerous other experts and professionals as a team. If you read the previous chapters in this book, you probably know more about investments than 80 percent of the advisors you will ever meet or work with. Knowledge is power.

Is your advisor a financial doctor or just a salesperson pushing you to buy his/her product? Is your current advisor a jack-of-all-trades and master of none who thinks he/she can handle everything?

There is a lot of confusion in our industry, and I will be discussing several designations such as CFP® (Certified Financial Planner) and the fact the CFP board has finally approved public disclosure of CFPs who have filed bankruptcy in the last five years. I have been a member of the Financial Planners Association (FPA) for over five years and I am not a CFP. I wish they would add full disclosure to their code of ethics.

If financial advisors have ever filed for bankruptcy, they need to disclose that to anyone whose hard-earned dollars they invest. Why would any professionals be allowed to call themselves Certified Financial Planners when they have been through a bankruptcy? Most members of the FPA and those who are CFPs feel that no one who has gone through a bankruptcy should be allowed to use the CFP designation, or that person should at least be required to disclose this information to prospective clients. What do you think?

Aside from CFP, there are a couple of accredited designations—Certified Retirement Financial Advisor™ (CRFA) and Certified Senior Advisor (CSA)—that require full disclosure when dealing with clients and prospective clients. In full disclosure, I am proud to be a charter member of the CRFA and a member of the CSA as well.

Does your advisor have one of these designations accredited by the National Commission for Certifying Agencies and recognized by the FINRA?

- Certified Retirement Finanial Advisor (CRFA)
- Certified Financial Planner (CFP)
- Certified Retirement Counselor (CRC)
- Certified Senior Advisor (CSA)

Advisors who have one or more of these designations must follow ethical standards or they will not be allowed to use the designation. They have annual educational requirements to stay up to date. This is the least you should expect from your advisor.

If advisors don't have a designation, what is their training and what is their continuing education? What are the ethical standards they have to follow in dealing with the public?

The point is, there is no class on ethics or honesty and there is no degree or designation that guarantees an advisor will be honest. People need to check out their advisors at their state insurance department and at the FINRA's BrokerCheck search service.

If you want to invest your savings, it makes sense that you would want someone to help you. After all, we've seen that building a portfolio and investing can be complicated.

What are your options for advisors who can help? They include:

- Financial planners
- Estate planners
- Bank representatives
- CPAs
- CFPs, CRFAs, CSAs, CRCs
- CLUs
- Insurance agents
- Credit union representatives
- Investment advisors
- Investment consultants
- RIAs (registered investment advisors)
- IARs (investment advisor representatives)
- Insurance consultants
- Stock brokers
- Wealth managers
- Financial advisors

I am sure I have missed many more options, but what's the one thing they all have in common? It's simple. They want your money. The problem here is that a university degree or a fancy designation such as CFP, CPA, CSA, or CRFA or CRC after someone's name does not guarantee that person has your best interest at heart. Just because advisors may work at banks and credit unions does not mean they are going to put your needs in front of their employer's. We will discuss fiduciary responsibility later.

Unfortunately, there is no educational degree or class that can predict honesty or ethics. Bernie Madoff had many degrees and served on several college boards, and he was a very educated crook. The sad truth is most crooks in the financial industry are very well educated, which means you can't rely on credentials or education as proof of integrity and honesty. Madoff, who was a stockbroker, financier, investment advisor, and nonexecutive chairman of the NASDAQ, was also a white collar criminal, as we all now know. His Ponzi scheme was the largest case of financial fraud in US history. The only thing worse is what the US government has done with our Social Security deductions, but no one is going to prison yet. Why didn't anyone check out Bernie? This is an important lesson for us all.

All of the advisors trying to sell you their products and services are paid in different ways, so how do you know which one is best for you? Let's take a look at how they are paid:

INSURANCE AGENTS

They are licensed to sell life insurance and annuities and they are paid only on commissions. There is nothing wrong with commissions, but you need to understand the commission is directly related to how long your funds are tied up.

If the insurance agent recommends you sell your brokerage account or your managed account or your bonds or stocks, make sure the agent has had the proper training and the knowledge to advise you on investments. To help you with your investments, the agent should be licensed for securities, in addition to an insurance license—and agents are not always licensed. Always ask what training the agent has to discuss the stock market or investing. Shouldn't you know if the agent has the training or not?

Ask if the agent is licensed to sell anything in addition to life insurance or annuities. Annuities are not investments; they are insurance contracts, with the exception of variable life annuities (variable annuities), which are handled by securities licensed agents who are paid for these products on commission.

FINANCIAL ADVISORS/ REPRESENTATIVES (SERIES 6)

Financial advisors with a Series 6 license are licensed to sell mutual funds, variable annuities (VAs), and variable life insurance policies (VLs), and they are paid on commission. They may be licensed for life insurance and annuities as well. If they want you to get out of your bonds or stocks or fee-based accounts, make sure they have the proper knowledge to give such advice since they are not licensed to do so. To buy a mutual fund, you either pay a commission upfront or you pay it deferred. Most advisors have ongoing costs, but they have to if they are to stay in business. Check that your advisor's training is in stocks, bonds, and fee-based accounts, knowledge of mutual funds, and recovery time in volatile markets.

STOCK BROKER (SERIES 7)–FINANCIAL PLANNERS/FINANCIAL ADVISORS/ FINANCIAL CONSULTANTS

Advisors with a Series 7 license are licensed to advise on stocks, bonds, mutual funds, and variable annuities. They are not licensed to discuss fee-based accounts and may not be trained in life insurance and annuities. They are usually paid on commission. Check your advisor's training in FIAs, EIAs, and fee-based accounts. Ask for a breakdown of the percentage of your advisor's business that is for securities and the percentage for annuities or life insurance.

FEE-BASED RIAS, IARS, WEALTH MANAGERS, FINANCIAL PLANNERS (SERIES 65 OR 66)

Advisors with a Series 65 or 66 license offer advice for fees and many receive no commissions. They can be licensed for life insurance and annuities and securities. Always ask prospective fee-based advisors what percentage of their business in the last 12 months was fee based and what percentage was from annuities or life insurance sales or commissions. Why would that be good to know? You will find out what they are really selling. We have many RIAs and IARs in our area who are licensed for fee-based transactions but make 90 percent of their income from annuity sales and only 10 percent from fees. They are really just annuity salespeople in disguise as RIAs or IARs. This is why you need to ask.

FIDUCIARY RESPONSIBILITY

Fiduciary responsibility is a hot question right now in the financial services industry. If your advisor is an employee at a bank or credit union, or at many of the large broker-dealer firms, your advisor is an employee. Is that advisor's first responsibility to you, the client, or is it to the broker-dealer employer? Shouldn't you know?

The same could be said of advisors at a broker-dealer firm who are supposedly independent. They actually have to sell you whatever their broker-dealer approves, regardless of whether it is best for you. Many broker-dealers restrict sales of FIAs that might actually benefit the client, in my opinion.

In many ways, even if independent, advisors are still at the mercy of the FINRA or their broker-dealer to decide which products and services they are allowed to offer and advise you on. This can be good and bad.

The registered investment advisor (RIA) can be associated with a broker-dealer, in which case the broker-dealer determines what can and cannot be offered for sale. Agents who are independent RIAs can offer or sell whatever they want. However, if they are not affiliated with a broker-dealer firm, they cannot offer variable annuities, variable life, stocks, bonds, or REITs unless they are in a fee-based account.

Is this complicated enough for you?

Ask prospective agents if they have a fiduciary responsibility to you, the investor. Do you come first, or their employer? Ask if they are employees or if they are independent advisors. Is their fiduciary responsibility to their broker-dealer, or to their employer (bank or credit union), or to you, the investor?

EIGHT QUESTIONS TO ASK YOUR FINANCIAL ADVISOR

Now that you know what a financial advisor is, it's time to choose the right one for you. Take this list with you when you interview your next prospective financial advisor.

1. **Have you ever filed for or gone through bankruptcy?** This is the very first question you need to ask. You should do your homework and check advisors out at BrokerCheck.com. You can also check advisors out at the state insurance department to see if they have been through a bankruptcy. There may be many reasons to go bankrupt, but you should know if you are going to entrust your life savings to someone, shouldn't you? After all, if advisors can't handle their own funds, do you really want them investing yours?

2. **Have you ever had a complaint or had to pay a fine for something you did in your professional life?** This can also be checked with your state insurance department or at BrokerCheck.com. If there are any problems, they will show up there. Follow-up questions: If the advisor has received complaints, what was the outcome? Has the advisor ever been fined by any of the agencies, state or federal?

3. **How do you get paid?** It's a good idea to know ahead of time how your financial advisor is paid. The choices are:

    Commissions: If the advisor is paid on commission, are the commissions taken up front or are they spread out so the advisor has an incentive to help you in later years? Many annuities advisors have a choice to take a larger commission upfront, such as 7 percent, or they can take a lesser commission, such as 3 percent, and get, maybe, 0.25 percent for the later years. With the second option, the advisor still has an incentive to keep advising you. Be sure to ask questions. If it's all up front, how much? Is there a fee, commission, or charge if you cash out? I can't tell you how many times I have seen agents get an upfront commission and the client never sees them again. Is that the investment advice you want?

Fees: If the advisor is paid through fees, how much are the fees? Does the advisor take them up front or per year? What is the track record of the managed portfolios on offer and what are their net returns for the past 10 years, by each and every year? Remember that Average Annual Return is NOT the same as Real rate of Return, do you know the difference?

Combination of both: If the advisor gets both commissions and fees, ask all of the applicable questions for commissions and fees.

Salary: If the advisor is paid with a salary alone, you have every right to be skeptical. Ask, "You mean you have absolutely no incentive for selling me something?" In my 42 years in this industry, I have never met anyone who works on a salary with no incentive of any kind. Watch out for bank advisors and credit union advisors. They will usually fail on the ethics test because they are trained this way. They will tell you they get a salary and they are just there to help you. So, is their job based on sales or not? If the banks or credit unions didn't require sales, they would go broke, and we all know they are in business to make money.

4. **Which license do you have?** You should make sure that your financial advisor has solid credentials. It also helps if you know whether the advisor is biased in favor of one particular asset class over others. The choices are:

   Life insurance or annuity licenses: This category limits the advisor to selling fixed annuities, fixed indexed annuities (FIAs), and life insurance.

   Securities: A license in securities could refer to a wide range of possible investments:

   - Series 6 covers mutual funds, variable annuities, and variable life.
   - Series 7 means a stockbroker is licensed for stocks, bonds, and REITs, along with everything a Series 6 covers.
   - Series 24 is a registered principal license and, usually, the holder is in a supervisory position.
   - Series 65 or 66 covers fee-based business.

   Many advisors have them all, but the thing you are looking for is whether they have an incentive to avoid recommending something to you that they can't get paid for.

5. **What is the breakdown of the percentage of your sales in the following services for the past 12 months?**
   - Annuities (all types)
   - Life insurance
   - Mutual funds
   - REITS
   - Stocks
   - Bonds
   - Managed portfolios (fee based)

6. **What accreditations, like CRFA, CFP, CSA or CRC do you have?** If, not why not?

7. **What do you do for your continuing education every year?** Do you follow economist like Harry S. Dent or do you stay current with latest tax laws for retirement like Ed Slott, CPA and Company? If not, why not?

8. **Is your Fiduciary responsibility to your client or to your employer?**

These are just some of the questions you should ask a prospective financial advisor. You want to know if this advisor is an annuity pusher or actually sells investments and offers a planning service. First of all, you need to understand that the word investment means there is a risk and a reward. If you invest your money, there is no guaranteed investment that will return 100 percent of your principal and 100 percent of the growth of the market without some kind of downside or some kind of risk.

I have explained in previous chapters all the investments I am aware of and how the advisor gets paid, so you now have the knowledge to ask the right questions and know the answer before you ask the question.

The biggest question of all: Is this advisor looking to sell to you or to actually help you?

Here are some points you need to know so you can make educated evaluations of advisors:

1. Do they ask to review your current beneficiaries before trying to sell you anything, including all your insurance policies, retirement plans, and brokerage accounts or bank accounts?
2. Do they review your tax return for ideas and strategies?
3. Do they offer to review your current portfolio and give you an evaluation in writing before asking you to buy anything?
4. Do they work with attorneys and tax advisors you can call to ask questions about this advisor and find out how long they have all worked together?

If you can answer yes to these four questions after your first meeting with your new advisor, you have someone who wants to be of service and value to you, not someone who just wants to sell your something the majority of the time. There are exceptions to every rule, but this is a good starting point.

FEES

This is a good time to talk about fees. The lowest fees are not always the best. For example, if you purchased a no-load fund, do you really believe anyone would invest your money for free, with no transaction fees and no operating expenses?

How would that person stay in business? You are smarter than that because you have read this book.

If you invested $100,000 and it cost 1 percent, but you made a profit of $5,000 (5 percent), would you be happy? Of course you would. However, what if there was a similar investment that cost 2.75 percent and returned you a net profit of $9,000 (9 percent), including the fees? Which investment would you want?

The point is that lower fees do not automatically mean higher overall returns. It is far more important to employ a strategy with a good track record in various market conditions. Are you looking to make money or to pay low fees? If you can do both, that is great.

No matter how capable you are, though, it can always help to have a professional opinion when you are charting a course to retirement. It's the reason why many smart investors and business people have money managers and financial advisors. You can benefit from this wisdom as well. Here is a rundown of the various people who can help you create a financial plan or provide some valuable advice:

1. Yourself (knowledge is power)
2. Fee-based financial advisor or planner
3. Fee-based money manager
4. Financial planner
5. Stock broker
6. Bank or credit union representative
7. Insurance agent

Many people gain positive results by getting help from a fee-based financial advisor or planner; these are professionals who either provide you with advice and accept a fee amounting to a percentage of the assets they manage for you, or work on an hourly basis. Many advisors and planners work with money managers, and they can help you pick the one who's right for your needs and risk tolerance.

While you can get good help from banks, credit unions, insurance agents, and stockbrokers, it is important to remember that these advisors often receive commissions from what they sell or from meeting monthly sales quotas. This means that you may not always be steered in a direction that is best for you and your unique goals and risk tolerance.

Some financial planners also receive commissions from products they get you to invest in. You can find a fee-based financial planner at www.napfa.org or www.finra.org. Also, check with your state insurance department or state securities department to confirm that your chosen advisor or agent has had no past problems and there have been no major complaints against that advisor.

Make sure your advisor is licensed to handle securities and investments. Many insurance agents discuss the stock market but are not licensed for, or trained in, investments. There are differences between opinion and fact, and you need to get facts.

Interview several advisors before you pick one. You are the boss, and you are paying for a service. It is up to you to decide who works for you. It never hurts to ask an advisor this powerful question: "Who do you represent?" Next, find out whether the advisor offers such benefits as regular financial reviews, tax efficiency reviews that include the tax implications of investments, educational and informative meetings, and newsletters with updates for clients.

Communication is the most important thing. Do you speak the same language as it relates to your values? Does the advisor talk with you or at you? Are you comfortable when talking to the advisor and able to share your true feelings and concerns? Always ask questions if you do not understand something. The only bad question is the one not asked.

Finally, try to ignore a lot of the hype in the financial press. These folks are professionals who earn their living in infotainment. The true nuts and bolts of a successful retirement portfolio are quite boring: You invest for the long haul, look for solid returns (even though they may be "only" average), and limit your risky investments.

No one wants to listen to a financial talk show host who makes things sound boring. We like to be entertained, and investment and financial shows that make finance sound like a sporting event are much more interesting. However, you need to remember that these talking heads are paid when their ratings go up, and nothing sells like abject panic or unrestrained optimism. The truth, usually, is much more boring and somewhere in the middle.

Instead of being swayed by the noise you hear in the financial media, create a retirement plan and work on building your portfolio in a way that is deliberate and measured. A good financial planner can help you chart a course that is likely to provide you with enough capital for your retirement, provided you start early and stick to your plan.

You have seen that history favors investments in the long term, especially if you are sufficiently diversified. While you might need to adjust the plan a little bit over the years, chances are good that it will suffice over the long haul, regardless of whatever gas shortages, bombings, and political upheaval occur in the short term.

CHAPTER 15

RETIREMENT CHECKLIST

It can be helpful to have a checklist of things you should be doing in the years leading up to retirement. Here's what you can do to stay on track for a comfortable and satisfying retirement. We all know the earlier you start your retirement planning, the better.

Most people, however, do not start their retirement planning 30 years before they retire; instead, most people really get into the nuts and bolts of retirement planning around 15 years before they plan to retire.

THE 15-YEAR RETIREMENT CHECKLIST:

First, you must remember not to count on Social Security; it will be changing, and not for the better for you, especially if you have 15 years to go to retire or longer. You absolutely should still be on the 80/20 Rule until 5 years prior to retirement, then go on the 90/10 Rule. Below are some things to do during this time to maximize your chances of the retirement you want.

- **Double-check your company retirement plan:** Are you taking full advantage of the match that is available, and are you putting in the maximum you can? Adjust your contributions to your company retirement plan to reflect your ability to set money aside, aiming to, at a minimum, max out the company match—the more the better.

- **Check your beneficiaries:** Make sure you have primary and contingent beneficiaries on all of your accounts, including your retirement accounts; do not leave this to chance!

- **Move to managed portfolios that have preservation of principal:** You cannot afford a five-to 10-year period without earnings on your retirement funds; it is time to get conservative with your risk, especially in your retirement plans. If your employer doesn't have one, ask them, why not? Remember, they have a fiduciary responsibility for the plans they offer to their employees, and this is why most employers now offer managed portfolios for their employees.

- **Do *not* leave large amounts in any mutual fund or retirement plan that is not managed for preservation:** Reposition large principal amounts by dollar cost averaging them from a cash or money market account and invest on the dips. Do not get stuck in a five-to 10-year recovery of a fund or stock.

- **Review your estate plan or arrangements:** Review your estate plan or your will or your living trust and health-care directives, as well as powers of attorney. You are not a kid anymore; it is time to take responsibility for yourself and for your heirs. If you don't decide who gets what, the courts will. Do you really want to be the person who didn't take care of this?

- **Consider opening retirement plans in addition to your employer-sponsored plan:** If possible, open a traditional IRA, or better yet, a Roth IRA. If you are self-employed, you can open some sort of self-employed retirement plan as well. Depending on your situation, it might be a good time to plan how you can max out your retirement plan contributions. You might put in what you can at the company to get the maximum match and then max out the Roth IRA or max out any other IRAs you have; once you have maxed out your deductions, then the Roth IRA is the cherry on the top!

- **Build your emergency savings:** Now is a good time to build an emergency fund. If you have an emergency fund, put it into a high-yield savings account, CD ladder, or relatively liquid money market fund. Once you have accumulated enough, you can invest into a managed preservation of principle account to max out your earnings potential. If something unexpected comes up, you won't have to borrow from your retirement account, which would limit your growth potential and future retirement needs.

- **Begin paying down debt:** Now is also a good time to begin paying down debt so that you do not have any when you retire. Look into what you can do to create a debt repayment plan that will have you mostly clear by the time you retire. If you are really ambitious, you can make sure that your mortgage is paid off by then as well.

THE 10-YEAR RETIREMENT CHECKLIST

Time is still mostly on your side at this point, but this is a good time to evaluate your retirement plan and make sure you are still on track.

- **Max out your retirement accounts:** Hopefully, you have been paying down debt and freeing up some capital. If you can max out your contributions to your retirement accounts, do so! The more money you have in tax-deferred and tax-free investments, the better. Make sure they are in a managed preservation of principal portfolio and avoid market risk and having to play catch-up. You cannot afford five to 10 years with no earnings.

- **Do not leave large amounts in any mutual fund or retirement plan that is not managed for preservation:** Reposition large principle amounts by dollar cost averaging them from a cash or money market account and invest on the dips. Do not get stuck in a five-to 10-year recovery of a fund or stock.

- **Make catch-up contributions:** If you qualify and if you are over the age of 50, now is a good time to be taking advantage of catch-up contributions. The fact that you can contribute beyond the normal limits is a great gift, and you should use it to the greatest degree possible.

- **Begin looking at your asset allocation:** Now is a good time to rebalance your investment portfolio to a preservation of principle portfolio and reduce the risk in your plan. It is better to be in preservation of principle than to be diversified at this point in your life; you can not afford playing catch-up for five to 10 years for being aggressive.

- **Think about what you want from retirement:** If you haven't been seriously thinking about what you want from retirement, now is the time to do so. Consider what you would like to accomplish, and what you would like to do. Now is the perfect time to estimate how much that might cost you and double-check to make sure you are on track to generate the income you need to secure the retirement you want.

- **Consider long-term-care options:** You can also begin evaluating long-term-care options; the sooner you start paying premiums, the lower they will be. If you can swing it, think about the possibility of getting a good policy while you can do so at a lower price.

- **Be aware that Social Security benefits are likely to be reduced sometime in the future:** Do not count on the amount of income shown on your statement. We recommend that you not even consider it when making plans. Anything you get from Social Security is a bonus or spending money, not a source of income for living expenses.

- **Maintain the 80/20 Rule:** Keep your expenses to about 80 percent of your income, the remaining 20 percent left over should be going toward savings and investments.

- **Check your beneficiaries:** Make sure you have primary and contingent beneficiaries on all of your accounts, including your retirement accounts

- **Review your estate plan or arrangements:** Review your estate plan or your will or your living trust and health-care directives as well as power of attorney. If you haven't done this, what are you waiting for? This is your job; get it done!

THE 5-YEAR RETIREMENT CHECKLIST

This is the time to make sure things are ready for retirement.

- **Make sure you are still on track:** Do an honest evaluation of where you are. Figure out whether you really can meet your retirement goals. Do you need to tack on another five years of work, or will you be fine if you retire on schedule?

- **Think about Social Security:** No, you aren't even close to taking Social Security benefits, but it is a good time to start thinking about it. See what you need to do to put off taking payments until you are at least 65 years of age, if possible. The longer you can wait, the more you will get each month, so carefully plan it to get through the first few years of retirement without it—if you plan to retire before 65, that is. Realize there will be changes in Social Security over time, so do not plan to rely on this amount for your future years. Currently, if you delay taking the benefit, it will increase each year you wait. From age 62 to 66 the benefit goes up by 6 percent each year and from age 66 to 70 goes up another 8 percent per year. That is a minimum of 56 percent more at age 70 than at 62 and it just depends on how long you will live.

- **Triple-check your health insurance:** This is the time to make sure that everything is in order for health-care insurance and other similar needs. Find out what you will need to do in order to make sure that you are properly covered and ready to go.

- **Start living on 90 percent of your expected retirement income:** This is a great time to see if your planning has worked and it gives you five years to adjust if your numbers don't come out as you thought they would. Once you retire, there is no going back. Even though you are working, just live on the amount you will get in retirement and see if it works.

- **Try to finish paying off debt:** If possible, try to wrap up the rest of your debt. Ridding yourself of obligations that drain your income away and require you to pay interest rather than earn it should be a high priority at this point.

- **Check your beneficiaries:** Make sure you have primary and contingent beneficiaries on all of your accounts, including your retirement accounts.

- **Review your estate plan and arrangements:** Review your estate plan, your will or living trust, your health-care directives and your power of attorneys and review your funeral plans or start making them! This is not fun, but it is the adult thing to do.

THE YEAR BEFORE RETIREMENT

It's go time. Now is the time to check on all of your last-minute agenda items, making sure that everything is ready to roll as you approach zero hour.

- **Evaluate your position:** Make sure you really are ready to retire. Do you have enough income streams to support your desired lifestyle? Is your nest egg large enough to generate the income that you need? Remember that you should withdraw only 4 percent to 5 percent of your assets each year in order to increase the chances that your money will outlive you.

- **Get your retirement portfolio in place:** Finalize your retirement in a preservation of portfolio. You should have income investments as your base, but depending on your tolerance for risk and your investment objectives, a significant portion of your portfolio should be in a managed preservation of principle portfolio—yes, this is contrary to many! You must preserve your principal in retirement.

- **Check with human resources:** Find out what you need to do in order to smoothly transition your company's retirement plan into your control into a self-directed IRA. Find out everything you need in order to transfer your retirement plan into a self-directed IRA, and get familiar with the paperwork.

- **Check your estate planning:** Visit with a financial professional who can help you begin making updates on your estate plan. Plot out your possible retirement course with respect to what will happen to your assets when you pass on. Make sure everything is order. You should review your estate plan every three years, as well as when a life-changing event occurs. Verify your primary and contingent beneficiaries for everything you own.

- **Long-term care:** If you don't already have long-term-care insurance, now is the time to seriously consider it. Think about facilities that you might be interested in, and find out what you might need in order to get there. It's much more pleasant to be able to plan ahead and choose your own facility than settle for whatever is available and affordable when you are forced into a decision, or when someone is forced into making that decision for you.

- **Make sure that everything is set:** Double-check all paperwork, all insurance policies, and all trusts documents, and make sure everything is the way you want it. Have you planned your funeral yet?

DURING RETIREMENT

Your retirement planning doesn't stop just because you are retired. You still need to evaluate your position every so often and keep on looking ahead. Most people spend more time planning their yearly vacation than their retirement. Once you are retired, you have no excuses. You need to schedule one or two days every year to review everything and every three yars to review your estate plan with your attorney.

1. **Do you like what you are doing?** Consider your life as a retiree. Do you enjoy what you are doing day to day, or is there something else you would rather be occupying yourself with? Think about how satisfied you are with your life and whether you want to make any changes.

2. **Do you need more income?** Take a hard look at your habits, and the effect that your spending and inflation are having on your retirement portfolio. Do you need to adjust your priorities? If the economy is going through a rough patch, do you need to take on part-time or consulting work? Perhaps you need to cut back or downsize your lifestyle.

3. **Remember the 90/10 Rule?** It is for *life*. Even in retirement you want to continue saving and investing at least 10 percent of your income. Strive to always live below your means, and you'll continue to grow wealth.

4. **Maintain your money manager review.** Every six months at a minimum, you should meet with your fee-based money manager (as opposed to commission-based). In your meetings, review how your investments are being managed. If your money manager is not getting the job done, you may need to change managers, but remember to have realistic expectations. You need to have the majority of your funds in a preservation of principal managed portfolio.

5. **Do annual reviews of all annuities or insurance policies.** If you own income annuities, demand to meet once a year with your agent and find out how that agent is recommending the repositioning of the subaccounts. This is as important for your finances as the income benefit is in the long run and is usually tied to the market value of the account.

6. **Continue estate planning and review it every 3 years.** Make sure that your estate is structured the way you want it and if you are considering a trust, now is a good time to switch it over. Don't forget to review your plan every three years or when a life-changing event occurs. Remember, in most states the power of attorneys and health-care directives need to be updated every 3 years.

7. **Evaluate your insurance coverage every year.** Throughout your retirement, make sure that you carefully evaluate your insurance coverage and adjust it as needed.

8. **Don't be that grumpy old person.** Think young, get a smile on your face. Yes, you have been there, done that before, but the people sharing their experience with you have not. Be excited for someone who hasn't had your

experience in life, but listen to them and if they ask your opinion, then give it. This is the time in your life you get to be the sage and wise advisor for the rest.

Most of all, enjoy your retirement. If you have planned properly for it, it truly should be one of the best times of your life. Now, you are the boss.

WORDS OF ADVICE ABOUT RETIREMENT

Doing well financially in retirement requires you to understand the basics of investments and how to manage money. You should have a basic grasp of concepts related to risk, as well as how to maximize your returns within your accepted risk tolerance and minimize your taxes. In fact, if you have a basic understanding of most of the concepts in this publication, it is likely that you could actually create your own retirement portfolio using online sources with a little guidance from a financial planner or advisor.

THE RIGHT RETIREMENT ATTITUDE

The right attitude is everything when it comes to enjoying life as a retiree; even if you are financially stable, you can be unhappy and unfulfilled. There are many who might be considered "poor" who are rich in enjoyment and other ways, so you need to approach each day with a sense of happiness.

Enjoy your life and the rewards from working hard and saving and investing and remember there is no cost for a smile and a good attitude!

Try new things because you are never too old to learn, and never stop asking questions and never stop reading or listening to others.

Engage in life and all that it holds because you only get one shot at it, so make it count.

THE FOLLOWING APPENDICES ARE PROVIDED BY OTHER PROFESSIONALS WHO SPECIALIZE IN AREAS I DO NOT.

AT MY FIRM WE HAVE WORKED WITH ALL OF THEM FOR THE THE BENEFIT OF OUR CLIENTS OR THEIRS WITH NO EXCHANGE OF FEES OR COMPENSATION.

IF YOUR FINANCIAL ADVISOR IS A "FINANCIAL DOCTOR,"THEY SHOULD NOT HAVE A PROBLEM IN PROVIDING A LIST OF OTHER PROFESSIONALS THEY WORK WITH.

APPENDIX A

THE FOUR PRINCIPLES OF RISK-INTELLIGENT INVESTING

Jerry Murphey

Today most investors agree that in the same way that everyday products continue to get smarter, so should investment portfolios. The "Four Principles of Risk-Intelligent Investing" is a guide to help investors maintain appropriate perspective, and it provides a road map to survive and prosper, not only in calm and rising markets but in volatile and declining markets as well.

These are amazing times for investors. The financial services industry is going through a profound transformation, and the greatest breakthroughs in portfolio construction have yet to be fully realized. There is no doubt that we are faced with what can sometimes seem like insurmountable challenges to deeply complex problems throughout every aspect of humanity. Many of these challenges pose a direct risk to our financial success.

With these challenges come great opportunities and great responsibility. Fortunately, innovations in risk mitigation, portfolio diversification, and investment selection are making their way to normalized and broad applications. This is good news for the financial advisors who embrace innovation, and not such good news for those who cling to old ways of the past.

Investors are right to expect their modern portfolios to be smarter. "The Four Principles of Risk-Intelligent Investing" identifies the characteristics of financial professionals who build portfolios that benefit in volatile and declining markets, as well as markets that are calm and rising.

QUESTION TRADITION

Over 400 years ago, Sir Isaac Newton gave us a way to organize the universe and simplify its nature for our understanding, leading mankind to bring order to many complex natural systems in a mechanical way. His work has led to huge technological advancements, such as mass production in manufacturing and, in many ways, is responsible for the quality of life we enjoy today.

Let's fast forward to 1955, when Harry Markowitz received a PhD degree from the University of Chicago with his thesis on portfolio theory that ultimately won him the Nobel Prize in economics in 1990. In the early 1960s, Eugene Fama, a 2013 Nobel Prize winner, defined the conversation on efficient markets, which concluded that a person cannot consistently achieve returns in excess of average market returns on a risk-adjusted basis, given the information available at the time the investment is made.

Harry and Eugene's contributions to the science of investing evolved into modern portfolio theory, mean variance optimization, and efficient market hypotheses, all of which are the foundations of today's most widely used methods for portfolio construction and asset allocation. A simplistic way to think about these bodies of work is that they are based on pricing and algorithms used to identify the optimal mix of assets for a particular risk level within a portfolio.

However, as is the case with most good ideas, overapplication is inevitable. Financial institutions wholeheartedly adopted the theory that individual investment success can be achieved by focusing on the averages of a number of different experiences, including some bad and some good. Further, they decided that as long as we all focus on the average experience, we will be okay by the end of our investment horizon.

Here's an analogy to illustrate this idea: If you stand with one foot on a block of ice and one foot over a fire, your average temperature should be just right. The average of a diverse range of experiences looks good in theory, but in reality it is a different story altogether, especially within an investment horizon that happens to have many periods of extreme market volatility.

There is no doubt that Sir Isaac Newton's system of classical mechanics and Harry Markowitz's modern portfolio theory are great systems, helping bring control and order to an ever-expanding, dynamic, and chaotic universe. However, people are not institutions, and the mechanical solutions of the past have paved the way for smarter technologies in virtually every area of our lives.

This is especially true with investing. In the same way that the cars we drive today have evolved to make driving safer and more efficient in navigating roads and highways, we should expect our investment portfolios to better adapt to changing market conditions.

Out of modern portfolio theory, mean variance optimization, and efficient market hypotheses, we've seen dramatic advancements in portfolio construction, such as progressive portfolio theory, full scale optimization, and adaptive market hypothesis. A smarter portfolio construction process has evolved.

Even in today's challenging times, and with empirical evidence of the shortcomings of traditional methods, some financial advisors cling to older schools of thought. Many investors understand this because they remain in the same portfolio system that dramatically eroded their wealth in 2000 and 2007. By now, most portfolios have recovered from those extreme market events, and many experts believe another crisis is simply a matter of time.

This is a good time to ask your financial advisor what is being done that is different from what was done in the past to guard against the next big financial crisis. Use their response to decide if you are with the right financial advisor, or if you're relying on traditional methods based on 400-year-old technology to achieve meaningful investment results today and in the future.

TRAVEL A PATH OF DEEPER UNDERSTANDING

If a tree falls in the woods and nobody is around to hear it, does it make a sound? If risk exists in your investment portfolio that you are unaware of, can it harm you?

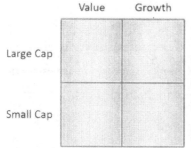

Back in 1994, Morningstar created the style box which conveniently categorized investments by their market capitalization and relative price.

This system provided a simple way to observe and understand different investments in an effort to achieve diversification. The idea is that different investment classes and categories perform differently during different parts of the market cycle. By blending these various asset classes and categories, investors can lower their exposure to volatility and achieve better investment results over time.

For the most part, this method of style-box asset allocation has served investors well and remains the most popular investment method today. However, during times of extreme market declines, the diversification between different asset classes and categories fails. Throughout history, this down-market diversification failure has been a primary cause for significant portfolio losses.

This is because the benefits of blending low correlating investment categories are dramatically diminished in an extreme market downturn. Back in the 1990s, blending two low-correlating asset classes, such as large cap growth (Russell 1000 Growth) and value (Russell 1000 Value), was common practice in building a diversified portfolio. However, the extreme down-markets we experienced between 2000 and 2002, as well as 2007 and 2008, rendered this method ineffective. The result was dramatic erosion of portfolio value (see chart below).

300,000

200,000

100,000

■ Russell 1000 Growth TR USD   ■ 5050 Russell Growth Value   ■ Russell 1000 Value TR USD

1997   1998   1999   2000   2001   2002   2003   2004   2005   2006   2007   2008

Returns represent past performance, are not a guarantee of future performance, and are not indicative of any specific investment. Returns of one year or longer are annualized.

Fortunately, innovation in investment design and major techno-logical advancements are making it possible for financial advisors to access investments that combine distinct up and down-market strate-gies to dramatically reduce the effects of down-market diversification failure. A great example of this is how Navellier & Associates, Inc., a leading equity asset manager, has incorporated a technical overlay that seeks to identify price inflection points with the ability to shift assets to fixed income exchange-traded funds (ETFs) staggered across the yield curve when markets begin to deteriorate. This is only a single example of how industry thought leaders are creating new methods of combining distinct up-and-down market philosophies into a single investment, making their way to widespread practice and distribution.

The old days of relying on asset categories and classes based on price and market capitalization are leading to a new way of building portfolios that can systematically adapt to changing markets. Ulti-mately, whether or not a tree falling in the woods actually makes a sound when nobody is around to hear it, it is clear that misunderstood risk and diversification failure during down-markets can devastate a financial system—and an individual investor's portfolio too.

Your portfolio's health depends upon a financial advisor who raises questions regarding observation and knowledge of today's economic reality. Be sure to carefully choose an advisor who is aware of these new realities, and your path to deeper understanding will inevitably lead to more meaningful results for you and those in your care.

KNOW THE EFFECTS OF
EMOTION AND BEHAVIOR

There is a story of a young girl who hears a tap on the window, evoking images of a scary monster, and cries for her father. Dad walks in, opens up the curtain, shows her it is only a branch tapping on the window and assures his daughter there is nothing to fear. Later that night, the child hears the tap again and is comforted by the belief that the sound is only a branch when, this time, a big scary monster is actually standing at the window. The moral of the story is that our emotions might encourage thoughts and behavior that aren't entirely grounded in reality.

Just like the father in our story, large financial institutions tell us to be rational and not to let emotions affect our thinking. This is because traditional portfolio construction methods rely on the idea that, on average, investors are rational. It implies that extreme down-markets such as the dot com bubble (2000–2002) and the credit crisis (2007–2008) can be overcome simply by not reacting and staying the course.

In November 2013, at the time I am writing this chapter, this theory has worked pretty well. It is true that most investors have fully recovered from the past two extreme down-market events. However, many investors worry about several scenarios that have the potential to be even more frightening than the past two extreme market events, while they worry that they do not have 13 years for their portfolios to recover. The biggest fear is that even if you remain what I call institutionally rational, emotional crowds react irrationally, and scary events can dramatically reduce your wealth, requiring years to recover.

The trouble is traditional investment methods fail to recognize that people are not institutions, and most conventional economic theories rely on the assumption that all participants behave rationally. On an individual level, rational behavior doesn't always mean receiving the most financial benefit, because the potential satisfaction 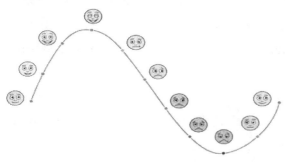 could be purely emotional. For example, while it would be more financially lucrative for you to keep your job rather than retire early, it would still be considered rational behavior for you to take early retirement if you believe that the benefit of retirement is greater than the benefit of a paycheck.

The disconnect is between individual and institutional rationality, and there are volumes of evidence showing that investors are emotional and do react to market disturbances in ways that are considered irrational from an institutional perspective. Eugene Fama's efficient market hypothesis (EMH) is one of the most popular methods utilized for portfolio construction today. It concludes that the market is efficient, and a person cannot consistently achieve returns in excess of average market returns on a risk-adjusted basis, given the information available at the time the investment is made.

According to EMH, scary market events should be ignored and treated with the same level of concern as all other events. It statistically normalizes events that can actually harm our ability to achieve investment objectives and potentially miss opportunities to make meaningful advancements toward our financial goals. What happens when you are institutionally rational and subscribe to the belief the market is efficient, while the investing population overreacts and pulls its money out of the market? You pay the price. Does this sound familiar?

The good news is that there have been huge advancements in the area of behavioral finance. Robert Shiller (2013 Nobel Prize winner in economics, along with Eugene Fama and Lars Hansen) has produced significant evidence that extreme market movements cannot be entirely explained by rational decision making and, instead, reflect the irrational behavior of market participants.

Another behavioral finance thought leader, Andrew Lo, created the adaptive market hypothesis (AMH), which can be viewed as a new version of Fama's EMH and incorporates counter examples to economic rationality: loss aversion, overconfidence, overreaction, and other behavioral biases. These advancements are empowering financial advisors to incorporate traditional methods with the effects of human behavior to build portfolios that can adapt to changing markets, especially scary ones.

Unfortunately, what many investors are missing is a financial advisor with the knowledge, tools, and resources to factor in the effects of behavior on the overall market and on an individual's investment portfolio. It is important to ensure that the financial advisor you're working with understands how emotion affects market behavior and has the skill and ability to incorporate this understanding into an investment process to help you survive scary events and achieve your financial goals.

PUT RISK FIRST

Risk is an inescapable feature of living a full and meaningful life. It's true that there is risk in everything we do. Understanding investment risk and making it the first thing we consider is paramount to success, especially in these turbulent times. In investing, when we talk about risk, we are really talking about the potential for loss. Traditional investment methodology tells us that to achieve a specific unit of reward, we must endure a specific level of risk.

A reasonable person knows that we should be able to remove risk in times of volatility and add risk when markets are calm and clear. A simple clothing analogy might illustrate this rational expectation: We add layers of clothing to our bodies when it's cold and remove layers as the temperature increases. We don't use a single item of clothing to satisfy all weather conditions, nor should we average out the risk and reward of an investment experience as traditional investment methods would dictate, because it requires us to experience extreme events from which it could take many years to recover.

Many experts believe that the investment environment has changed and extreme market events such as the dot com bubble (2000–2002) and the credit crisis (2007–2008) are now a permanent part of our investment climate. Evolutionary biologists have a theory called punctuated equilibrium, which suggests that extreme shocks to the environment can permanently alter our ecology, causing some species of plant life to go extinct while paving the way for entirely new species to emerge.

Similarly, extreme shocks to the investment environment can render certain investment products and processes ineffective, and advancements in investment management research are producing a host of new products that are better suited for today's extreme investment climate. For example, there are exchange traded funds (ETFs) that didn't exist 10 years ago but that are engineered to meet almost any investment scenario imaginable.

THE FUTURE OF INVESTING

At my company, FolioMetrix, our research team collaborates with industry thought leaders to advance the science of portfolio construction. This helps financial advisors deliver portfolios that can add risk when markets are calm and rising and remove risk during times of volatility and downturns. We identify investment managers and strategists who prove that they produce results during these different market scenarios.

Through a proprietary 39-attribute research model, our team is diametrically combining distinct up-and-down market strategies into a series of risk-intelligent mutual funds. Our research shows that adding these hybrid investment products to a traditional asset allocation portfolio can reduce the impact of an extreme down-market event, while producing quality relative returns in an up-market.

It is now possible for investors to own a portfolio that combines different risk-intelligent funds, using an optimization process that separately views normal market conditions from times of market stress. It's based on the idea that optimal portfolios must factor in the impact of extreme market events on the effectiveness of traditional methods. Today, we can focus on creating an efficient portfolio that reduces the risk of sudden short-term losses, as well as the risk of not meeting long-term investment goals.

If it is true that the future will include more volatile times, then it is better to think of risk in terms of thresholds of losses. From here, new technology allows unacceptable losses to be represented by different input parameters and/or portfolio constraints. This process can be repeated until an allocation is produced which maximizes growth potential, while minimizing the probability of losses.

This means financial advisors can now offer a blend of risk-intelligent mutual funds for a specific objective and risk level. Serving as the center of influence between you and your investment goals, the right financial advisor can coordinate and implement a risk-intelligent portfolio solution to help fulfill your expectations and investment policy.

What has made America a great country is our undying optimism about the future and the potential of what might be. This optimism can put risk in a purely negative light, but successful investors know that there is great opportunity in assuming the right amount of risk. Today, more than ever, it is critical to think of risk first. If we do not, we are destined to repeat the same mistakes over and over.

THE 90S ARE CALLING—THEY WANT THEIR PORTFOLIOS BACK

If you believe that investment portfolios should evolve at the same pace as other products in our lives, you are right. I hope The Four Principles of Risk-Intelligent Investing serves as your guide to understanding the future of investing. Many of the recent breakthroughs in portfolio construction have yet to be fully realized by many financial institutions and advisors. The key is to be sure you are working with a financial advisor who can help you question tradition, take a path of deeper understanding, know the effects that emotion and behavior have on your portfolio, and most importantly, always put risk first. Follow these principles and you will be a risk-intelligent investor.

ABOUT THE AUTHOR

 Jerry Murphey is the cofounder, president, and CEO of FolioMetrix, LLC, a provider of asset management products, programs, and consulting services to financial advisors, broker-dealers, and institutions across the United States. Jerry began his career over 20 years ago on Wall Street. He was the cofounder of Mutual Data Incorporated, a boutique research and consulting firm, and headed up the worldwide operations for Dearborn Financial Institute.

As a leading catalyst, he helped many of the nation's largest independent broker-dealers deliver their first in-house managed money platform solutions through his work at Prudential Investments. He has spoken at numerous national and regional broker-dealer events, and is responsible for the development and delivery of over 80,000 hours of continuing education directly to financial professionals throughout the world.

FolioMetrix LLC, a wholly owned subsidiary of Uptrade Research Associates LLC, is an Investment Advisor and the advisor to the Starboard Investment Trust's RiskX mutual fund series. Please request

Form ADV Part II for a complete description of FolioMetrix, LLC's management services. Always be aware of the specific risks associated with any investment product and always read the prospectus before investing, As such, your investments may lose value or you may lose the principal investment.

An investor should consider the investment objectives, risks, and charges and expenses of the Fund carefully before investing. The prospectus contains this and other information about the Fund. A copy of the prospectus is available on the website at www.riskxfunds.com or by calling Shareholder Services at 1-800-773-3863. The prospectus should be read carefully before investing.

All information contained herein is for informational purposes only and does not constitute an offer to sell, or a solicitation of an offer to buy, securities or advisory services. It is not our intention to state or imply in any manner that past results and profitability is an indication of future performance. All materials are compiled from sources believed to be reliable. However, accuracy cannot be guaranteed. Before making an investment decision, prospective investors should carefully read all material provided.

APPENDIX B

ESTATE PLANNING

Contributed by Carl Jepsen
Estate Planning Attorney and Partner
in Warren Allen LLP Law Firm

The thing about estate planning is that it is for your heirs. You won't see what happens to your money when you are gone. For some retirees, that is just as well, since poor estate planning can result in a large chunk of money being excised out of your estate for tax purposes.

If you are more concerned about making sure you live comfortably in retirement, but aren't overly concerned about passing on a large inheritance, then estate planning becomes less important. However, if you want to be able to provide the maximum amount possible to your heirs, it helps to engage in a little estate planning.

ESTATE TAXES

When you die, the government wants its cut of the estate that you pass on to your heirs. (Never mind the fact that you have already paid taxes on your property, your income, and in some cases, your capital gains.) Estate taxes contain a great deal of wrenching about by Congress, with rules constantly changing.

In fact, we are right in the middle of an interesting transition. For a long time, up to $1.5 million in an estate's assets was exempt from the tax. Then, a new exemption was enacted, raising the threshold to $3.5 million. The good news is that it is now $5.12 million, meaning a husband and wife can leave an estate worth $10.24 million with no federal estate taxes.

However, many states now have an estate tax too. For example, Oregon starts at $1 million and goes up to $5.12 million, and Washington State starts at $2 million and goes to $5.12 million. You need to know what your state's estate tax is. We have provided a list of states that have an estate tax in the Appendix.

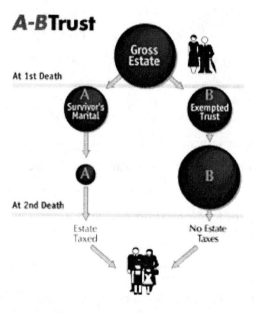

A-BTrust

TRUSTS

One of the most popular ways to minimize taxes and avoid probate is through the use of trusts. A trust is considered a separate entity from you. The trust can control assets, doling them out to the proper beneficiaries. To protect your estate, you change the name of your assets to those of the trust. If you have a living trust, you can even be one of the beneficiaries while you are alive.

You can also structure a trust so that you still have a great deal of control over your assets, and so that your express wishes are carried out should you become incapacitated.

A trust also means that all of the assets inside of it bypass probate upon your death. Instead of having the estate tied up in court, and subject to court and legal fees, the trustees just keep distributing the assets to the beneficiaries, as expected. A living trust can also help reduce your estate taxes, when it is structured as an A-B trust. This diagram from SaveWealth.com illustrates how an A-B trust works, shielding a portion of the estate from taxes:

It is important to pay attention to the structure of your trust, though. You should consult with a knowledgeable estate planner who can help you understand the differences between a revocable trust and an irrevocable trust, as well as living trusts and testamentary trusts. There are many other subtleties associated with trusts, including what is known as a bypass trust, so it is important to carefully consider your options and use a trust in a way that makes sense for your situation.

PAYING ESTATE TAXES WITH LIFE INSURANCE

Another estate planning tactic is to purchase a life insurance policy with the intent that its payout can be used by your heirs to pay any estate taxes owed. In this scenario, you estimate how much your estate will be worth when your life expectancy is up. This can be tricky, but you can use a financial planner or online calculators to help give you a reasonably good idea of how long you can expect to live, and how much your estate will be worth in that time.

If you determine that estate taxes will be right around $350,000, you can do a little research and see how much it would cost for such a policy on you and your spouse, if you have one. Let's say it would cost about $10,000 per year in order to insure you for that amount. (Your actual premium will be based on a number of different factors, and may be higher or lower.) You can set up a separate irrevocable life insurance trust for this process (incurring costs and reducing the size of your estate), or you can just have the policy purchased. It is important that this particular policy not be included as part of your estate. Your children should own this type of policy.

Now, instead of just paying the insurance premium right out, you gift money to your children. Since you have your gift tax exclusion, you can gift this money to your children, and reduce the size of your estate, thereby reducing your taxes. Your children then use the money to pay the insurance premium for you and your spouse.

The whole thing is set up so that your children own the policy, not you, and it is completely separate from your estate. Once both you and your spouse are dead, your children can take the tax-free money from the life insurance policy and use the money to pay the estate taxes, allowing the estate to pass to them relatively unencumbered. The total cost depends on the premiums paid. However, in our example, if you died before 35 years were up, you would actually have set things up so that you get $350,000 for the estate taxes without having to put in the full amount.

You can see why the wealthy take the time and spend the money to structure their estates. The initial outlay is more than worth it when you consider the hundreds of thousands of dollars that can be saved for your heirs. If you are interested in making sure that more of your hard earned wealth goes to your progeny, instead of to the government, it's a good idea to consult a competent estate planning attorney. There are many complex issues associated with estate planning including planning for incapacity.

The following are some of the most common tools used by estate planning attorneys:

1. **Living Trust** - The living trust is a document that functions as a will substitute with the primary benefit of avoiding the need for probate.

2. **Power of Attorney** - A "durable power of" is a document that allows someone else, your Agent, to act on your behalf when you become incapacitated and are no longer competent to manage your financial affairs.

3. **Will** - A will is a set of legal instructions that explains how to give away your property after your death, and to nominate guardians for your minor children.

4. **Conservatorship/Guardianship** - (Conservatorship and guardianship are terms that describe court proceedings to appoint some third party to manage your property and money, and/or your personal decisions like health care and living arrangements, if you become legally incapacitated.)

5. **Special Needs Trust** - A special needs trust is a document that allows you to provide support to a disabled beneficiary without jeopardizing any government benefits, such as Medicaid, that the beneficiary is receiving.

An estate planning attorney can help you preserve as many of your assets for your heirs as possible. For best results, have your financial advisor and attorney work as a team to coordinate your estate plan. Paying an attorney to do your estate plan the right way will save a lot of heartache, confusion, and expenses for your loved ones after you die. This is one place where you should pay enough to get the right advice.

Here are ten questions you should ask when interviewing a prospective estate planning attorney:

1. How much of your practice comprises estate planning?
2. How long have you been practicing?
3. Do you have any experience in litigating estate planning or probate issues? An estate planning attorney with related litigation experience may have enhanced insight into potentially troublesome issues.
4. Can you give me an estimate of your fees? The attorney may not be able to give you an estimate until after he has had a thorough discussion with you about your estate assets and estate planning goals.
5. How are your fees charged?
   - Flat fee
   - Hourly rate
   - Hourly rate with a capped maximum
6. How are your fees to be paid?
   - Upfront
   - Retainer upfront, with the rest upon signing
   - Upon signing, you pay a deposit
7. Do you send me draft documents I can review before signing?
8. What assistance do you provide in transferring assets to a living trust?

9. Do you have any follow-up procedures after my estate planning documents are signed to make sure any tasks I have to do have been completed?

10. After my estate planning documents have been signed, will you charge me if I call you occasionally for information about how my planning documents work

APPENDIX C

FINDING AND HIRING A CPA

Contributed by Keven Steege, CPA

Aside from brain surgery or nuclear fusion, it's possible to do most things on your own. You can certainly learn to prepare your own tax returns. However, just as with brain surgery and nuclear fusion, some things are much more costly than others when they go wrong.

Paying more money than you are legally required to pay, increased IRS scrutiny, penalties and interest, and reading and responding to IRS inquiries are just some of the joys of incorrectly filed tax returns. Even well-meaning taxpayers have subjected themselves to criminal prosecution and large fines by something as simple as failing to disclose certain assets. The Internal Revenue Code has more than tripled since 2001 with a complexity that has allowed honest taxpayers to fail in compliance, while providing sophisticated taxpayers with loopholes to potentially avoid paying taxes altogether.

Whether you're a high net worth individual, are well into your retirement years, or are just beginning to save your first dollars, just about every taxpayer can benefit from hiring an experienced, competent tax professional. Your tax bill will almost assuredly be your single largest lifetime expense—possibly taking 25 percent to

40 percent or more of your income during life and even more after death.

Not hiring someone who is working specifically for you and your success is penny wise but pound foolish. You're not just replacing off-the-shelf tax prep software; you are hiring a business advisor that should be tapped for insight, recommendations, counsel, and feedback. The more you know about your personal financial situation, the more value you will get from your tax professional. As you ask questions and your advisor begins to understand you and your finances, you will begin a lifetime dialogue that should continue to provide more and more value to you throughout the years. That person or firm should become one of your first stops when considering a major transaction or life move.

With this in mind, it is extremely important to find the right person. Look for someone with specialized experience or competency in your area. Look for someone who uses technology efficiently, is timely and ethical, has the ability to communicate in a way you can understand, and is successful in their own business.

Probably your most important resource will be referrals from business colleagues and co-workers, family members, and friends. Getting a reference from someone you trust who has found value in a firm or advisor (or can help you avoid a bad firm or advisor) will save you a lot of time and headache. It also ensures that you won't have to keep starting over again with someone new in a couple of years.

10 THINGS TO ASK BEFORE YOU HIRE A CPA

Once you have found a firm or advisor that seems promising, here are 10 things to ask that will help you determine if they are suitable to be your trusted business advisor:

1. **How long has your firm been in business and what is its reputation?** A firm should have a long-standing presence and reputation in the community and have few, if any, complaints or disciplinary action with the state board of accountancy. Websites such as LinkedIn, Yelp, Google+, or Angie's List may provide beneficial information on positive or negative user reviews, along with an inquiry to the Better Business Bureau. Enrollment in the American Institute of Certified Public Accountants and the state Society of CPAs usually indicates that the professional is subject to the highest professional standards, and possibly even independent peer review.

2. **Do you specialize in my area of business or tax issue?** Your trusted business advisor should have broad tax exposure and be knowledgeable in many different areas, but should have specific experience and knowledge with multiple clients in your area of need. The American Institute of Certified Public Accountants provides a list of local CPAs that specialize in specific areas.

3. **How do you bill for your services?** It's important to understand which services the CPA will be providing you and how they will bill you. This is usually done through an engagement letter provided by the accountant. Some firms bill by the hour, while others bill a flat rate or by the form. National firms will usually be the most expensive

and tend to utilize new college graduates supervised by an experienced CPA. Single-accountant firms usually bill at a lesser rate, but even the best can have difficulty maintaining quality control without additional staff.

4. **What is your turnaround time for a project?** Services must be provided in a timely manner and the firm should be staffed appropriately in order to meet deadlines. Outdated information becomes less and less relevant, and missed due dates lead to penalties and interest from taxing authorities.

5. **Can we work together remotely?** With changing times and globalized technology, there are many benefits to utilizing these tools. A brick and mortar presence is no longer as necessary as a proactive approach to information handling and security. The firm should be flexible enough to adjust to your level of tech savvy.

6. **What kind of IT security and confidentiality policy do you have?** You will want someone who not only utilizes technology to protect your information from criminal attempts at identity theft, but who also has an active and firm policy on how your information is released to legitimate third-party sources. A confidentiality or privacy policy should be obtained for your review and should provide third-party disclosure only upon your express written authorization.

7. **What is your availability after tax season?** While a seasonal tax preparer can help you with your annual filing obligations, that's not all you're looking for. Having someone who is available to discuss an upcoming transaction, idea, or life change—and to help plan the

financial as well as tax implications—is much more valuable. At some point, you are going to need on-the-spot advice or an emergency copy of your tax return, and a seasonal preparer simply won't be around to help when that happens.

8. **Who will be working on my account and what licenses or credentials do they have?** It's important to know the other members of the team, if any, whom you will be working with and who will be knowledgeable about your financial activities. For example, you probably don't want your CPA calculating your weekly payroll for your business, but they should have competent professionals that you enjoy working with.

9. **Are you conservative or aggressive in your interpretation of the tax code?** There is nothing wrong with resolving an issue and reporting a transaction in the taxpayer's favor. Often, there are unusual circumstances that warrant an aggressive position. However, a preparer that continually takes an aggressive stance may get flagged with the IRS. Additionally, a good firm will stand behind its work and will pay penalties and interest for errors or mistakes they made on your behalf. If there is a gray area, you should be notified of the issue and be allowed to make the decision. Ultimately, the responsibility and accuracy of your tax filings rests with you.

10. **What is your experience with the IRS?** The CPA designation is a good starting point for looking for a qualified tax advisor, but you should continue to vet out their experience. They should have good standing with the IRS, be proficient in the IRS processes available only

to the professional preparer, and have worked various correspondence and in-person audits.

An audit can happen to even the most conservative taxpayer and preparer, and statistically you will be subject to at least one during your lifetime. Having someone who knows the environment and how to effectively represent you can be an extremely valuable asset throughout the audit process.

APPENDIX D

HIDDEN VA BENEFITS

Contributed by Mei Wong, Senior Resources Today
5257 NE ML King Jr Blvd., Suite 201
Portland, OR 97211
Office Phone: (503)869-9538
Cell: (971)998-3667
E-mail: mei@seniorresourcestoday.org
www.seniorresourcestoday.org

"Veterans have earned this benefit by their service to our nation," said Secretary of Veterans Affairs Jim Nicholson. "We want to ensure that every veteran or surviving spouse who qualifies has the chance to apply."

The Aid and Attendance pension benefit may be available to wartime veterans and surviving spouses who have in-home care or who live in nursing-homes or assisted-living facilities. Although this is not a new program, not everyone is aware of his/her potential eligibility.

Many elderly veterans and surviving spouses whose incomes are above the congressionally mandated legal limit for a VA pension may still be eligible for the special monthly Aid and Attendance benefit if they have large medical expenses, including nursing home and assisted-living expenses, for which they do not receive reimbursement. To qualify, claimants must be incapable of self support and in need of regular personal assistance.

The basic criteria for the Aid and Attendance benefit include—but are not limited to—the inability to feed oneself, to dress and undress without assistance, or to take care of one's own bodily needs. People who are bedridden or need help to adjust special prosthetic or orthopedic devices may also be eligible, as well as those who have a physical or mental injury or illness that requires regular assistance to protect them from hazards or dangers in their daily environment.

For a wartime veteran or surviving spouse to qualify for this special monthly pension, the veteran must have served at least 90 days of active military service, one day of which was during a period of war, and be discharged under conditions other than dishonorable. Wartime veterans who entered active duty on or after September 8, 1980, (October 16, 1981, for officers) must have completed at least 24 continuous months of military service, or the period for which they were ordered to active duty.

If all requirements are met, VA determines eligibility for the Aid and Attendance benefit by adjusting for un-reimbursed medical expenses from the veteran's or surviving spouse's total household income. If the remaining income amount falls below the annual income threshold for the Aid and Attendance benefit, VA pays the difference between the claimant's household income and the Aid and Attendance threshold.

The Aid and Attendance income threshold for a veteran without dependents is now $20,795 annually. The threshold increases to $24,652 if a veteran has one dependent, and by $2020 for each additional dependent. The annual Aid and Attendance threshold for a surviving spouse alone is $13,362. This threshold increases to $15,940 if there is one dependent child, and by $2020 for each additional child. Information is also available on the Internet at www.va.gov or from any local veteran's service organization.

WARTIME SERVICE REQUIREMENT

For eligibility to improved pension to exist, the veteran must meet the minimum active duty and wartime service requirements.

The veteran is considered to have met the wartime service requirement if at least one day of the veteran's active duty was served during a wartime period. The following table provides the beginning and ending dates of qualifying periods of war for pension benefits.

PERIOD OF WAR	BEGINNING AND ENDING DATES
MEXICAN BORDER PERIOD	May 9, 1916 through April 5, 1917 for veterans who served in Mexico, on its borders, or adjacent waters
WORLD WAR I	April 6, 1917 through November 11, 1918; for veterans who served in Russia, April 6, 1917 through April 1, 1920
WORLD WAR II	December 7, 1941 through December 31, 1946
KOREAN CONFLICT	June 27, 1950 through January 31, 1955
VIETNAM ERA	August 5, 1964 through May 7, 1975; for veterans who served "in country" before August 5, 1964, February 28, 1961 through May 7, 1975
GULF WAR	August 2, 1990 through a date to be set by law or Presidential Proclamation

Reference: For information on developing for wartime service, see M21-1MR, Part III, Subpart iii, 2.D.23.

Benefit Calculations – 2013 Thresholds

Aid and Attendance Maximum Annual Pension Rate (MAPR) Category If you are ...	Basic Pension MAPR	5% of Basic Pension MAPR The amount you subtract from medical expenses...	Annual Aid and Attendance Pension Rate Your yearly income must be less than...
Single Veteran	$12,465 ($1,039 per month)	$623	$20,795 ($1,733 per month)
Veteran with Spouse/ Dependent	$16,324 ($1,360 per month)	$816	$24,652 ($2,054 per month)
Two Veterans Married to Each Other	$16,324 $1,360 per month)	$816	$32,115 ($2,676 per month)
Surviving Spouse	$8,359 ($697 per month)	$417	$13,362 ($1,114 per month)
Surviving Spouse with One Dependent	$10,942 ($912 per month)	$547	$15,940 ($1,328 per month)

APPENDIX E

LONG-TERM CARE

Contributed by Rick Dimick

These are considered to be the 7 essentials for long-term care planning:

KNOWING YOUR RISKS

By not planning today for your long-term care, are you risking not receiving the proper care you may need in the future? Do you need long-term care insurance protection? Maybe you do or maybe you don't – this is, of course, a personal decision. Experience dictates that the best way to make an intelligent decision is to look at the facts:

- How likely are you to need long-term care?
- What would you be placing at risk if you did need long-term care?
- Can you afford the insurance?
- What's the likelihood you will need long-term care?

The odds are very good you will be affected by long-term care at some point in your life. Rosalyn Carter, former first lady, has a famous quote on the impact of long-term care on each family:

"There are four kinds of people in the world: Those who have been caregivers, those who currently are caregivers, those who will be caregivers, and those who will need caregivers."

According to the US Department of Health and Human Services, "At least 70 percent of people over age 65 will require some long-term care services at some point in their lives."[21]

The agency also warns, "Contrary to what many people believe, Medicare and private health insurance programs do not pay for the majority of long-term care services that most people need -- help with personal care such as dressing or using the bathroom independently. Planning is essential for you to be able to get the care you might need."[22]   Once they've reached the age of 65, 3 out of 4 Americans will need-long-term care.[23]

Think that long-term care is just for elderly people?

Think again. Young men and women also need long-term care for a variety of reasons, including accidents, multiple sclerosis, strokes, and other debilitating conditions. In fact, 40 percent of the people receiving long-term care are working age adults between the ages of 18 and 64.[24]

What will you pay for nursing home care?

Although nursing home care is the care most commonly associated with long-term care, this is only one venue that could be required. Other venues include home care, adult day care, and assisted living

---

21(US Department of Health and Human Services. www.longtermcare.gov)
22(US Department of Health and Human Services. www.longtermcare.gov/LTC/Main_Site/Paying_LTC/Costs_Of_Care/Costs_Of_Care.aspx#Who)
23(US Department of Health and Human Services. What is Long-term care? 2009.)
24(ARS-AFM Administrative and Financial Services, Retirement & Benefits, LTC Care Basics Q&A article, Section: It Can Happen at Any Age, January 7, 2003.)

care. Right now, the national average rate for a private room in a nursing home is $219 a day, or $79,935 annually.

That equals $223,818 for the average nursing home stay of 2.8 years. In some parts of the country, it can cost over $100,000 a year. If we assume that nursing home costs will continue to reflect recent trends, then by the year 2021, the average rate will have risen to about $480 a day, or $175,200 annually.[25]

Given these statistics and the potential risk to your savings, long-term care insurance has become commonly referred to as "Estate Planning 101".

Consider Who Will Care for You

Many people plan in advance for long-term care to protect assets or to maintain independence and dignity, while others just want peace of mind. Increasingly, more people are planning for potential long-term care needs so that they don't burden family and friends. Thirty years ago, it was common for an unpaid family member to provide care for a loved one in the home.

These days, many households are dual income families or single parents with competing priorities like earning a promotion at work or raising young children. A 40-hour work week plus raising a family leaves little time to be a primary caregiver. If you are thinking about planning for long-term care, ask yourself these questions:

- Who will care for you?
- Will your son or daughter be able to quit their job to care for you?

25(The MetLife Market Survey of Nursing Home & Assisted Living Costs, 2009.)

- Would you want them to do the type of work that caregiving requires (bathing, dressing, toileting)?
- How would caregiving affect your daughter's or son's health, physically and emotionally?
- What would that mean for their future and the future of their children?
- If you hire a professional caregiver, how will you pay for it?

These are all important considerations when deciding who will care for you when you need long-term care and where that care will be provided. Your options for long-term care services include home care, assisted living, adult day care/community care services, and nursing home care.

You don't have to be limited. A broad long-term care plan will offer various choices as to where and how care is provided. Most long-term care plans offer home care built into the base policy. Some plans reduce home care services to 50 percent or 75 percent, but that reduction doesn't always translate into big savings. Consider 100 percent home health care to ensure the most flexibility in your plan. Some long-term care plans allow for care to be provided by a family member or friend.

For home care, this generally depends on someone who is not duly licensed to provide care services. If this is an important consideration for you, then be sure to ask your specialist if your plan provides that option. While it may sound good now, family may not be the best option.

Assisted living is an option for when the care required is more than can be provided at home. You can negotiate the cost of your care based on what you need. These facilities are similar to an apartment or condominium with amenities like laundry, meal services, and social activities. One and two bedroom apartments are available, providing different levels of care services. The more care you need, the higher the monthly fees.

Adult day care is an option for those who have a family caregiver who is available in the evenings. Day care services are much like that of a child care facility with daily activities, exercise, and meals at mealtime. These services are often provided at community activity centers and senior centers in most cities.

Nursing homes can provide skilled care services when you need 24-hour care by a doctor, nurse, or therapist. Due to advances in technology, many people who need long-term care are utilizing assisted living, or staying at home and avoiding the nursing home altogether. Keep in mind, however, that round-the clock home care is more expensive than a nursing home.

Considering who will care for you and where you will receive care is crucial when planning for your future long-term care needs. Design a plan that will cover care in all venues so that you can make the right choice when the time comes.

PAYING FOR LONG-TERM CARE

Knowing your risks and the cost of care are two crucial elements of planning for long-term care, but what are your options for paying for services should you need long-term care tomorrow? Well, there are three primary methods of paying for long-term care services today.

SELF-INSURING

Most people are self-insured by default because they have not educated themselves on the issues. If you need long-term care tomorrow, how will you pay for it? Will savings and investments suffice? Will you have to liquidate stocks and retirement accounts at the bottom of the market? What about paying taxes on those retirement funds? These questions and more loom very large when you haven't planned in advance for long-term care expenses.

Often, family becomes the "insurance" plan and loved ones are thrust into caregiving roles for which they are not qualified or prepared. Family caregivers often provide this care at a significant cost to income, career advancements, and physical health.

MEDICAID

Medicaid is a state and federally funded program designed to pay for health care, long-term care, and other needs of those who cannot afford to pay themselves. In order to qualify for Medicaid, you must "Spend Down" assets to required levels to qualify for benefits. Medicaid will take a snapshot of your financial situation and determine how much of your income and assets you can keep (usually less than $10,000).

In addition, all financial transactions for 5 years prior to application for Medicaid will be scrutinized. If transfers were made from accounts during that period, you could be declined eligibility. If you are single, you must spend the equity in your home along with retirement plan assets and any cash value life insurance. If you are married, the community spouse is permitted to keep the home (as long as you live in it) and half of the jointly held assets up to $110,000 (indexed for inflation).

After that, the balance of the assets must be spent on the spouse in the nursing home before Medicaid will pay. Estate recovery is required when the spouse at home passes away. Remember, Medicaid is designed to pay for long-term care, only after you qualify financially. Most people do not plan to use Medicaid, nor should they. Consider it the last resort.

MEDICARE

Medicare is health insurance for people 65 and older and was never designed to pay for long-term care expenses. Medicare does cover limited long-term care services provided by a skilled professional such as a doctor, nurse, or therapist. In order to qualify for Medicare's skilled care payments, the following must occur:

- Must have three consecutive days in the hospital, not counting the day of discharge.
- You must be admitted to a nursing facility within 30 days of being discharged from the hospital.
- You must be showing improvement in order to continue to receive benefits for up to 100 days.

Medicare will pay 100 percent of your expenses for the first 20 days, provided that you are receiving skilled care. For days 21-100, you are responsible for a deductible or co-pay of $137.50 or more per day—Medicare picks up the balance of the daily costs. Every few days, Medicare will evaluate your progress to make certain that you are moving towards recovery. If you are not progressing, then Medicare stops paying. Regardless, after day 100, you are responsible for all costs. The bottom line is, Medicare was never designed to pay for long-term care and at best will cover 20 to 100 days of skilled care.

DO YOUR HOMEWORK: RESEARCHING LONG-TERM CARE PLANNING

A broad LTC plan will allow you to leave your options open, helping you to use your plan wherever you, your doctor, and your family see fit. Whether you are buying a home or searching for the best college for your child, researching your options for a major purchase is extremely important. The same is true for long-term care planning.

You may own this plan for many years before you need it, so it's important that you do your homework and buy a plan that fits your needs now and in the future. There are three very important considerations when searching for a long-term care insurance company:

1. Plan options
2. Financial strength and experience in LTC
3. Premium for the selected benefits

Most people who are planning for their future long-term care needs are seeking a plan that will pay for home care, assisted living, community care services, and nursing home care. While home care is what most people prefer, no one has a crystal ball to tell you what the need will be twenty or thirty years down the road. A comprehensive LTC plan will ensure that you have some choices at your disposal.

Company financial strength is important when shopping for a long-term care plan. Insurance companies are graded by independent rating services such as AM Best, Moody's, and Fitch. These rating services grade insurance companies based on whether the company offers good financial security and has the resources to deal with a variety of adverse economic conditions.

For example, AM Best's rating of A++ Superior is assigned to insurance companies that have, based on a variety of measurements, a superior ability to meet their ongoing obligations to policyholders. In addition to financial strength, it is also important to consider how long the company has offered long-term care insurance to consumers. The size of the baby boomer generation has created a wave of Americans who will live longer and healthier lives and therefore have a greater need for long-term care.

Beware of companies that have just entered the market, and research their history thoroughly. It is recommended to consider companies that have a history of at least 10 years of offering long-term care plans to consumers. This experience allows for a better picture of the company's claims paying ability, customer service, and adaptation to the changing long-term care market.

Finally, when researching your options for long-term care insurance planning, be sure to compare apples to apples. There are four basic components that make up a long-term care plan, but there are dozens of optional riders and features that can add to your premiums unnecessarily, without providing you much additional value. An unusually low premium usually means one of those four basic components of a long-term care insurance plan is missing. A good rule of thumb is if it sounds too good to be true, it probably is. A specialist can help you compare plan offerings.

DESIGNING THE RIGHT PLAN FOR YOU: PUTTING IT ALL TOGETHER

Designing a long-term care insurance policy that is appropriate for you is really not as complicated as it may seem. You simply have to keep a few important points in mind. Determining the cost of your coverage is based on the following four components.

1. **Monthly Benefits** - The first and most important decision is to determine how much of the average monthly cost of care you will want your policy to cover. In most cases, you should make sure that your benefits are available for home, assisted living, and nursing home care. Keep in mind that nearly 80 percent of claims are for home health care, which can be less expensive than nursing home care.

   In that case, make sure you are not buying more coverage than you may actually need. Be sure to consider interest on savings, dividends, Social Security, or pension income to supplement expenses and design a plan that pays for 80-100 percent of care costs in your area of the country.

2. **Elimination Period** - As with other types of insurance, long-term care insurance policies offer the choice of several different elimination periods. The elimination period represents the number of days you agree to pay out of pocket before benefits begin. Unlike other types of insurance, most long-term care policies require only one elimination period for the life of the policy. Logically, the bigger the elimination period, the lower your premiums. Working with a specialist will allow you

to view exact cost comparisons with various elimination periods and help you maximize your premium dollars.

3. **Benefit Period** - Long-term care insurance policies are designed to create an account with a maximum amount of money over the life of the policy. This is referred to as a "benefit period" and is determined by using a simple calculation. For example, a policy that pays for 5 years of care (the benefit period) at $5,000 monthly would have a face amount of $300,000. ($5,000 x 60 months = $300,000). When you need long-term care, you can draw money from your account until your policy is exhausted.

4. **Inflation Protection** - Today, most people who are shopping for long-term care insurance are under the age of 70. If you fall into this category, it is highly recommended that you consider some type of inflation protection option in your policy. When you have a future claim, your policy will pay you back a higher dollar amount to keep pace with inflation.

Be sure you understand all of the inflation options on the market today and the benefits of each option.

DO YOUR RESEARCH: FINDING THE RIGHT CARRIER

Like any other business, insurance companies are in business to make a profit. However, these same insurance companies are lawfully permitted to discriminate based on health profiles provided at the time of application. Many carriers provide wide choices for comprehensive coverage, with few exclusions and limitations, and stable premiums.

Additionally, there are insurance companies willing to consider the health challenged, such as those with diabetic conditions with complications, or co-morbid combinations including height/weight issues, tobacco use with heart/circulation complications, recent cancer treatments, etc. Of course, these plans may cost more and offer less in return. Benefits will likely be limited and more difficult to obtain.

With this in mind, you may find a considerable number of varying options between the different long-term care insurance companies. Many couples with health disparities between them have found the best combinations of benefits and premiums by applying to two different companies (similar to two drivers in the same household, one with a "preferred" and the other with an "assigned risk" classification.) Carrier benefits include domestic partner discounts and domestic vs. international coverage.

In some states, some carriers offer "partnership" plans in conjunction with the state, assuring additional levels of asset protection. While most plans are based on reimbursement models requiring the submission of expenses, several carriers indemnify a specific cash benefit, regardless of actual expenses, to be used however you choose. There are plans more suited to couples by virtue of "shared" benefits as well as those that offer discounts for couples—both traditionally married or domestic partner relationships.

For the educated consumer, the ability to compare insurance companies side by side is essential in making the right decision. Having choices ensures that you'll find optimal benefits, affordable premiums, and the confidence that you have made the right decision for your situation and needs.

WORK WITH A SPECIALIST

When considering long-term care insurance, consumers are typically challenged by a multitude of decisions to be made:

- How much coverage do I actually need?
- Which benefits are most meaningful to my specific needs?
- Which insurance company is best for my situation?
- What are "partnership plans", and should I consider one?

The value of dealing with a "specialist" cannot be overstated. Increasingly, financial advisors, legal consultants, and even general insurance brokers advise their clients to seek out licensed agents who are long-term care specialists dealing exclusively with this product. A specialist will have access to many major carriers, including state partnership plans (where available), so the concerned consumer can be assured all options are considered on their behalf. Carriers have different policies regarding domestic vs. international claims, independent care providers vs. agency caregivers, discounts available when only one spouse applies, and nontraditional relationships, as well as for group and professional affiliations.

Most significantly, insurance companies decide insurability based on health profiles provided at the time of application, and companies differ on what health conditions they will accept. This is reflected in premiums or even the ability to obtain a policy. One other consideration is, when is a group offering (open enrollment) better than an individual plan?

A specialist will consider your specific needs and situation and is experienced in gathering all relevant data. The LTC specialist will then make recommendations pertaining to a long-term care plan design and appropriate carrier, based on your needs. Working with a specialist allows many more options compared to a general insurance agent who may have limited carrier access and minimal plan design. With only a few options, you may not get exactly what you need.

As improved lifestyles, advances in medical technology, and the continued development of carrier benefits affect the dynamics of long-term care issues, we believe that only a long-term care specialist can provide the education, plan design, and comparisons best suited to your needs.

SOME FINAL THOUGHTS

Most states have over 20 approved long-term care insurance policies on the market. To complicate matters, premiums and coverage can be different in each state. With all of these factors to consider, where do you begin? Fortunately, it isn't necessary for you to review every policy yourself. Speak to an experienced long-term care insurance specialist.

You have every right to question the experience of any person with whom you are considering working. Find out whether the agent is familiar with all the policies and carriers doing business in your state, how long they have been selling long-term care insurance, and how many policyholders they have obtained coverage for.

If you are considering long-term care insurance, you want to make the right decision. Take the time to speak to a long-term care insurance specialist to discuss your options. In the end, you will be that much wiser and better equipped to make the right decision for you and your family.

ABOUT RICK DIMICK

Rick consults with individuals, financial advisers, attorneys, CPAs and small business owners on the importance of long-term care planning for themselves, their employees, and/or their clients. Rick explains very precisely and succinctly how long-term care insurance can often be the most cost effective way to pay for probable long-term care needs.

"It is my responsibility to help people understand the emotional, physical, and financial consequences associated with providing or paying for care over an extended period of time. It is essential they have this information so they can take action to protect those they love while they have options. I am committed to helping my clients create an appropriate plan to meet their specific needs."

Rick has extensive family experience with long-term care situations at all levels of care, including his mother's dementia disease, which has progressed over 5 years. He believes totally that everyone needs to ask themselves 2 vital questions:

1. What is my written plan if I lose my independence and my family needs to take care of me at home or in extended care?
2. How will I pay for that care?

Rick can address your questions and issues, determine if this coverage is appropriate for you, help qualify you for a plan, design an appropriate plan, and help you shop for the best company, coverage, and price for your specific situation.

Rick Dimick
Life Insurance
Linked/hybrid Benefits &
Long term care specialist
rdimick@usa.com
503-908-0845

APPENDIX F

REVERSE MORTGAGES

Contributed by Mark Eshelman, CSA

Did you know that using a variety of assets can help you get the most out of your retirement dollar? I'd bet most people know their IRA is an asset, and they're most likely aware that their 401(k) is an asset too. However, when it comes to retirement planning, most people don't think of their home equity as an asset to be utilized.

Your home equity is indeed an asset and it can be utilized in retirement. Often, it's the most valuable asset in your retirement portfolio. If that's the case, why do some people ignore their biggest asset when they are developing their retirement plans? I'm happy to say there's a new way of thinking about your home equity in retirement.

GARY AND ANNA'S STORY

Consider this retirement success story:

Gary and Anna, both 64, have a little over $400,000 saved up between them in their 401(k)s and IRAs. They also own a home worth $375,000 that they recently paid off. They plan to retire after they both turn 65. In order for Gary and Anna to make sure they have enough cash to live the lifestyle they've grown accustomed to and have money available for emergencies in their retirement years, they decided to get a reverse mortgage now rather than waiting until their retirement savings ran out.

Gary and Anna have a reverse mortgage that's federally insured called a Home Equity Conversion Mortgage (HECM). They chose the HECM Saver option because it had lower closing costs, even though it doesn't tap as much of the home equity available to them (In this case, about 10 percent less equity than the HECM Standard option).

In October 2013, it's expected that the FHA will make some adjustments to the HECM Saver and HECM Standard programs. It is anticipated that the two programs will be merged and one new program will be available. Many of the reverse mortgage functions will remain unchanged, but there will be new guidelines that impact the amount of money that can be withdrawn with the initial draw of a new HECM reverse mortgage.

In Gary and Anna's case, their home appraised at $375,000 and they received a Line-of-Credit (LOC) for $173,906. The HECM Line-of-credit has a unique growth feature: the unused portion of the LOC grows at the "credit line growth rate," which is equal to the compounding rate of interest plus the mortgage insurance rate.

If Gary and Anna leave their LOC unused over the next 10 years, it will grow in borrowing capacity up to $333,535. In 20 years, the LOC borrowing capacity will grow to $639,686, if left untouched. Please see the details for Gary & Anna's example with the Amortization Schedule in the Appendix at the end of the chapter.

Because the borrower pays mortgage insurance, the FHA guarantees that money is available for their use, even if their property value declines. In Gary and Anna's case, the mortgage insurance costs would only total $1,504 after 10 years and would be just $4,315 after 20 years.

Keep in mind, this is just one of the many ways a reverse mortgage can help you in retirement.

THE REVERSE MORTGAGE

Using your home equity as a part of your financial strategy can stretch your retirement dollar. In a 2010 study conducted by The Center for Retirement Research at Boston College, it was discovered that the National Retirement Risk Index (NRRI) increased by 10 percentage points when home equity is not utilized through a reverse mortgage as part of a retirement strategy. The risk is that you might outlive your retirement savings.

Too many retirees are neglecting or ignoring a valuable retirement planning tool known as a reverse mortgage. It's important for you to understand the benefits of a reverse mortgage because as baby boomers retire, most will retire without a defined benefit pension from their employers. This is affecting the oldest boomers right now.

According to the Stanford Center for Longevity, 75 percent of older adults (65+) have annual incomes, including Social Security, of less than $34,000. However, 9 out of 10 of the oldest baby boomers are homeowners with an average home value of $254,000. Most people have heard the term "reverse mortgage," but many don't truly understand how they work. If you find that you don't completely understand all of the benefits and details of reverse mortgages, don't feel bad. You're not alone.

A reverse mortgage is a unique financial instrument designed to extend the cash flow of qualified homeowners in their retirement years, starting at age 62. To better understand a reverse mortgage and how it differs from a traditional "forward" mortgage, let's take a look at the basic features of each mortgage.

REVERSE MORTGAGE VS. TRADITIONAL MORTGAGE

With a traditional forward mortgage, a bank lends people money to buy a home. The borrower then agrees to pay the bank back the principal amount borrowed plus any interest and mortgage insurance that accrues. The borrower makes monthly installment payments that are applied to the accrued interest, mortgage insurance (if applicable), and toward the principal loan amount for a specified period of time. Typically, the time periods for a mortgage are 15, 20, or 30 years.

The only way a homeowner can access the equity in their home is by selling the home, refinancing the original loan, or taking out a home equity loan. The refinance option, as well as the home equity loan option, still requires the borrower to make monthly installment payments. On top of that, the borrower needs to meet all of the income, credit, and home equity requirements in order to use the money from their home equity. Please note that not everyone qualifies for a traditional mortgage.

The reverse mortgage is different from a traditional forward mortgage in that qualified borrowers age 62 and older can remain in their home, stay on the title of their home, and receive tax-free money from their home equity without making monthly mortgage payments. The borrower only needs to live in the home, maintain the home, and pay the annual property taxes and insurance, which are things most homeowners do anyway.

With a traditional forward mortgage, as you continue making on-time monthly payments, your loan balance goes down and your home equity can grow. The loan must be paid off by the end of a pre-specified period of time, such as 15, 20, or 30 years. It's different with a reverse mortgage.

Since a reverse mortgage does not require monthly mortgage payments and the borrower can draw from the reverse mortgage line-of-credit, the loan balance grows over time and the home equity typically shrinks. With the reverse mortgage, the loan is not paid back until the borrowers no longer live in the home as their primary residence, or when the home is sold.

THE REVERSE MORTGAGE
LANDSCAPE IS CHANGING

In 2012, *The Journal of Financial Planning* published two articles illustrating the benefits of using a reverse mortgage as part of your retirement plan. The first article was written by Dr. Barry H. Sacks and Dr. Stephen R. Sacks, and it is titled, "Reversing the Conventional Wisdom: Using Home Equity to Supplement Retirement Income." This report goes into detail about how properly using a reverse mortgage along with your liquid retirement assets can stretch your money further in your retirement years.

Their strategy is based on using a reverse mortgage line-of-credit in conjunction with your retirement portfolio, which includes the IRA, 401(k), etc. As part of the plan, you would use the funds from your retirement portfolio to live on during the good years when your portfolio is meeting the desired growth rate and the returns you need. In years when the portfolio is not performing to the standards you need, such as during a bear market, you stop drawing funds from those retirement accounts and instead draw from the reverse mortgage LOC.

This allows you to preserve your retirement portfolio and gives it a chance to recover, which should make those funds last longer in retirement. In several probability models, the authors show the retirement cash flow survival rate was increased between 10 percent and 30 percent using their reverse mortgage strategy.

The second article in the *Journal of Financial Planning* was written by Dr. John Salter, Shaun Pfeiffer, and Harold Evensky. Their report is titled, "Standby Reverse Mortgages: A Risk Management Tool for Retirement Distributions." Their report goes a step further than the

Sacks' research, by implementing a borrowing and payback methodology with a reverse mortgage LOC within a three-bucket strategy.

One bucket is for Cash Flow Reserves (CFR), another bucket is for the investment portfolio, and the third bucket is for the HECM Standby Reverse Mortgage (SRM). The SRM is to be used in a bear market when the cash bucket is low or empty. The article states, "The SRM bucket provides an alternative to refill the cash bucket with no transaction cost, no tax consequences, and possible tax-deductible interest upon repayment. This strategy also allows a reduction in the Cash Flow Reserve holdings, from as much as 24 months down to 6 months, because of the 'standby' source of readily available cash in the reverse mortgage line-of-credit."

The article goes on to illustrate that when their client reached age 92 using the Standby Reverse Mortgage method, his portfolio went from having a positive value of 52 percent all the way up to 82 percent, when compared to not using the Standby Reverse Mortgage. This may not be how your grandparents used their reverse mortgage, but you can see that when combining a reverse mortgage with your other retirement assets, you can successfully extend your cash flow in your golden years and live a more comfortable retirement.

SAFETY NETS

A reverse mortgage is designed with several "safety net" features to protect the homeowner. One is called a Non-Recourse feature. This protects the borrower from owing more than their home is worth. The Department of Housing and Urban Development (HUD) defines it this way: "Non-recourse" means that if a lender takes legal action against the borrower for default on the loan, the lender can look only to the property to satisfy the loan, as opposed to holding the borrower personally liable for the debt.

Note: This repayment standard also applies to the borrower's heirs or estate when the property is sold to repay the outstanding loan. The lender cannot hold the heirs or estate personally liable for the balance. However, if the heirs or the estate wish to keep the property, they are personally liable for the full balance of the loan.

Another "safety net" on all reverse mortgages is the requirement for HUD certified third-party counseling to be completed by the borrower prior to applying for a reverse mortgage. The counseling session is used to make sure the borrower fully understands the reverse mortgage and how it may impact their specific situation. Also, the reverse mortgage counselor will explore other options that may be available to a prospective applicant in lieu of getting a reverse mortgage. This helps make sure that only people who will truly benefit from a reverse mortgage obtain this type of loan.

As with any primary residence refinance loan, a reverse mortgage also has a three-day right of rescission after the loan is signed to allow the borrowers an opportunity to change their minds prior to the reverse mortgage being funded.

TAX-FREE FUNDS

The money received from a reverse mortgage is not taxed. There are several reasons for this, but the main reason is because the home equity is an asset that's already yours. A reverse mortgage just converts your home equity into usable cash. In addition, the money received from a reverse mortgage cannot be taxed because it's still considered a loan, and loan proceeds from a primary residence are not taxable.

Reverse mortgage proceeds are not considered income for tax purposes, nor should they affect your Social Security Retirement Benefits or Medicare. However, you should note that lump sum distributions from a reverse mortgage may impact a person's eligibility for Medicaid, Supplemental Social Security Income (SSI), and other government need-based income or support.

WAYS TO USE YOUR REVERSE MORTGAGE FUNDS

Here are just a few ways a reverse mortgage can be used to benefit retirement life:

- Supplement your monthly retirement income.
- Pay off an existing mortgage or credit card debt.
- Pay for medical expenses or in-home care.
- Make home improvements or modify your home to meet your current and long-term living needs.
- Travel.
- Gift to children or grandchildren.
- Purchase long-term care insurance.
- Avoid foreclosure.
- Buy a boat or RV.
- Pay for rising property taxes and homeowner's insurance.
- Secure a cash reserve for emergencies.
- Purchase a new primary residence that better meets your needs.
- Maintain your financial independence.

ELIGIBILITY REQUIREMENTS

In a nutshell, here's what you need to know about qualifying for a reverse mortgage:

- The home must be the borrower's primary residence.
- All borrowers on title must be 62 years of age or older.
- The amount borrowed is based on the youngest person's age.
- Currently, there are no credit or income qualifications for most reverse mortgages.
- All liens reporting on the home's title must be paid or satisfied at closing.
- Borrower must have equity in their home, generally between 24 percent and 47 percent.
- Older borrowers can use a higher percentage of their home's equity.

5 REASONS NOT TO CONSIDER A REVERSE MORTGAGE

Reverse Mortgages can help solve many problems for seniors, but there is no one-size-fits-all loan product that can solve every problem. Here's a short list of reasons you should think it through before opting for a reverse mortgage.

1. **Risky Investments** - If someone is telling you to get a reverse mortgage in order to invest your money into one of their financial products or "business ideas," it may be time for you to turn the other way and run. They may be trying to get you to spend your hard-earned money on their risky investments. Most seniors don't have the financial recovery

time to recapture any money lost on bad investments.

2. **Annuities** - The Department of Housing and Urban Development (HUD) has done a good job of implementing rules to eliminate the practice of selling annuities to people who seek a reverse mortgage. In the past, unethical insurance agents and financial advisors urged reverse mortgage applicants to purchase an annuity with their loan proceeds. This practice has been illegal since 2008. Today, the borrower can purchase an annuity with their loan proceeds, but it cannot be part of the reverse mortgage loan process.

Purchasing an annuity with reverse mortgage proceeds is not necessary because the loan program already has a built-in annuity feature. A borrower can choose the "term" or "tenure" pay-out option with their reverse mortgage and save themselves the expense of paying a commission to their insurance agent or financial advisor.

3. **Short-term Uses** - This one can get tricky. Using a reverse mortgage can be costly for short term needs, so it's not typically recommended for someone who only plans to stay in their home for few years.

In some cases, though, the short-term use of a reverse mortgage may be the only option. For example, I worked with a client in Portland, OR who had a terminal illness. He still had a decent sized mortgage to pay on, but he also had a pile of medical bills and medical treatments to pay for. He didn't qualify for Medicaid, so a reverse mortgage gave him the monthly mortgage payment relief he needed, as well as a $60,000 line-of-credit to use as he needed.

Again, a reverse mortgage is not specifically designed for short-term needs, so be sure to check out all of your options before making a decision. This is one of the "safety net" benefits of the required reverse mortgage counseling mentioned earlier.

4. **Loans to Friends and Family Members** - Borrowing money against your own home to pay for someone else's debt is seldom ever a good idea. Be careful in avoiding untrusted or irresponsible friends and family members talking you into a reverse mortgage so that they can use the benefits for themselves. This type of situation rarely ends on a happy note for either party.

5. **Non-Borrowing Spouse Taken Off Title** - This part of a reverse mortgage does create some questions. Be sure to work with a loan officer that understands the impact of taking a spouse off title with a reverse mortgage. Also, it's imperative that both spouses seek legal guidance before deciding to remove a spouse from title. If the FHA rules do change in regards to the non-borrowing spouse, it's very important for you to know the long-term impact this may have on you.

THE NON-BORROWING SPOUSE STORY OF GENE AND FRANNIE

Gene and Frannie lived in Everett, WA. Gene wanted to retire early at the age of 62. Frannie was already a retired school teacher, but she was only 59 years old. Both of them wanted to spend their retirement years close to their children and grandchildren in central Oregon. They sold their home in Everett with a nice profit of $190,000, but the home in central Oregon that they wanted to buy was about $285,000.

Their goal was to retire with no mortgage payment. They were able to accomplish this by doing a reverse mortgage purchase. They paid about $183,000 for a down payment and closing costs and now have the home they've wanted all of their lives. It was a single-story home on 5 acres with a big view and a barn for horses. Perfect.

However, Frannie was only 59, so she didn't qualify to be on the reverse mortgage. This meant that in the event of Gene's death, Frannie would need to either sell the home or refinance the loan to pay off the reverse mortgage in Gene's name. The good thing was that if Gene happened to precede Frannie in death, she had no plans to stay on the 5 acres all by herself.

She was okay with selling the home if Gene died, since she wasn't on the reverse mortgage. However, their circumstances are a unique occurrence, so always consult carefully with your reverse mortgage loan officer when at least one of the people on title of the home is under the age of 62.

OTHER TAX BENEFITS WITH A REVERSE MORTGAGE

When you have a reverse mortgage, you're not required to make that monthly principal and interest payment. If no interest payments are made, there won't be any mortgage interest to deduct on your tax return. This is important to remember for those that depend on receiving that tax deduction each year. However, a borrower can choose to make payments on their reverse mortgage. If/when a payment is made, it's applied to the outstanding accrued mortgage insurance, then accrued interest, and lastly the principal balance.

The interest and mortgage insurance that's accruing on a reverse mortgage is being deferred to a later date. It'll be paid when the home is actually sold. Depending on how many years a reverse mortgage is in place, the amount of deferred interest and mortgage insurance can accumulate to a substantial amount. In the year the home is sold and the reverse mortgage is paid off, there could be a huge tax deduction waiting for you. Here's an example of how this works.

THE STORY OF DAVE AND ANGELA AND THEIR BIG TAX DEDUCTION

Dave and Angela took out a HECM Reverse Mortgage back in 2005, when they were both 66 years old. Their home was in Wilsonville, OR and was worth $275,000. They used most of the proceeds of their reverse mortgage to pay off their traditional forward mortgage and some other debt.

Now that Dave and Angela are 74 years old, they've changed their plans about living the rest of their lives in Oregon. They want to sell their home and move to Arizona to live in the sun year round. They plan to by a luxury condo in a retirement community and take it easy playing golf and sitting by the pool. Not a bad plan, in my opinion.

When Dave and Angela sell their home with the reverse mortgage, they will have a mortgage interest, mortgage insurance, and loan origination fee tax deduction of approximately $94,900 for their 2013 tax return. They're selling their Wilsonville home to their son, who's a developer, at a deep discount. They'll only have sale proceeds of about $50,000 available to use as a down payment on the Arizona condo. Down the road, their son will pay them back the money they had to forgo with the reduced sale price. However, that could take two to three years.

The purchase price on the Arizona condo is $320,000. Dave and Angela have decided to use the reverse mortgage purchase program to finance the condo, so they still won't have a monthly mortgage payment. Based on their age of 74, they'll need about $124,000 to cover the down payment and closing costs.

With the $50,000 from the sale of the Wilsonville home, they'll be about $74,000 short, but remember that $94,900 tax deduction that's waiting in the wings? This would be a great year to pull the remaining down payment of $74,000 out of their IRA and pay almost no income tax for doing it because of their big tax deduction.

Dave and Angela's Condo Purchase Breakdown:

Arizona Condo Purchase Price	$320,000
Reverse Mortgage Loan Amount	- $196,000
Amount for Down Payment & Closing Costs	$124,000
Down Payment & Closing Costs	$124,000
Sale Proceeds from Wilsonville Home	- $50,000
Amount Needed from IRA Withdrawal*	$74,000

*This withdrawal from Dave and Angela's Traditional IRA will be a tax-free withdrawal because of the $94,900 tax deduction they received from paying off their old reverse mortgage on the Wilsonville home.

In summary, Dave and Angela will have avoided depleting their retirement nest egg by not making monthly mortgage payments. They gave their son a huge break with a low price on their Wilsonville home, and they saved a good chunk of change on income taxes. By using a reverse mortgage correctly, all of these benefits were possible.

As you can see, a reverse mortgage is a flexible financial tool that can stretch your retirement dollar and allow you to live the kind of life you worked so hard to achieve. Your golden years should be a reward to you, because you deserve it. Make sure to use all of the tools and options available to you to get the most out of the assets you already have. You only live once, so make it count.

Mark Eshelman
Reverse Mortgage Loan Officer
NMLS #913042
15640 NE 4th Plain Blvd, Ste. #120-A
Vancouver WA 98682
Phone: 360.910.7710
Email: MEshelman@BannerBank.com

6 QUESTIONS YOU NEED TO ASK YOUR REVERSE MORTGAGE LOAN OFFICER

1. **Does your company offer other types of home loans beyond reverse mortgages?** - The reason this is important is because a reverse mortgage isn't right for everyone. Like I said before, there is no one-size-fits-all loan product. If the loan officer you're working with works for a company that only offers reverse mortgages, you might want to shop around to make sure you're getting the best mortgage for your specific needs.

   Reverse mortgages are a great loan with many flexible options, but it may not meet all of your needs. Make sure that your loan officer has the ability to get you the right loan for your particular situation.

2. **How many reverse mortgages do you close each year?** - Many mortgage brokers can offer just about every loan under the sun, which can be great in some instances. However, putting together a reverse mortgage is considerably different from every other loan product on the market. If your mortgage professional does fewer than five reverse mortgages per year, they probably don't have the expertise to give you sound advice as to whether a reverse mortgage is best for you, or as to which type of reverse mortgage would suit your needs the best.

3. **What sort of background or experience do you have that's relevant to your work as a reverse mortgage loan officer?** - If your reverse mortgage loan officer doesn't have experience working on other types of mortgages, they may not be aware that a different loan product may solve your needs better than a reverse mortgage. Also, it's good to find out if your loan officer or mortgage broker works with senior homeowners frequently.

Working with first-time homebuyers is significantly different than working with a seasoned senior homeowner. One thing I've noticed in working with seniors is they prefer to take their time gathering and evaluating information prior to making a decision. That's a good thing. If someone is causing you to feel rushed to make a decision about a reverse mortgage, take a step back and pause. It's not a race. Use the time you need to make the best decision for yourself.

4. **How often will you contact me to let me know the status of my reverse mortgage loan in process?** - Getting a good answer from your loan officer on this question gives the customer a great opportunity to hold their loan officer accountable throughout the entire loan process. Any good loan officer should return all phone calls and e-mails within one business day, preferably taking no more than 4 hours to get back in touch with you.

As a customer, you shouldn't have to put up with long delays in getting your questions answered. Hold your loan officer accountable. If they don't call you back in a reasonable time frame, tell them you'll take your business elsewhere. It's amazing how fast a loan officer calls back when they get that message.

5. **Are you licensed to sell other financial or insurance products? If so, which type of products do you sell?** - My opinion is that it's hard to be a jack-of-all-trades, master-of-none and still be able to correctly advise a client through the process of a reverse mortgage. Sadly, I know this from experience. When I was in my late twenties, I had my insurance licenses and securities licenses, along with being a mortgage loan officer. I wanted to be all things to all people. Needless to say, I was overwhelmed. It was just too much information to keep organized accurately in one person's head.

If it's a reverse mortgage you're looking for, find a specialist who can focus on just doing that for you. Remember, it's still okay to ask your financial advisor, accountant, and attorney to look over the information you receive from your reverse mortgage loan officer. Second opinions can be worth their weight in gold.

6. **How does the loan officer get paid for closing my loan?** - It's important to make sure that your reverse mortgage loan officer does not get paid a higher commission based on the type of reverse mortgage loan option you choose. In addition, you should ask the loan officer if they make a higher commission based on the interest rate you get.

In some cases, a loan officer can make more money off your loan when they sell you on taking a higher interest rate. By asking these questions first, you hold your loan officer accountable to getting the best deal for you, not them.

⌂REVERSEVISION

1620 5th Avenue, Suite 725 | San Diego, CA 92101
Web: www.reversevision.com

Amortization Schedule - Annual Projections
The amortization schedule on the next page is based on the following circumstances:

Borrower Name/ Case Number:	Gary and Anna Sample	Refinance	No
Age of Youngest Borrower:	62	Initial Property Value	$375,000.00
Interest Rate (Expected / Initial):	5.280% / 2.434%	: Beg. Mortgage	$8,343.45
Maximum Claim Amount:	$375,000.00	Balance: Expected	4.000%
Initial Principal Limit	$182,250.00	Appreciation: Initial	$173,906.55
Initial Advance	$0.00	Line-of-credit: Monthly	$0.00
Lien Payoffs with Reverse Mortgage:	$0.00	Payment:	$0.00
Financed Closing Costs	$8,343.45	Monthly Servicing Fee: Mortgage Insurance (MIP)	1.25%

Note: Actual interest charges and property value projections may vary from amounts shown. Available credit will be less than projected if funds withdrawn from line-of-credit.

This illustration is an example of a reverse mortgage amortization schedule and annual projections. It shows how it can be used to assist with a financial plan, if it fits your personal situation and needs. You should always consult with your tax advisor, as well as your financial advisor, when considering a reverse mortgage.

YR	AGE	SVC FEE	CASH PAY	MIP	RATE	INTEREST	LOAN BALANCE	LINE-OF-CREDIT	PROPERTY VALUE	EQUITY
1	62	$0	$0	$107	5.280%	$454	$8,905	$185,609	$390,000	$381,095
2	63	$0	$0	$115	5.280%	$485	$9,504	$198,098	$405,600	$396,096
3	64	$0	$0	$122	5.280%	$517	$10,144	$211,429	$421,824	$411,680
4	65	$0	$0	$131	5.280%	$552	$10,826	$225,656	$438,697	$427,871
5	66	$0	$0	$139	5.280%	$589	$11,555	$240,840	$456,245	$444,690
6	67	$0	$0	$149	5.280%	$629	$12,332	$257,046	$474,495	$462,162
7	68	$0	$0	$159	5.280%	$671	$13,162	$274,343	$493,474	$480,312
8	69	$0	$0	$170	5.280%	$716	$14,048	$292,804	$513,213	$499,166
9	70	$0	$0	$181	5.280%	$764	$14,993	$312,506	$533,742	$518,749
10	71	$0	$0	$193	5.280%	$816	$16,002	$333,535	$555,092	$539,090
11	72	$0	$0	$206	5.280%	$871	$17,079	$355,979	$577,295	$560,217
12	73	$0	$0	$220	5.280%	$929	$18,228	$379,933	$600,387	$582,159
13	74	$0	$0	$235	5.280%	$992	$19,454	$405,498	$624,403	$604,948
14	75	$0	$0	$251	5.280%	$1,059	$20,764	$432,784	$649,379	$628,615
15	76	$0	$0	$267	5.280%	$1,130	$22,161	$461,907	$675,354	$653,193
16	77	$0	$0	$285	5.280%	$1,206	$23,652	$492,988	$702,368	$678,716
17	78	$0	$0	$305	5.280%	$1,287	$25,243	$526,162	$730,463	$705,219
18	79	$0	$0	$325	5.280%	$1,373	$26,942	$561,567	$759,681	$732,739
19	80	$0	$0	$347	5.280%	$1,466	$28,755	$599,355	$790,068	$761,313
20	81	$0	$0	$370	5.280%	$1,565	$30,690	$639,686	$821,671	$790,981
22	83	$0	$0	$422	5.280%	$1,782	$34,959	$728,672	$888,720	$853,760
24	85	$0	$0	$481	5.280%	$2,030	$39,822	$830,036	$961,239	$921,417
26	87	$0	$0	$547	5.280%	$2,313	$45,362	$945,501	$1,039,676	$994,314
28	89	$0	$0	$624	5.280%	$2,634	$51,672	$1,077,029	$1,124,514	$1,072,842
30	91	$0	$0	$710	5.280%	$3,001	$58,860	$1,226,853	$1,216,274	$1,157,414
32	93	$0	$0	$809	5.280%	$3,418	$67,048	$1,397,518	$1,315,522	$1,248,474
34	95	$0	$0	$922	5.280%	$3,894	$76,375	$1,591,925	$1,422,869	$1,346,493
36	97	$0	$0	$1,050	5.280%	$4,435	$87,000	$1,813,375	$1,538,975	$1,451,975
38	99	$0	$0	$1,196	5.280%	$5,052	$99,102	$2,065,631	$1,664,555	$1,565,453

APPENDIX G

MEDICARE—THE BIG UNKNOWN

Contributed by Karen Kane, August 30, 2013

Here are my 10 Tips on how to plan for health insurance now and into retirement:

1. Planning for Health Insurance into Retirement

Retirement is that time in your life when you get to do all those things you didn't do while you were working. Unfortunately, as you plan for all of those things, it's easy to overlook your potential medical costs. Most people will become responsible for their own insurance and medical costs, planning, and decisions in retirement. In fact, they may already have had to do this if they were self-employed.

It used to be that you retired when you turned age 65, and Medicare was your primary source for health insurance. These days, it's very different. Some people are in their 50's or in their 70's when they retire. Health care is getting more expensive all the time, as is health insurance, to the point where it's a big part of your monthly and annual budget. You should ask questions about the cost of care and coverage before you commit to retirement, because it might influence your decision.

Most health insurance decisions are made annually on a calendar year basis. You will choose your plan to serve your needs from January 1st through December 31st. An insurance plan's deductible is likely based on a calendar year too.

It's a good idea to assess your medical services. What kinds do you use and how frequently? What do you anticipate for the next year? Are you considering surgery? Will there be tests or physical therapy? How many prescriptions do you take regularly? Medical and prescription out of pocket costs are accumulated separately by the insurance plans, so you should keep those separate too.

2. Non-Medicare (Under Age 65)

Now, it's possible to select and enroll in an individual insurance plan to cover you until age 65. As of January 1, 2014, health insurance plans have been available to everyone regardless of pre-existing health conditions. This is helpful because it gives everyone a broader choice for health care. Just remember that paying a higher monthly premium doesn't always means you are getting better insurance coverage.

You would expect that the more you pay upfront per month, the lower you should have to pay later when you need it. Do a quick analysis of the total annual premium plus the insurance plan's total maximum out of pocket amount given a worst-case scenario. The insurance plan's description may or may not include the annual deductible amount. You need to ask whether the maximum out of pocket includes the deductible or not. Important factors to consider include the provider network, your medical care needs, the types of services you use and the frequency, your annual budget or premium, and health-care services.

3A. Medicare Part A

Hospital insurance is typically free if you or your spouse paid taxes while you worked. It is also available for a monthly premium. There are deductibles and co-pays you are expected to pay for each hospital stay or skilled nursing facility stay. These costs can change yearly. There are limits to the number of days Medicare Part A covers. Medicare covers only $250 for medical care received for foreign travel.

3B. Medicare Part B

Medical insurance covers doctor's services, such as office visits, tests, and surgeries. Part B usually costs you a monthly premium that's determined each year. Qualified low-income Medicare beneficiaries can reduce their premium for Medicare Part B and other medical costs, while above average income earners may pay a higher monthly premium. The insurance coverage is the same for everyone, covering 80percent of Medicare allowable fees after an annual deductible. This includes office visits, diagnostic tests, and surgeries. Medicare insurance leaves gaps that could be costly.

Additional insurance to help pay amounts not covered by Medicare includes relatively low premiums and comes in a wide range of choices. Most people purchase another insurance plan known as a Medicare Supplement or Medicare Advantage plan.

4. Medicare Supplement Plans

Medicare Supplement plans are a secondary insurance plan to Medicare. That means that Medicare must pay its benefits first and then the secondary insurance can pay. As you can imagine, this causes delays in payments to providers. Providers do not have to accept Medicare patients. Ideally, consider a plan that has a predictable co-pay or limit to your cost.

An unlimited co-insurance such as 20 percent indefinitely leaves exposure to a significant risk of financial loss in today's environment. You could have thousands of dollars left to pay after a serious medical event. Compare the total annual premium for a Medicare Supplement plan that covers everything 100 percent. Rates and benefits depend on your age and location. However, the premiums for these plans may be higher than alternative choices, like a Medicare Advantage plan.

5. Medicare Advantage Plans

Medicare Advantage plans generally are offered as a PPO or an HMO. This means they have a provider network that you are expected to stay within, along with predictable co-pays. These plans come with prescription drug benefits and may include vision, dental, and complimentary alternative care.

The monthly premium is usually lower than some Medicare Supplement plans because you will have co-pays when you incur services in exchange for a lower monthly premium. All plans have a maximum out of pocket limit which protects you against catastrophic loss when unexpected medical events happen. The healthier you are, the less you will spend for your insurance and health care on a Medicare Advantage plan.

Like prescription drug plans, Medicare Advantage Plans have an annual enrollment period (AEP) October 15 through December 7 every year. Your new insurance plan will provide your benefits from January 1 through December 31 of the next year. You are "locked-in" to that plan and cannot change plans during the year, unless you experience a qualifying event giving you a Special Election Period (SEP).

6. Standalone Prescription Drug Plans

A standalone prescription drug plan is a necessary purchase for those covered only by Medicare Part A and Part B—even if they are choosing to not have additional medical insurance—as well as for those enrolled in a Medicare Supplement plan, because Medicare Supplement plans do not cover prescriptions. It's necessary because Medicare and Medicare Supplement insurance don't cover prescription drugs, and Medicare will charge you a penalty later when you do purchase prescription drug coverage.

The penalty for not enrolling in prescription drug coverage is dependent on how long you went without the coverage. Once you are enrolled, you will shop and enroll in plans during the annual enrollment period (AEP), October 15 through December 7, just like the Medicare Advantage plan members do.

As with medical insurance, you should try to calculate the cost for a worst-case scenario, and then consider a best-case scenario. This gives you the parameters by which you are planning your budget. Again, it costs less for least usage, which essentially rewards those with better managed health.

Prescription drug plans, whether included with a Medicare Advantage plan (MAPD) or a standalone Prescription Drug Plan (PDP), are modeled to CMS's (Medicare) standard of coverage. Whether you are paying for a most costly plan or a least costly premium plan, they follow the standardized model of cost-sharing in the initial coverage, reduced purchase price for drugs while you are in the Coverage Gap, and optimum coverage in the Catastrophic Coverage.

It is difficult to calculate precisely if and when you will enter the Medicare Coverage Gap. Generally, if you take a few generic drugs, you will not likely enter the Coverage Gap. Brand drug retail costs vary so widely, you will need to know the retail price of each to get a better idea of whether you should plan for the Rx Coverage Gap. With Medicare plans, it is a balancing act between costs for medical care and costs for prescription drugs. You hope to protect your finances from large medical care expenses while planning and managing the costs of your ongoing prescription drug needs.

7. Provider Choice

Medicare Advantage plans usually have a Provider Network associated with the plan, like a PPO or an HMO. This is an important factor in your research and plan selection. It is usually the first question I ask to help narrow down the list of plan options. Which doctors and hospitals will you use for your care?

Your first choice is a PPO (preferred provider organization). A PPO gives you the freedom to go to providers that are in the network or use providers outside of the network. You will generally pay higher co-pays when using providers out of the network, but you don't have to get any permission.

Your other choice is an HMO (Health Maintenance Organization). The HMO requires you to select and utilize a primary care provider to receive benefits. You must get a referral from your primary care provider to see a specialist within in the network. Generally, services obtained outside of the provider network or without obtaining a referral from your primary care provider are not a covered service, unless it is a bona fide medical emergency.

It is helpful to first ask your doctors which "Medicare Plans" they accept. Be careful not to just ask if they accept Medicare – they may think you are only inquiring about original Medicare and Medicare Supplement plan coverage. By referring to Medicare Plans or Medicare Advantage Plans, you make it clear that you're asking under which plans they are a participating provider.

8. Travel, Secondary Residence, and "Snowbirds"

Health issues can happen anywhere, of course – and even away from your home service area. It's important to understand the consequences of getting care outside of your network before you travel from your area. If you are covered by a PPO, the PPO plan may be part of a larger provider network which gives you access to in-network providers in other places. In addition, since a PPO covers you whether your providers are in-network or out-of-network, you should be able to find a provider.

An HMO will only cover you for urgently needed medical care, which leaves it open to subjective interpretation. You might have to give details about why you needed to get certain medical care while you were away. An HMO is not recommended for someone who travels for extended periods because they will be denied coverage for follow-up care. Outside your service area, HMO plans cover urgent and emergency care only.

9. Rules and Exceptions

There are always rules for enrolling in and cancelling plans. There are specific time frames in which you can enroll and cancel coverage, submit claims for reimbursement, file a claims appeal for a rejected claim, and more. You need to find out the rules. Always ask the customer service department at your insurance company.

Customer service is trained to advise you about your benefits, limitations and exclusions and how to file claims and what to expect. They can review your claims and see how your plan's benefits were paid. Ask for a clear explanation. Remember their name. If you are not satisfied with the explanation provided, ask for clarification until you are satisfied. You can also ask to speak to a supervisor or manager, or talk to your insurance broker for further assistance. An insurance broker has experience and knowledge and is familiar with insurance contract terms. A broker can give a valued independent perspective and provide guidance in dealing with the insurance company.

10. Resources: Whom Do You Call?

You can learn all about Medicare and Social Security from their websites and their publications. Each insurance company can help you with their specific plans. An insurance agent may be employed by a company to represent that company's plans. An insurance broker represents many plans and is often employed independently. They are paid by the insurance companies for assisting with enrollment applications and providing assistance. You pay the same premium whether you have a broker or not.

Your insurance agent or broker is an advisor, advocate and consumer educator. Your agent or broker can help you compare plans, fill out an insurance company application and assist with claims issues. Agents and brokers are held to a standard of ongoing training, licensure and continuing education.

The laws governing health insurance are detailed and complex. Sometimes the rules are vague or even contradictory. Getting them wrong can have serious legal and financial consequences.

APPENDIX H

PROTECTING YOUR ASSETS

How do you invest when you are retired? Very carefully. You need to know how to protect your assets. Many smart people have planned so diligently for retirement by investing wisely, sacrificing immediate pleasures for long-term returns, and setting aside money for their later years in life. However, it is not uncommon for many of these same people to overlook their immediate insurance needs in a way that leaves the potential for destruction of all they have worked hard for.

Wise retirement planning must always take into account your immediate needs, not just the desires of the future. Who in their right mind would want to allow the possibility for their assets to be taken away as a direct result of poor planning? The key to avoiding catastrophe is to make certain that your insurance coverage is adequate and appropriate for your situation.

HOME INSURANCE
Contributed by Greg Ford

Natural disasters in the United States, which used to be fairly rare, seem to be more and more common these days. Whether it's hurricane Katrina in 2005, the tornados in Joplin, Missouri in 2011, or Superstorm Sandy in 2012, people are confronted regularly with the fact that their homes are underinsured.

For many people, insurance is a commodity that is "forced upon them." They simply make a choice and never think about it again until there is a problem. It's not uncommon for someone to have a home owner's insurance policy that was last evaluated 20 or more years earlier. Without taking inflation into account, many victims of the above listed natural disasters wound up getting reimbursed only a portion of what their home was worth because they neglected to review their insurance on a regular basis.

To avoid such a scenario, meet with your insurance agent once every year or two to make sure that your assets are insured properly. For your home, it is important to make sure your replacement cost would rebuild your current home in the event of a total loss. Many companies today provide periodic increases in your home replacement cost to keep up with inflation, but if you have done major upgrades or contributed anything that adds value to your home, it is extremely important to let your agent know about them.

Also make sure you have enough liability insurance on your home policy so that if someone sues you for something that happened on your property, you're covered. Liability insurance will help pay for court costs associated with a claim against you, as well as any judgment ruled against you, up to the liability limits you have chosen.

Liability insurance is quite affordable for what it offers you. Any increase of your coverage amount to higher limits is often not much more expensive in terms of premiums, but provides substantial coverage for your assets if something happens. Remember that fire, flood, and earthquake insurance are all usually separate from a regular homeowner's policy and require additional premiums. Make sure you understand what is covered in the policy that you purchase. Many homeowners are unclear as to what is and isn't covered.

On top of picking a plan carefully, it is incredibly important to keep records of what is in your home. In the event of a major loss at your home, your insurance company is going to ask you to account for what property needs to be replaced. If you wind up forgetting a lot of items or have no tangible proof of your assets, you will never get reimbursed for the items you owned before the loss.

It is always advisable to take an inventory of what you own in your home. If possible, take a video tour of your home and its contents and keep this in a safe place. You could keep this video file stored online, with another family or friend, or in a safe deposit box. Many insurance companies today are also providing content record applications for smart phones too. By taking this one small step, you put a record of what is in your home—and the value of these objects—in a place where it won't be destroyed if something should ever happen to your home.

AUTO INSURANCE
Contributed by Bill Russell

As with homeowner's insurance coverage, you don't want to overlook some key aspects of having adequate and appropriate auto insurance. When you insure a car, go over the details of the policy with your agent to make sure it accounts for all your needs.

Perhaps the most important thing to keep in mind is your liability limits. Many states offer low minimum liability limits, which appeal to people due to the more affordable rates. However, those low limits of liability could quite easily come back to haunt you and cause you to lose your assets if they are not enough to cover you. Your liability insurance will help you pay for court costs related to a claim against you, as well as any judgment ruled against you, up to the liability limits you have chosen.

If you still have an auto loan, then you know that it is important to have comprehensive coverage so that if something happens to the car, you are compensated for the loss and can use the money to buy a new car, if needed. You might also want to consider having uninsured/ underinsured motorist coverage to compensate you if an uninsured or underinsured driver with no assets causes an accident. Many states now actually require this coverage to coincide with the liability limits you have chosen for yourself. Consult with your agent to make sure that you have more than enough to cover such instances.

PERSONAL LIABILITY UMBRELLA INSURANCE
Contributed by Bill Russell

A personal liability policy, commonly called an umbrella policy, serves as a last line of defense against lawsuits. When your home, auto, or personal watercraft insurance has reached its limit of liability, an umbrella policy will pay claims up to the amount covered beyond your regular policy.

Without an umbrella policy, your assets and future earnings may be taken away from you to cover the difference. This extra liability coverage may also cover you for things like slander, libel, or false arrest. It often extends coverage for you when you are visiting other countries.

The average premium ranges from about $200 to $500 annually. Some people consider this coverage to be unnecessary, due to the extremely slim odds of ever needing to use it. However, most financial advisors believe it is certainly an affordable way to prevent you from losing all you have worked so hard to amass in life.

PROTECTING YOUR BUSINESS
Contributed by Janelle Markovich

For those who own a business or multiple businesses, there are key items you will want to review and have in place as you plan for retirement. We all get into the day to day grind and when it comes to planning for the future or taking care of ourselves, we often say: "It's on my list – I will get to that...." Another year or two can go by and that item is still on your list.

The business you have worked so hard to build up over the years not only has valuable assets, but is also a valuable source of income. Whether you plan to sell the business or transfer it to a family member or partner, you need to be prepared to protect what you have built. It is important to have your portfolio reviewed annually not only for your current coverage, but also let your agent know what your business plan is for the next few years and advise you if your operations change in any way.

As technology continues to be a large part of our lives, it has also brought changes to the way we do business. Consequently, your business is now vulnerable to more problems that are not typically covered under a basic business insurance policy. For example, there's more exposure to theft due to the volume of online transactions today.

It's unfortunately common to hear that $100,000 to a $1 million was stolen from a business. The perpretrator is often a bookkeeper, long-time employee, or outside hacker. Most business policies do not provide coverage for this, so your business would need coverage under a separate policy for Crime/Fiduciary.

Some of the fastest growing claims against businesses recently are wrongful termination allegations, wage/labor claims, and claims of sexual harassment. These claims typically run in the range of $250,000 and up. Some carriers are adding a little bit of coverage now, but it's truly not enough coverage to help defend and pay for these kinds of claims. It's advisable to purchase a separate, dedicated policy to protect your business.

Many business owners today don't think of purchasing an umbrella/excess policy to provide liability protection. Most insurance policies only provide up to $1 million limit for any one claim, which is quite low considering recent awards to plaintiffs. Fortunately, your umbrella/excess limits can extend your liability protection well beyond the basic policy limit for minimal additional cost.

As you prepare your business plan, one of the items to put on your to-do list is the buy/sell agreement. This will protect the business in the event of an unexpected death of an owner/partner. It is important to your business' long-term solvency to have your attorney set up a buy/sell agreement. Note that it can be funded with a life insurance policy.

Janelle Markovich
Propel Insurance
Sales Executive
Commercial Insurance
888 SW 5th Avenue, Suite 1170
Portland, OR 97204-2025
503.467.2828 Direct
866.577.1326 Fax

APPENDIX I

PLANNING YOUR FUNERAL

Contributed by Michael Dougherty

Death. No one likes to talk about it, especially when it comes to themselves. That is why the vast majority of people don't know what to do when a death occurs. I know I didn't.

My mom was diagnosed in February of 2008 with an aggressive form of cancer. One month later, she was gone. We should have been thinking during that time what we would do when she passed. We didn't. When she did pass, we had no idea what to do. Fortunately, I have a friend who's been in a related business and knew whom to call.

I've been told that 128 decisions need to be made in the first 24 hours. It was certainly a blur at the time. Even now, I don't remember most of it. Deciding what my mom would have wanted for her funeral and the other decisions during a time of grief was so hard on my family.

Knowing what to do at the time of a loved one's passing, or your own passing, will relieve your family from that burden. Here are a few ways to help the ones you love and those that love you.

1. **Take Responsibility for Your Arrangements** - Just as estate planning and creating a will are responsible actions,

planning your final arrangements in advance makes emotional and financial sense, and protects your loved ones from the burden of planning services for you.

A way to do that is to take these steps:

Step 1: Reflect

While so many of us ask big questions about what happens when we die, we often forget to ask questions that will capture the way we lived and help our friends and family celebrate our life and honor our memory.

Take time to think about the type of funeral and cemetery services that you would want to celebrate or otherwise memorialize your life. Consider the tone and atmosphere of the services. Are they somber? Traditional? Celebratory?

Will they reflect your unique interests and personality? What will the experience be like for the guests? Answering these questions will help you begin to make the funeral and cemetery selections that are right for you.

Step 2: Record

Once you've reflected on and determined your wishes for your final arrangements, actually recording your wishes is the best way to ensure they will be carried out. Whether stored on paper or electronically, your recorded wishes will allow your loved ones to act on your behalf. Ultimately, just as you keep your will and financial documents updated, you should review and update your funeral and cemetery plans when necessary as well.

Step 3: Share

After you've recorded your funeral and cemetery plans, it's important to share them with loved ones so they'll be able to carry out your wishes.

Keep your funeral plans safe but accessible. It's a common mistake to store them in a safe deposit box. At the time of your death, a safe deposit box only in your name may not be accessible to others until the legal matters of your estate have been settled. This process may not be resolved until after your final arrangements are carried out.

Instead, there are several ways you can make your plans accessible. Notify your family of its location or provide them with their own copy. If you have selected a funeral provider and made arrangements with them, your provider will also keep your plans on file.

Step 4: Support

Finally, support your plans with funding if you choose. By relieving your family of the need to pay for your funeral or cemetery services at the time of your death, you may prevent additional stress for them at an already difficult time.

Funding your plans also provides protection against inflation. By locking in today's prices, your loved ones will not have to pay more for your selected merchandise and services at the time of your death.

Ask the funeral provider for estimates of what your selections would cost today as well as what they are likely to cost in the future.

It's important to work with your provider to understand the laws and regulations that protect pre-need funds in your state. No matter what your wishes are for your funeral and cemetery plans, recording them and sharing them with your loved ones will help ensure that your final arrangements will be what you want, while easing the burden on your family and friends.

2. Eliminate Guesswork for Your Family

When you prearrange your funeral and cemetery services, you'll help alleviate your family's burden of having to make difficult decisions during an already difficult time. With your wishes recorded, they won't be left to guess what you would have wanted.

3. Personalize Your Service

Making your final arrangements in advance allows you to influence all elements of your services, including songs, readings, or other personal details that are important to you. It's your funeral—it should celebrate your life, your way.

4. Avoid Emotional Overspending

By communicating exactly which merchandise and services you want, you can keep your family from purchasing unnecessary additions to your services.

5. Find the Value and Quality You Want

Investigating different funeral homes and cemeteries is an important part of making final arrangements. Comparison shopping allows you to find the value and quality of service that's right for you.

6. If Possible, Lock in Today's Prices

If you choose to fund your prearranged funeral plans, you can lock in today's prices for products and services that likely will be more expensive in the future. It is important to work with a funeral professional to understand your options.

Whether you simply want to ensure that your wishes are carried out, or you want to protect your family from being forced to make difficult decisions at a time of loss, planning your final arrangements in advance is an important responsibility, and one of the greatest gifts you can give your loved ones. Don't wait. Start planning now. It's something you simply must do.

Mike Dougherty
Preplanning Advisor
Dignity Memorial
503-936-2373
michael.dougherty@dignitymemorial.com

THE INDUSTRY IN TURMOIL

Unfortunately, consumers are caught in the middle of a war between the states and two government agencies: the SEC and FINRA.

There has been a big fight between the SEC and FINRA against the state insurance departments on the control of the fixed indexed annuity (FIA or EIA). These agencies couldn't stand that the US Congress actually declared that the fixed indexed annuity is not a security. It is NOT an Investment in the true sense of the word. There is no risk to the consumer or purchaser.

Because of this, the FINRA circumvented the law and said they still need to supervise their advisors that offer this annuity, even though it is not legally a security. I wonder if it had anything to do with the additional revenue created for the broker dealers and fees paid to FINRA on the earnings of the advisors and broker dealers? This is not a new move for FINRA. It is also done with various long-term care policies and life insurance policies that are clearly NOT securities. Anyone say Patriot Act.

The large broker dealers are just another extension of the government. They are self-governed by FINRA, which in my opinion is governed by overpaid politically motivated appointments to supervise the industry. Few of these people have ever worked on Main Street directly with consumers. Instead, most have been in management or are right out of Wall Street firms.

There is a total disconnect between the SEC and FINRA as related to the individual investment advisor or stockbroker. This is why the trend is for advisors to give up their securities license that is regulated by FINRA and go to an RIA (Registered Investment Advisory Firm), regulated either by the state securities departments or directly with the SEC.

Why should you be concerned? In my opinion regulation costs about 10 percent to 20 percent of your investment return, whether you make money or lose it. So how do you like Regulations now? With your help, we can change this, but you have to take action. Go to www.AsktheFinancialDoctor.com and sign our Petition to FINRA and the SEC.

GLOSSARY

FINANCIAL TERMS 101

-- # --

10-5-3 Rule - A rule of thumb useful for asset allocation, stating that stocks will earn 10 percent, bonds will earn 5 percent, and cash will earn 3 percent each year.

30 Year Treasury - Long-term and low-risk government bond used to keep your money safe.

401(k) Plan - A pre-tax qualified retirement account provided by an employer, used to grow your money while deferring taxes.

403(b) Plan - The equivalent of a 401(k) plan, provided for people working in a public education or non-profit organization.

90/10 Rule - A rule stating that 90 percent of your income goes toward living expenses, while 10 percent of it works for you through savings and investments.

80/20 Rule - A rule stating that 80 percent of your income goes toward living expenses, while 20 percent of it works for you through savings and investments.

-- A --

Average Annual Return (AAR) - A misleading term that's supposed to describe how much your money grew per year on average.

Annuity - Financial product offered by insurance companies that's useful for providing a steady income in retirement. An Annuity is not an Investment; it is an Insurance Product. Only a Variable Annuity is actually an Investment and is considered a Security.

Immediate Annuity is designed to pay an income for a Lifetime or for a defined period like 10 or 20 years.

Deferred Annuity is designed to grow sheltered from taxes. You or your heirs pay taxes on the earnings when the funds are withdrawn.

Fixed Annuity

A fixed annuity is one in which your principal is guaranteed. You are offered a set interest rate for the entire length of the contract, usually between 3 percent and 5 percent. You have a guaranteed period, which can be as short as a month to as long as several years, in which the interest rate does not change. At the end of each period, the rate is adjusted according to the market.

Fixed Index Annuity or Equity Indexed Annuity: They Are the Same.

It is also worth noting that the increasing array of financial and investing products has given rise to a number of products that combine aspects of different types of annuities. One of these is the fixed index annuity (FIA), also called the Equity Indexed Annuity (EIA). This product guarantees[26] your principal while still allowing you to take advantage of market changes.

Your premium is guaranteed not to go down due to market fluctuations, while you are able to potentially earn a higher rate of interest that is determined by changes in a predetermined stock market index or in a guaranteed interest account. This type of annuity is tax deferred, allowing your money to grow faster, since you don't pay taxes on your earnings until you withdraw[27].

Your FIA / EIA also comes with an option that is common to variable annuities: Guaranteed lifetime income. This is an option that allows you to specify that your annuity be used to provide you with an income stream for life after a certain point. When you go with a non-qualified plan, a part of your annuity payment is actually a return of premium—which isn't taxed, lowering your overall tax liability.

26Guarantees are based on the claims paying ability of the issuing insurance agency. Annuities are products of the insurance industry, and are not guaranteed by any bank or insured by the FDIC. Annuities are long term retirement planning products, which may contain surrender charges during the early years of the contract. If you surrender your EIA during the surrender schedule, you will pay a surrender charge that may reduce or eliminate any return and could cause a loss of principal.

2710 percent Penalty on funds removed prior to age 59½.

Variable Annuity[28](VA) (Investment that is a Security)

If you have a bit more risk tolerance, a variable annuity is an option. Variable annuities are long-term investment vehicles issued by insurance companies designed for retirement purposes. With these types of annuities, your principal is not guaranteed, and neither is your rate of interest yield return. You should also realize that variable annuities may contain contingent deferred sales charges, mortality and expense risk charges, administrative fees, and annual contract fees. You have to rely on market conditions.

Keep in mind that investment returns will fluctuate and the principal value, when redeemed, may be worth more or less than the original investment. If equity markets go up, though, you get to take advantage of the earnings, and you get growth benefits through subaccounts which use pooled investment portfolios similar to mutual funds. You can choose from investment options for variable annuities, as well.

Although variable annuities offer investment features similar in many respects to mutual funds, a typical variable annuity offers three basic features not commonly found in mutual funds:

1. Tax-deferred treatment of earnings.

2. A death benefit.

3. Annuity payout options that can provide guaranteed income for life or a Variable

4. Payment based on performance.

Generally, variable annuities have two phases:

1. The "accumulation" phase when investor contributions (premiums) are allocated among investment portfolios (subac counts) and earnings accumulate.

2. The "distribution" phase when you withdraw money, typically as a lump sum or through various annuity payment options.

28Withdrawals of earnings are subject to income tax and, if made prior to age 59½, may be subject to an additional 10 percent federal tax penalty. Withdrawals can reduce the living and death benefits. Withdrawals, for tax purposes, are deemed to be gains out first.
Withdrawals or surrenders may be subject to contingent deferred sales charges which may reduce any return to the investor as well as causing a loss of principal.

If the payments are delayed to the future, you have a deferred annuity. If the payments start immediately, you have an immediate annuity. As its name implies, a variable annuity's rate of return is not stable, but varies with the stock, bond, and money market subaccounts that you choose as investment options.

There is no guarantee that you will earn any return on your investment and there is a risk that you will lose money. Because of this risk, variable annuities are securities registered with the Securities and Exchange Commission (SEC). The SEC and FINRA also regulate sales of variable insurance products.

-- B --

Bankruptcy – The state of an individual or organization unable to repay the debts that it owes.

Bond – Asset where you lend money to an organization in exchange for interest.

Bond Rating – From AAA to CCC, it represents the safety of a bond, based on the reliability of the borrower to repay a loan.

Broker – A professional who helps you buy and sell assets like stocks, usually for a commission.

Brokerage – An organization that employs brokers, and the term for online services that serve the same role as a broker.

-- C --

Capital – Financial funds that are used for the basis of investing.

Certificate of Deposit (CD) – A fairly liquid interest-bearing financial product provided by banks and credit unions.

Collateral – Something of value that's pledged to help you secure a loan.

Company Match – An employer benefit where your company will match the contributions you make to a retirement account, sometimes granted over a vesting period.

Compound Interest – Exponential growth from interest added to your principal and future interest applied to that greater sum.

Credit – Financial capital lent out with the expectation of repayment plus interest.

Credit Union – A financial institution owned and controlled by its members.

-- D --

Debt - Money that you've borrowed and are obligated to pay back.

Depreciation - The loss in value of an asset over time.

Deposit - The placement of funds in a financial institution.

Diversity - The balancing of different asset classes in a portfolio to manage risk.

Dividend - Payment from a company to its shareholders, usually to distribute profit.

Dollar Cost Averaging - A method of investing where you regularly contribute a predetermined amount of money into a fund, buying more shares when the price is down and fewer shares when the price is up.

Down Payment - The initial money you pay ahead of securing a loan for an expensive item like a house or a car.

-- E --

Equity - The amount of value or ownership interest held in an asset like a home—also, another name for a stock.

Equity-Indexed Annuity (EIA) - A hybrid annuity that guarantees your principal while still allowing you to benefit from market changes.

Estate Planning - The process of deciding what will happen to your money when you die, including distribution of an inheritance and attempting to minimize losses due to estate tax, often through the use of a trust.

Estate Tax - The government's tax on an estate after someone has died, taken before the estate is distributed to heirs.

Exchange Traded Fund (ETF) - A hybrid between a mutual fund and a stock, it contains a basket of individual investments like a fund, but can be traded on the exchange like a stock.

-- F --

Federal Deposit Insurance Corporation (FDIC) - Federal agency that insures deposits at financial and lending institutions against loss or default, currently up to $250,000.

Fee Based Advisor - A financial advisor who makes money based on an hourly fee or a percentage of assets being managed, rather than commission.

Financial Industry Regulatory Authority (FINRA) – The most prominent private securities regulation organization in the United States; a counterpart to the government-based Securities and Exchange Commission.

Financial Planning – The process of determining the best way to grow your money while mitigating risk.

Fixed Annuity – An annuity where your principal is guaranteed, but your interest payments of 3 percent to 5 percent are fixed for the length of the contract and can be reset each year by the Insurance Company.

Fixed Indexed Annuity - Has a guaranteed principal that has an earnings portion tied to an index like the S&P and the Owner can get a portion of the rate for their account

Fixed Rate – A rate that remains unchanged for the length of a contract, regardless of market conditions. It can apply to assets like bonds, as well as liabilities like home equity loans.

-- H --

Home Equity Line of Credit (HELOC) – A loan you take out that's secured by the equity in your home as collateral.

-- I --

Income Stream – A source of income, usually combined with others as a means of supporting yourself in retirement.

Index - A segment of the market that measures the value of stocks, such as the S&P or the Dow Jones Industrial Average.

Index Fund – Technically a mutual fund, but different in that it's a collection of funds tied to a particular index.

Individual Retirement Account (IRA) – A qualified retirement account that helps you accumulate funds for retirement, mainly through tax-deferred or tax-exempt gains, and with contribution limits.

Inflation – The rising prices of goods and services in the economy over time.

Insurance – A financial product that offsets your risk in exchange for payment— examples include life, long-term care, homeowner's, and health.

Interest – Payment that a borrower makes in exchange for the usage of someone else's financial capital.

Interest Rate – The rate at which a borrower pays for using money from a lender.

Internal Revenue Service (IRS) - The organization responsible for collecting taxes in the United States.

Investing - The act of buying assets like stocks and bonds with the intention of growing your money.

Investment - Something where you're invested, such as real estate or a stock, that's intended to make you a profit.

-- K --

Keogh Plan - The original retirement vehicle for self-employed individuals, available as a defined benefit or defined contribution plan.

-- L --

Liability - A debt or obligation that you owe, representing negative value in your portfolio.

Liquidity - How accessible your money is in a particular asset class—real estate isn't very liquid, while savings accounts are highly liquid.

Loan - Money given to someone in exchange for repayment, usually with interest.

Long-term Care Insurance - A policy that helps you cover the costs of long-term care, including comprehensive care or facilities.

-- M --

Margin - Collateral that you put down in order to cover some or all of the risk of borrowing for an investment.

Medicaid - A United States federal program providing health resources for low-income individuals and families.

Medicare - A United States federal social insurance program primarily designed to provide healthcare to Americans 65 and older.

Money Manager - An individual or organization that you hire to manage your investment portfolio or a subset of it.

Money Market Fund - A mutual fund investing in short-term debt securities that's not insured by the FDIC, but generally provides a higher yield than bank accounts.

Mortgage - A loan you take out for a home using the real estate as collateral.

Mutual Fund - An investment of a group of individual investments that's managed by professional money managers for a fee.

-- N --

Net Income - The money you have left over after paying the taxes you owe—in business, it's the company's earnings or profit after covering expenses. After all fees and expenses, it is what you have left

Net Worth - How much you have, found by subtracting your liabilities from your assets.

-- P --

Pension - Regular income provided to employees by a company or the government during retirement, often calculated as percentage of their ending salary.

Portfolio - A collection of your investments.

Profit Sharing - A plan in which the employer is the sole contributor, putting a portion of company profits into your retirement plan as an employee.

Principal - The initial sum of money in a deposit or investment.

Purchasing Power - The value of your money, or how much it can buy—this is negatively impacted by inflation.

-- R --

Real Estate - An asset class of physical property like houses and commercial buildings.

Real Estate Investment Trust (REIT) - Investment in a company that owns income-generating properties, useful as a way to invest in real estate without having to own property outright.

Real Rate of Return (RR) - An accurate way of determining how much your money is returning each year, adjusted for inflation and other negative factors.

Retirement - The period of time after you've quit working.

Retirement Plan - The way you pay for your living expenses during retirement—also refers to retirement vehicles like the IRA or 401(k).

Return - The amount or percentage of money you gain (or lose) from an investment.

Reverse Mortgage – A financial instrument that helps individuals secure a stable income in retirement, based on the equity in their home.

Risk – The possible extent to which you can lose money in an investment.

Risk Tolerance – How much money you're willing and able to lose in order to get a potentially higher return.

Roth IRA – A variation on the IRA vehicle for retirement that requires you to contribute after-tax dollars, but lets you accumulate and distribute any gains without paying any further taxes.

Rule of 72 – A rule that helps you determine how long it will take your money to double if you divide your expected return into 72.

Rule of 100 – A rule that helps you determine your risk tolerance by subtracting your age from 100; the result is the percentage of your portfolio that would be in risky investments.

-- S --

Savings – Money you've set aside from your income, some of which goes into investments.

Savings Account – A low-interest account at a bank or other financial institution.

Securities and Exchange Commission (SEC) – United States Federal agency that regulates the financial and securities industries.

Self Employment Plan (SEP IRA) – Similar to the traditional IRA, but with higher contribution limits and restricted to individuals who are self-employed.

Social Security – A federal program that provides a retirement income to seniors based on what they paid in, funded through the collection of payroll taxes.

Stock – An asset based on equity stake in a company.

Stock Market – Public entity that facilitates the trading of stocks and securities.

Stockholder – An individual who owns a stock, which represents a stake in a company.

Stock Option – A company stock benefit provided to employees as part of their compensation, and an incentive for employees to perform well to improve the value of the company.

-- T --

Tax Credit – An amount that's directly cut from total taxes owed.

Tax Deduction – A reduction in the income you owe taxes on, with examples that include contributions to charity and home mortgage interest.

Tax Deferred – Refers to funds or retirement vehicles where taxes that you accrue on earnings are delayed or deferred until distribution.

Tax Exemption – An elimination of the taxes that you would otherwise owe, such as on capital gains in tax-sheltered retirement vehicles.

Traditional IRA – The original IRA, where you contribute money before paying taxes and can accumulate earnings tax-deferred, only paying tax when you distribute the funds for retirement.

Treasury Bonds – US government bond that's backed by the US dollar and the American taxpayer base, considered a safe but low-yield investment.

Trust – Often part of estate planning, it's a separate entity that you can establish to help minimize taxes and avoid probate.

-- V --

Variable Annuity – Long-term investment vehicle issued by insurance companies for retirement, where your principal and yield is not guaranteed.

Volatility – Refers to how risky and unpredictable an asset or asset class is.

-- W --

-- X --

-- Y --

Let's get right to the 800-pound gorilla in the room and let's talk Social Security— or should we call it Social Insecurity? The politicians have borrowed in excess of $4 trillion (or is it $20 trillion?) and they have never paid a penny back. However, I believe the government will always pay something, even if it is reduced or you must qualify through an earnings or assets test to receive your benefit.

Here is one of my favorite letters to Malcolm Berko, and his response:

You're Entitled

Dear Mr. Berko,

I have been a widower for four years and helped raise six children , each of whom is mostly self-sufficient. My wife and I were very active in raising our children. I began taking Social Security at 70. I really don't need this entitle-ment. Starting in 1968, I had a good job for 40 years. We lived within our means. We saved money. My wife worked part time as a legal secretary for 30 years. We did well with investments.

The checks have come in handy for paying for a new air conditioner, a large-screen TV, airfare, and gifts for my children and grandchildren. And I hope to help some of them with their college costs. I could spend less and bragged about this (shouldn't have) to my pastor. Now, he's nicely suggesting that I give up this entitlement so the government can give it to people who need it. And I'm almost embarrassed that I get $2,200 every month. I'm aware that Congress wants to reduce this entitlement and that there will be a means test to qualify. I would like to hear your thoughts. – SG, Oklahoma City

Dear SG,

Stop referring to Social Security as an "entitlement." SS is not an entitlement. Every time you or your spouse earned a paycheck, the employer sent Social Security 6.2 percent of it to an account under your or her name. And each time you or your spouse earned a paycheck, the employer also sent SS a matching amount to your account. That's 12.4 percent per paycheck, and your spouse never received a shilling of it. You earned it. You paid for it. It's your money. It's not an entitlement.

The word "entitlements" is government-speak for the federal programs from which lots of folks receive support that they don't pay for. However, Congress is ill advised to call Social Security an entitlement. Calling SS an entitlement is purposefully disparaging and places it on the same common field as food stamps, job training, free cell phones, etc.

As Congress continues to call SS an entitlement, folks like you with 40 years of contributions will begin to believe it's an entitlement. That makes it easier for Congress to take it from you.

Assume your average annual income between 1968 and 2008 was $35,000 a year. In those 40 years, you and your employer probably contributed $5,250 annually to your Social Security account. That's $210,000. If these contributions were compounded at 4 percent annually for 40 years, your SS account would be worth about $625,000.

Do you consider this an entitlement? I don't! It belongs to you! Some of it is even taxed. Entitlements are not taxed. In my opinion, you should take your checks as long as the Social Security Administration sends them to you, but remember that they're your money!

If you kick the bucket at age 83, then what hasn't been paid to you accrues to SS. Be mindful that the average life expectancy in the US is 79 years, so most retirees collect benefits for less than 15 years. And there's a lot left over. During the past 50 years, more than 100 million workers have been putting billions every year into the system. I've tried to find out how much all employees and employers have contributed to the Social Security trust fund since 1963.

The Congressional Budget Office can't tell me. The Social Security Administration either won't or can't tell me, either. However, an educated guess places the number between $53 trillion and $58 trillion. If a half-trillion a year has been paid out each year during the past 50 years (extremely high), then $18 trillion to $23 trillion is missing.

Ask your congressperson where the money is, because $18 trillion or $23 trillion is a lot of money! Meanwhile, I don't care for religious types who offer unsolicited financial advice. Tell the pastor you'll give up your earned Social Security income if he pledges not to accept private checks to the Pastor's Discretionary Fund and stops hiding income under Internal Revenue Service regulations that favor members of the cloth.

Please address your financial questions to Malcolm Berko, P.O. Box 8303, Largo, FL 33775, or e-mail him at mjberko@yahoo.com.

To find out more about Malcolm Berko and read features by other Creators Syndicate writers and cartoonists, visit the Creators Syndicate website at www.creators.com.

Take Action on Social Security

If the above letter doesn't make you mad as hell at our government and both political parties, then there is no hope left in America. You might as well just give up, get your gray uniform, and start marching.

Every American who has contributed to Social Security needs to demand the following:

1. Demand an accounting of the funds at the Social Security Administration.

2. Immediately tie all the salaries and retirement income of all retired employees of the Social Security Administration and the IRS (which collects the funds), as well as every president and member of Congress to Social Security payments. That's called accountability.

It was the politicians' duty to protect the American public's funds, and they need to be held accountable for what they failed to do. We can no longer allow our politicians to be above the law and steal our money just by having some kangaroo court decide it's okay to lie to the public.

If you are between 20 and 70 years old, you need to immediately join our cause and demand our politicians start being accountable to us. After all, they work for us, not the other way around. You paid for Social Security. If you paid into it for over 20 years, it is not an entitlement; it's your money. Do you like getting ripped off?

The really sad part is that politicians are counting on your apathy to roll over and let them keep taking your money by changing laws. They did it with your Social Security contributions, and who complained when they stole your money and your employer's matching contributions?

Join our petition at www.AskTheFinancialDoctor.com.

Also, we have a petition for a term limit of 15 years for the justices of the Supreme Court or any other federal judges who are appointed, since nobody should have a lifetime job with no accountability.

Over 50 percent of Americans have no clue what is going on in front of their eyes.

If you know people like that, give them a copy of my book and educate them. You will be helping your country and your children, grandchildren, and great grandchildren.

-- Z --